Wennink

D1541150

Transportation Statistics Annual Report
2000

**Bureau of
Transportation
Statistics**

U.S. Department of Transportation

Bureau of Transportation Statistics

Our mission is to lead in developing transportation data and information of high quality and to advance their effective use in both public and private transportation decisionmaking.

Our vision for the future: Data and information of high quality will support every significant transportation policy decision, thus advancing the quality of life and the economic well-being of all Americans.

To obtain *Transportation Statistics Annual Report 2000* and other BTS publications

Mail: Product Orders
            Bureau of Transportation Statistics
            U.S. Department of Transportation
            400 Seventh Street, SW, Room 3430
            Washington, DC 20590

Phone: 202-366-DATA [press 1]
Fax: 202-366-3197
Internet: www.bts.gov

Recommended citation

U.S. Department of Transportation, Bureau of Transportation Statistics, *Transportation Statistics Annual Report 2000,* BTS01-02 (Washington, DC: 2001).

Photographs

Chapters 1, 2, 4, 5—Marsha Fenn for Bureau of Transportation Statistics: Metro, Washington, DC; luggage carousel, Reagan National Airport, Washington, DC; MARC train at Camden Yards Station, Baltimore, MD; containers loaded on ship at the Port of Miami, FL

Chapter 3—National Highway Traffic Safety Administration

Chapters 6 and 7—Bureau of Transportation Statistics staff: Washington, DC, traffic; U.S. Coast Guard vessel, outside Baltimore, MD

For sale by the Superintendent of Documents, U.S. Government Printing Office
Internet: bookstore.gpo.gov Phone: (202) 512-1800 Fax: (202) 512-2250
Mail: Stop SSOP, Washington, DC 20402-0001

ISBN 0-16-050853-3

Acknowledgments

U.S. Department of Transportation

Norman Y. Mineta
Secretary

Michael P. Jackson
Deputy Secretary

Bureau of Transportation Statistics

Ashish K. Sen
Director

Rick Kowalewski
Deputy Director

Susan J. Lapham
*Associate Director for
Statistical Programs*

John V. Wells
Chief Economist

Wendell Fletcher
*Assistant Director for
Transportation Analysis*

Project Manager
Kirsten Oldenburg
(from January 2001)
Joanne Sedor
(through December 2000)

Editor
Marsha Fenn

Major Contributors
Felix Ammah-Tagoe
Charles Beene
Ron Duych
Bingsong Fang
Xiaoli Han
Deborah Johnson

Maha Khan
Marcello Leonardi
William Mallett
Lisa Randall
Steve Schamberger
Deepak Virmani

Other Contributors
Davida Baldwin
David Banks
John Bushery
Russell Capelle
Lillian Chapman
David Chesser
Michael Cohen
Martha Courtney
June Jones
Terry Klein
Marcus Mathias
Chip Moore
Michael Myers
Neil Russell
Bruce Spear
Matthew Sheppard
Nancy Swaim
Lynn Weidman

Cover Design
Dan Halberstein

**Report Layout and
Production**
Dorinda Edmondson

Table of Contents

CHAPTER 4   MOBILITY AND ACCESS TO TRANSPORTATION

CHAPTER 5   ECONOMIC GROWTH

CHAPTER 6   ENERGY AND THE ENVIRONMENT

CHAPTER 7   NATIONAL SECURITY

CHAPTER 8   STATE OF TRANSPORTATION STATISTICS

APPENDICES

INDEX

Preface

Congress requires the Bureau of Transportation Statistics (BTS) to report on transportation statistics to the President and Congress. *Transportation Statistics Annual Report 2000* is the seventh such report prepared in response to this congressional mandate, laid out in 49 U.S.C. 111 (j). The report discusses the extent and condition of the transportation system; its use, performance, and safety record; transportation's economic contributions and costs; and its energy and environmental impacts. All modes of transportation are covered in the report.

The report has a new format this year, intended to make it easier for readers to find the information in which they are interested. The BTS publication, *National Transportation Statistics* has more comprehensive and longer time series, tabulated data than could be accommodated by the new format. Another BTS report, *Transportation Indicators,* provides quarterly, monthly, and in some cases, weekly updates for over 90 indicators pertinent to transportation. Both of these documents are available online at www.bts.gov.

Chapter 1
Summary

Summary

This seventh *Transportation Statistics Annual Report* (TSAR) provides the reader with a broad array of information on the U.S. transportation system: its extent and condition, relationship to the nation's economic growth and national security, safety aspects, reliance on energy, environmental impacts, and contribution to mobility and accessibility.

Transportation System Extent and Condition

As the fourth largest country in land area, the United States has over 4 million miles of highways, railroads, and waterways that connect all parts of the country. It also has 19,000 public and private airports and over 400,000 miles of oil and gas transmission pipelines.

- There were 220 million vehicles in the nation's highway fleet in 1999, 22 million more than a decade earlier.
- Revenue vehicle-miles of transit grew by nearly 30 percent between 1991 and 1999, to over 3 billion miles.
- The number of aircraft operated by air carriers increased by more than 30 percent between 1990 and 1999.
- High-speed rail service improvements were made in the Northeast Corridor between Washington, DC, and Boston in 2000.
- More than 41,000 U.S.-flag vessels were available for service in U.S. maritime trade as of December 1999.
- The condition of the nation's airport runways, roads, and bridges has generally improved in the last decade.

Safety

Reducing transportation-related deaths, injuries, and property damage is a key goal of the transportation community. While much progress has been made in reducing the number of deaths, these numbers remain high. Crashes and incidents involving transportation vehicles, vessels, aircraft, and pipelines claimed nearly 44,000 lives in 1999 and injured more than 3 million people.

- Motor vehicle collisions account for about 95 percent of transportation-related deaths.
- Transportation incidents ranked as the seventh leading cause of death in the United States in 1998, but motor vehicle crashes are the leading cause of death for people between the ages of 6 and 27.
- Alcohol-related fatalities fell from 57 percent of all highway fatalities in 1982 to 38 percent in 1999, but still killed nearly 15,787 people in 1999. (The National Highway Traffic Safety Administration's 2000 early assessment estimates the death toll at 16,068.)
- Sport utility vehicles have the highest rollover rate of any vehicle in fatal crashes.
- More than 14 million tires were judged prone to tread separation and recalled in 2000.
- Of the 5,656 bicycle and pedestrian fatalities involving motor vehicles in 1999, 60 percent of them occurred in urban areas.
- Commercial aviation accidents claimed the lives of 92 people in 2000 while 592 people were killed in general aviation accidents.
- Most commercial maritime fatalities in 2000 involved fishing vessels.
- The fatality rate per million train-miles decreased 40 percent between 1993 and 1999.
- Transportation's share of occupational fatalities increased from 40 percent in 1992 to 44 percent in 1998.

Mobility and Access to Transportation

The transportation system enables people and businesses to overcome the distance between places. For travelers, this includes having easy access to modes of transportation that will get them between home and work, from store to store, and off on vacation. Businesses need to move both people and goods, increasingly worldwide.

- About 4.6 trillion passenger-miles of travel occurred in 1999, an annual increase of 2 percent since 1990.
- There were over 3.8 trillion ton-miles of domestic freight shipments in 1999, representing an annual growth of 2 percent since 1990.
- Annual vehicle-miles of travel in the United States rose by nearly 30 percent between 1989 and 1999 to almost 2.7 trillion miles.
- International overnight travel to the United States increased by 33 percent while the number of U.S. residents traveling out of the country rose 44 percent between 1989 and 1999.
- Light truck travel increased from 14 percent of all passenger-miles of travel in 1975 to 31 percent in 1999.
- One in four flights by major U.S. air carriers arrived late or were diverted or canceled in 2000.
- Air freight, the fastest growing shipment mode, increased 52 percent in value between 1993 and 1997.
- The U.S. waterborne container trade balance has shifted more toward imports by a gap of 4 million 20-foot equivalent container units (TEUs) in 1999, up from a gap of 1 million TEUs in 1993.

Economic Growth

Transportation is a vital component of the U.S. economy. As a sizable element of the country's Gross Domestic Product, transportation employs millions of people and consumes a large amount of the economy's goods and services.

- Demand for transportation-related goods and services represents about 11 percent of the U.S. economy and supports one in eight jobs.
- In-house transportation contributed $142 billion to the economy compared with $236 billion by the for-hire sector in 1996.
- Households spent an average of $7,000 on transportation in 1999, nearly 20 percent of their income and second only to the amount they spent on housing.
- U.S. international merchandise trade rose 10.3 percent to $1.7 trillion between 1997 and 1999, with Canada retaining its status as our top trading partner.
- Most transportation modes showed much higher productivity growth between 1955 and 1998 than did the U.S. business sector.
- Average gasoline motor fuel prices increased 59 percent between January 1999 and July 2000, but did not make a major impact on fuel consumption.
- The value of highway capital stock increased by 19.4 percent between 1988 and 1999.

Energy and the Environment

The many benefits of transportation are tempered by its environmental impacts. The sector's dependence on fossil fuels is at the root of many problems. However, construction and maintenance of transportation infrastructure and facilities, refining of fuels, and vehicle manufacturing, maintenance, and disposal also affect the environment.

- Transportation sector energy use has grown at 1.5 percent annually for the last two decades and in 1999 accounted for two-thirds of petroleum fuel demand.
- The average fuel efficiency of each year's new car fleet has not changed from 28.8 miles per gallon since 1988.
- The transportation sector greenhouse gas emissions of carbon dioxide have risen 14.9 percent since 1990.
- While most transportation air pollutant emissions have declined since 1970, emissions of nitrogen oxides have not.
- The percentage of the U.S. population exposed to excessive aircraft noise has been cut in half since 1992 but an estimated 680,000 people are still affected.
- An average of 1.8 million gallons of oil—over 50 percent of it cargo—was spilled annually into U.S. waters between 1994 and 1998.
- The U.S. Army Corps of Engineers dredges about 300 million cubic yards of sediments—some of it contaminated—from navigation channels each year.
- Almost all (93 percent) of the lead content of disposed batteries was reused in 1998, but only 24 percent of the 4.5 million tons of scrapped tires were recycled.

National Security

The nation's economic well-being and national security are dependent on a transportation system that can move people, goods, and military personnel and equipment without the fear of intentional disruption or damage by terrorists or other criminal elements.

- Prior to September 11, 2001, incidents of unlawful interference with civil aviation—primarily hijackings and sabotage—had been decreasing since the 1970s. In 2000, attacks against civil aviation worldwide claimed only 2 lives and wounded 27 others.
- Among all nations, the United States ranks 11th in merchant shipbuilding, just ahead of Romania but behind countries such as Croatia and Finland.
- The U.S. aerospace industry is the single largest U.S. net exporter, with a positive trade balance in 1999 of $37 billion.
- OPEC supplied about 46 percent of U.S. net imports, 25 percent of total U.S. oil consumption in 1999.
- The U.S. Coast Guard seized a record 111,689 pounds of cocaine in 1999, with an estimated street value of $3.7 billion, and interdicted 4,826 illegal aliens at sea.

This report was predominantly written prior to the September 11, 2001, terrorist attacks on the United States.

The State of Transportation Statistics

People and organizations make innumerable transportation decisions every day. In order for the transportation system to work effectively and efficiently, decisionmakers everywhere need good information. Much data are currently collected, analyzed, and disseminated by a variety of organizations, but whether or not these data will help the transportation community make good decisions is a concern.

- Under the new Department of Transportation (DOT) Safety Data Action Plan, activities are underway to improve the quality, timeliness, and relevance of transportation safety data.
- Data for DOT's performance measures will be supported by the best statistical practices for data collection.
- The Omnibus Survey generates a monthly report about the transportation system, how it is used, and how the users view it.
- The Intermodal Transportation Database will provide one-stop shopping for many databases maintained by DOT.
- BTS's *Transportation Indicators* provides decisionmakers with quarterly, monthly, and in some cases, weekly data.

Chapter 2
Transportation System Extent and Condition

Introduction

The U.S. transportation system makes possible a high level of personal mobility and freight activity for the nation's 281 million residents and nearly 7 million business establishments. In 1999, over 230 million motor vehicles, transit vehicles, railroad cars, and boats were available for use on the over 4 million miles of highways, railroads, and waterways that connect all parts of the United States, the fourth largest country in the world in land area. The transportation system also includes about 213,000 aircraft and over 19,000 public and private airports (an average of about 6 per county), and over 400,000 miles of oil and gas transmission lines. This extensive transportation network supported about 4.6 trillion passenger-miles of travel in 1999 and 3.8 trillion ton-miles of commercial freight shipments in 1999.

In general, the nation's transportation infrastructure has changed very little in recent years, while the number of vehicles has grown, in some cases dramatically. Road lane-miles, for instance, have grown by about 3 percent between 1980 and 1999, while cars and light trucks have increased by 40 percent. In air transportation, the number of aircraft operated by air carriers has increased by more than 30 percent since 1990, while the number of certificated airports (those serving scheduled air carrier operations with aircraft seating more than 30 passengers) has shrunk. The heavy use of the nation's infrastructure raises the specter of deterioration. Data show, however, the nation's roads, bridges, and airport runways, in general, improved in the 1990s.

As the level of traffic continues to climb and the amount of infrastructure remains the same, improved management of the system is one method being used to keep traffic flowing. The increasing use of information technology is important not only in commercial aviation, railroading, and waterborne commerce, but also in highway transportation, transit, general aviation, and boating. Information technology enhances the capability to monitor, analyze, and control infrastructure and vehicles, and offers real-time information to system users. These technologies have a great deal of potential to help people and businesses use the transportation system more efficiently.

Transportation System Extent

The widespread availability of a large variety of transportation options brings a high level of mobility to most of the nation's residents and businesses. Tables 1 through 6 provide a snapshot of the key elements of the U.S. transportation system.

To put the system into perspective, the system's 4 million miles of roads would circle the globe

Table 1
Highways: 1999 Data (unless noted)

Public roads
46,567 miles of Interstate highways
113,983 miles of other National Highway
  System (NHS) roads
3,771,462 miles of non-NHS roads

Vehicles and use
132 million cars, driven 1.6 trillion miles
75 million light trucks, driven 0.9 trillion miles
7.8 million commercial trucks with 6 tires or
  more and combination trucks, driven 0.2 trillion miles
729,000 buses (all types), driven 7.7 billion miles
4.2 million motorcycles, driven 10.6 billion miles

Passenger and freight motor carriers
4,000 private motorcoach companies
  operating in the U.S. and Canada, 860 million passengers[1]
511,000 interstate freight motor carriers[2] (2000),
  1.1 trillion ton-miles carried[3]

[1] American Bus Association, available at http://www.buses.org, as of Nov. 9, 2000.
[2] U.S. Department of Transportation, Federal Motor Carrier Safety Administration, *Motor Carrier Management Safety Information System Report LS50B901* (Washington, DC: March 2000).
[3] Eno Foundation, Inc., *Transportation in America, 1999* (Washington, DC: 2000).

SOURCE: U.S. Department of Transportation, Federal Highway Administration, *Highway Statistics 1999* (Washington, DC: 2000), tables HM-14 and HM-20.

Table 2
Air: 1999 Data (unless noted)

Airports (2000)
5,317 public-use airports
13,964 private-use airports

Airports serving large certificated carriers[1]
29 large hubs (69 airports), 458 million enplaned passengers
31 medium hubs (48 airports), 96 million enplaned passengers
56 small hubs (73 airports), 39 million enplaned passengers
577 nonhubs (604 airports), 17 million enplaned passengers

Aircraft
8,111 certificated air carrier aircraft,[2] 5.1 billion domestic
  miles flown[3]
205,000 active general aviation aircraft[4] (1998), 3.9 billion
  statute-miles flown[5] (1997)

Passenger and freight companies[3]
81 carriers
588 million domestic revenue passenger enplanements
13.9 billion domestic ton-miles of freight

Certificated air carriers (domestic and international)
Majors: 13 carriers, 650,000 employees, 552 million revenue
  passenger enplanements
Nationals: 30 carriers, 66,000 employees, 87 million revenue
  passenger enplanements
Regionals: 38 carriers, 9,000 employees, 11 million revenue
  passenger enplanements

[1] U.S. Department of Transportation, Bureau of Transportation Statistics, Office of Airline Information, *Airport Activity Statistics of Certificated Air Carriers, 12 Months Ending December 31, 1999* (Washington, DC: 2001).
[2] Aerospace Industries Association, *Aerospace Facts and Figures* (Washington, DC: 1999/2000).
[3] U.S. Department of Transportation, Bureau of Transportation Statistics, Office of Airline Information, *Air Carrier Traffic Statistics* (Washington, DC: 1999).
[4] U.S. Department of Transportation, Federal Aviation Administration, *General Aviation and Air Taxi Activity and Avionics Survey, Calendar Year 1998* (Washington, DC: 2000).
[5] U.S. Department of Transportation, Federal Aviation Administration, *General Aviation and Air Taxi Activity and Avionics Survey, Calendar Year 1997*, FAA-APO-99-4 (Washington, DC: 1999).

SOURCE: U.S. Department of Transportation, Bureau of Transportation Statistics, *National Transportation Statistics 2000* (Washington, DC: 2001).

more than 157 times, its rail lines 7 times, and its oil and gas pipelines 56 times. The average distance traveled by each car and light truck annually (about 12,000 miles) equals a journey nearly halfway around the world, or added together, about one-tenth the distance to the nearest star outside our solar system.

The capacity of the air and transit systems in the United States is also phenomenal. There are more than enough seats on airplanes operated by U.S. air carriers to seat the entire population of Delaware (population 780,000). And the number of cars in the New York City subway system alone is more than large enough for the entire population of Baton Rouge, Louisiana (population about 200,000), to have a seat at the same time.

Table 3
Rail: 1999 Data (unless noted)

Miles of road operated
120,986 miles by major (Class I) railroads[1]
21,250 miles by regional railroads[1]
28,422 miles by local railroads[1]
22,741 miles by Amtrak[2]

Equipment[1]
1.4 million freight cars
20,256 freight locomotives in service

Freight railroad firms[1]
Class I: 8 systems, 177,557 employees, 1.4 trillion revenue
 ton-miles of freight carried
Regional: 36 companies, 11,372 employees
Local: 510 companies, 12,454 employees

Passenger (Amtrak)[2]
25,000 employees, 1,894 passenger/other cars
378 locomotives, 22.5 million passengers carried (FY 2000)

[1] Association of American Railroads, *Railroad Facts: 2000 Edition* (Washington, DC: 2000).
[2] National Railroad Passenger Corp., *Annual Report 2000* (Washington, DC: 2000), also available at http://www.amtrak.com/news/00annualrpt.pdf, as of April 2001.

SOURCE: U.S. Department of Transportation, Bureau of Transportation Statistics, *National Transportation Statistics 2000* (Washington, DC: 2001).

Table 4
Transit: 1999 Data (unless noted)

Vehicles[1] **(1998)**
55,661 buses (also included in buses under highway),
 17.9 billion passenger-miles
11,357 heavy and light rail, 13.4 billion passenger-miles
5,535 commuter rail, 8.7 billion passenger-miles
97 ferries, 280 million passenger-miles
20,042 demand responsive, 513 million passenger-miles
7,654 other vehicles, 654 million passenger-miles

Transit agencies[2]
554 federally funded urbanized area agencies
1,074 federally funded rural agencies
3,594 federally funded specialized transportation agencies
753 other agencies
321,000 employees

[1] U.S. Department of Transportation, Federal Transit Administration, National Transit Database 1998, available at http://www.fta.dot.gov/ntl/databases/index.html, as of Oct. 23, 2000.
[2] American Public Transportation Association, *Transit Factbook 1999* (Washington, DC: 1999).

SOURCE: U.S. Department of Transportation, Bureau of Transportation Statistics, *National Transportation Statistics 2000* (Washington, DC: 2001).

(continued on next page)

Table 5
Water: 1999 Data (unless noted)

U.S.-flag fleet
Great Lakes: 674 vessels,[1] 57 billion ton-miles
  (domestic commerce)[2]
Inland: 33,970 vessels,[1] 305 billion ton-miles
  (domestic commerce)[2]
Ocean: 7,122 vessels,[1] 293 billion ton-miles
  (domestic commerce)[2]
Recreational boats: 12.6 million numbered boats[3] (1998)

Commercial facilities[4]
Great Lakes: 619 deep-draft, 144 shallow-draft
Inland: 2,376 shallow-draft
Ocean: 4,050 deep-draft, 2,118 shallow-draft

[1] U.S. Army Corps of Engineers, Water Resources Support Center, *Waterborne Transportation Lines of the United States: Calendar Year 1999* (Fort Belvoir, VA: 2000), also available at http://www.wrsc.usace.army.mil/ndc/veslchar.htm, as of April 2001.
[2] U.S. Army Corps of Engineers, Water Resources Support Center, *Waterborne Commerce of the United States 1999* (Fort Belvoir, VA: 2001). Domestic ton-miles include commerce among the 50 states, Puerto Rico, the Virgin Islands, Guam, American Samoa, Wake Island, and the U.S. Trust Territories. Domestic total does not include cargo carried on general ferries, coal and petroleum products loaded from shore facilities directly into bunkers of vessels for fuel, transport of less than 100 tons of government materials on government-owned equipment in support of U.S. Army Corps of Engineers projects. Fish are also excluded from internal (inland) domestic traffic.
[3] U.S. Department of Transportation, U.S. Coast Guard, *Boating Statistics–1998* (Washington, DC: 2000).
[4] U.S. Army Corps of Engineers, Navigation Data Center, *Geographic Distribution of U.S. Waterway Facilities,* available at http://www.wrsc.usace.army.mil/ndc/fcgeodis.htm, as of January 2001.

SOURCE: U.S. Department of Transportation, Bureau of Transportation Statistics, *National Transportation Statistics 2000* (Washington, DC: 2001).

Table 6
Pipeline: 1999 Data (unless noted)

Oil[1]
Crude lines: 86,000 miles, 336 billion ton-miles
Product lines: 91,000 miles, 287 billion ton-miles

Natural gas (estimates)[2]
Transmission: 254,000 miles of pipe
Distribution: 981,000 miles of pipe, 86 companies,
  142,000 employees

[1] Eno Foundation, Inc., *Transportation in America, 1999* (Washington, DC: 2000).
[2] American Gas Association, *Gas Facts* (Washington, DC: 1999).

SOURCE: U.S. Department of Transportation, Bureau of Transportation Statistics, *National Transportation Statistics 2000* (Washington, DC: 2001).

Restructuring and Consolidation of Transportation Industries

Aviation

The aviation industry has grown dramatically and changed since the Airline Deregulation Act of 1978. It has experienced consolidation, while at the same time, new-entrant, low-fare competitors have emerged. Some older, established airlines, such as Eastern, National, and Pan American, have disappeared, while others, such as Southwest Airlines, a former intrastate carrier, have become major airlines. As a result, the number of major airlines has changed relatively little since 1980, even though airlines have come and gone.

Deregulation created major opportunities for smaller airlines, known as nationals and regionals. Before deregulation, these smaller airlines tended to operate on the fringes of the service areas of the large commercial air carriers. The typical smaller airline was a fixed-base operator that provided scheduled air service to small communities using small aircraft that seated fewer than 30 passengers.

After deregulation, national and regional airlines became increasingly important sources for connecting traffic to major carriers. These connections led to the next significant trend to evolve from deregulation—the development of "code-sharing" agreements between the major and nonmajor air carriers. Code-sharing is a common industry practice in which one airline offers services in its own name for a particular city-pair, but some, or all, of the transportation is provided by another carrier. More recently, the larger air carriers began purchasing their smaller partners. The close relationship between the regional, national, and major air carriers continues to shape the industry today.

In 1999, the national and large regional carriers enplaned 84 million people, up from 51 million in 1980. The share of passengers enplaned by majors has increased over this period, however, going from 81 percent to 85 percent.

Rail

The freight railroad industry has consolidated greatly over the past 25 years. Today, there are only 8 Class I (major) railroads in the United States, down from 73 in 1975. Between 1975 and 1999, the Class I railroads increased their traffic (measured in ton-miles) by 90 percent, while their network (miles of road owned) declined by about 50 percent and the number of employees declined by about 60 percent. During this same period, Class I railroad industry labor productivity, measured by revenue ton-miles per employee, soared (figure 1). In 1975, Class I railroads owned approximately 192,000 miles of road (route-miles). By 1999, Class I companies owned about 99,000 miles of rail line. Many of

Figure 1
Class I Railroad Performance Indices: 1975–1999

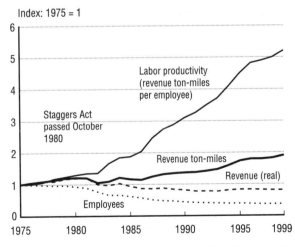

SOURCE: Association of American Railroads, *Railroad Facts* (Washington, DC: Annual issues).

the lines have been sold to new, aggressive regional and short-line railroads (Class II and III), especially since the Staggers Act of 1980 that encouraged sales to small railroads rather than abandonment. Today, these railroads operate a total of 50,000 miles of road [2].

Water

During the 1990s, the shipping industry underwent major consolidation in an effort to improve its efficiency and productivity. Some of the important mergers were P&O Container and Nedlloyd, Neptune Orient and APL Ltd., and Sealand and Maersk. Liner carriers[1] are currently using vessel-sharing arrangements with other carriers to improve productivity. As a result, individual companies have less need to provide direct services to multiple ports. Carriers can move cargo through a limited number of hub ports and use other modes, such as train, air, truck, or vessel feeder services, to connect the hub with the cargo's ultimate destination or origin. In the United States, the ports of Long Beach and Los Angeles in California are the largest container hub ports in North America.

The U.S. Congress deregulated the shipping industry in 1988 when it passed the Ocean Shipping Reform Act (OSRA). OSRA allows shippers and ocean carriers to enter, for the first time, into confidential service contracts that must be filed only with the Federal Maritime Commission. Previously, a system of conferences (voluntary associations of ocean carriers) set rates. Under earlier Acts, the carriers had to share rate information with all other shippers, who could then demand similar rates from ocean carriers. Now rates may be negotiated on a case-by-case, one-to-one basis between shippers and carriers. OSRA strengthens provisions that prohibit unfair foreign shipping practices and provides greater protection against

discriminatory actions. The Act could also lead to another round of consolidation in the industry.

Consolidation in the cruise line industry, through acquisitions and mergers, has provided the top companies with more financial strength and marketing muscle to promote their ships and control costs, contributing to the stability of the industry in the late 1990s. For instance, in 1998, the top four North American cruise lines controlled 82 percent of the North American cruise capacity, up from 61 percent in 1995. In fact, these companies controlled an even larger share of the market because their newer vessels tend to sail at higher percentages of capacity than those of smaller lines [3].

Motor Carriers

The motor carrier industry comprises truck and bus companies. In the mid-1970s, the motor carrier industry was regulated by the Interstate Commerce Commission (ICC), which controlled routes of service and rates through its rate bureaus. Startup companies were required to prove that their plan to provide new service was in the public's best interest. Only a limited number of truck and bus companies were authorized to provide service—18,000 truck companies in 1975 compared with nearly 500,000 companies in operation today [6]. Responding to concerns about the economic inefficiency of the trucking industry, ICC loosened the entry standards in the late 1970s. The Motor Carrier Act of 1980 further eased barriers to entry. In the early 1980s, the use of private carriers ("in-house" trucking fleets) declined as companies chose to take advantage of lower rates and improved service by for-hire carriers. Of the nearly 500,000 trucking companies providing service today, most have 6 or fewer trucks (table 1). About 3,200 carriers have more than 100 trucks [5].

Bus companies, too, were given authority to set rates and determine routes as a result of deregulation in 1982. Economic deregulation spurred strategic reorganization of the bus industry, creating conditions for improved serv-

---

[1] A cargo-carrying ship operated between specified ports on a regular basis for an advertised price, versus a chartered ship that operates for single deliveries to a variety of ports.

Table 1
Active Interstate Motor Carriers by Fleet Size: 2000

Fleet size (number of power units)	Number of carriers			
	Hazardous materials	Passenger carriers	All others	Total
1	9,083	5,927	204,269	**219,279**
2–6	17,249	4,535	139,021	**160,805**
7–20	9,028	1,470	32,058	**42,556**
21–100	5,194	832	9,799	**15,825**
101–5,000	1,644	147	1,417	**3,208**
Over 5,000	17	1	8	**26**
Unspecified	1,410	2,360	80,587	**84,357**
Total	**43,625**	**15,272**	**467,159**	**526,056**

NOTE: Data include intrastate hazardous materials carriers.

SOURCE: U.S. Department of Transportation, Federal Motor Carrier Safety Administration, *Motor Carrier Management Information System Report*, LS50B901 (Washington, DC: March 2000).

ices. In certain cases, however, deregulation resulted in diminished services.

Greyhound and Trailways merged in 1987 to provide a larger network of intercity bus service. This strategic agreement resulted in improved intercity service and better scheduling and fare information. In addition, new, smaller regional carriers have started providing service to specialized niche markets. These carriers not only serve geographic markets, but also sectors of the population, such as senior citizens, metropolitan commuters, vacation travelers, or luxury travelers. About 4,000 private motorcoach companies now operate in the United States and Canada, offering charters, tours, regular route service, and other bus services [1].

Following deregulation and with increasing competition from airlines and automobiles, bus companies eliminated many unprofitable routes and stops, particularly in rural areas. In 1982, more than 11,000 locations were served nationwide, down from 16,000 in the early 1970s [4]. Today, the number of locations served has fallen to just about 5,000, with much of the curtailed service in rural areas. The Transportation Equity Act for the 21st Century provides support for the intercity bus needs of rural residents.

Sources

1. American Bus Association, *Industry Profile: Motorcoach Industry Facts,* available at http://www.buses.org, as of July 26, 2000.

2. Association of American Railroads, *Railroad Facts* (Washington, DC: 2000).

3. Mathiesen, Oivind (ed.), *Cruise Industry News 1998 Annual* (New York, NY: Cruise Industry News, 1998).

4. U.S. General Accounting Office, *Surface Transportation: Availability of Intercity Bus Service Continues To Decline,* GAO/RECD-92-126 (Washington, DC: 1992).

5. U.S. Department of Transportation, Federal Motor Carrier Safety Administration, *Motor Carrier Management System Report LS50B901* (Washington, DC: March 2000).

6. ____. personal communication, Aug. 1, 2000.

Information Technology Use

From the telegraph used by railroads in the 19th century to radio and radar used in ships and planes at the beginning of the 20th century, information technology (IT) has enhanced the capabilities of our transportation systems. In recent years, these technologies have been integrated into all modes of transportation. Highway and transit applications of IT now are joining the other modes as new technology allows drivers to "navigate" roads.

Intelligent transportation systems (ITS) comprise a broad range of technologies, including those in the IT category, and help improve the efficiency, effectiveness, and safety of transportation. Travelers can obtain information and guidance from electronic surveillance, communications channels, and traffic analysis. ITS also boosts the capability to monitor, route, control, and manage information to facilitate travel.

The variety of technologies and approaches across the ITS spectrum, however, complicates the tracking of deployment. The U.S. Department of Transportation, Federal Highway Administration's ITS Joint Program Office conducted two surveys, in 1997 and 1999, to gauge urban implementation in 75 metropolitan areas in the United States [2]. The surveys collected data on deployment for nine ITS infrastructure components for highways, transit, and highway-rail grade crossings within the boundaries of metropolitan planning organizations (MPOs).

A single ITS component may utilize several technologies or approaches. For instance, electronic toll collection (ETC) technologies automatically collect payments through the application of in-vehicle, roadside, and communications technologies. Over 43 percent of the metropolitan areas surveyed had toll collection lanes with ETC capacity, up from 36 percent in 1997 [2].

Multiple ETC technology deployment highlights the growing importance of integrating ITS. Beyond measuring fixed ITS assets like vehicles, the ITS Joint Program Office also studies the integration among agencies operating the infrastructure. Federal officials define ITS integration as the transfer of information between three types of organizations: state departments of transportation, local governments, and transit agencies.

Traffic signal control and electronic toll collection are two of the top three highway ITS technologies currently being deployed (figure 1). These technologies directly benefit travelers by smoothing out trips on toll roads and signaled arterial roads. Highway-rail grade crossings have one of the lowest rates of deployment penetration, but a major federal initiative is providing funds to address this area (see the section on high-speed rail corridors elsewhere in this chapter).

The Global Positioning System (GPS) is being used in all transportation modes (even walking), although to what overall extent is uncertain. Thirty percent of the surveyed metropolitan areas showed some deployment of automatic vehicle location devices in fixed-route transit vehicles [2]. GPS is not only used for commercial aviation, but it is also used for general aviation. About 70 percent of corporate and over half of business-use aircraft have GPS devices, compared with about 40 percent of personal-use aircraft [1]. In 1996, the U.S. Coast Guard brought its Maritime Differential GPS (DGPS) online. Reference stations located every 200 miles along the coast and major rivers allow ships with the proper GPS receiving equipment to identify their positions within 5 to 10 meters, compared with 100 meters for other positioning systems. This is an important navigational aid, as some channels are less than 100 meters wide. The U.S. Department of Transportation is

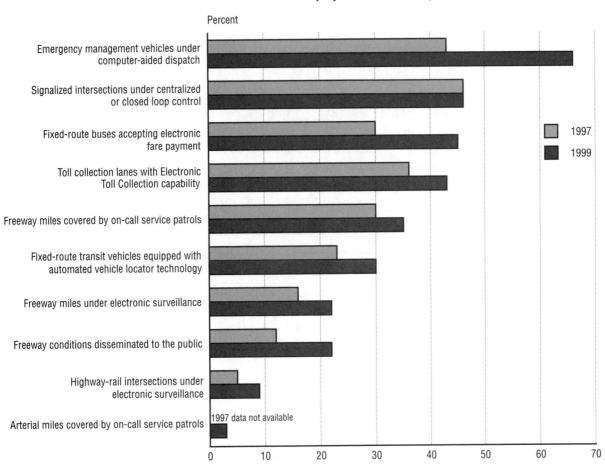

Figure 1
ITS Infrastructure Deployment in 75 Metropolitan Areas: 1997 and 1999

SOURCE: U.S. Department of Transportation, Federal Highway Administration, ITS Joint Program Office, *Tracking the Deployment of the Integrated Metropolitan Transportation Systems Infrastructure in the USA: FY 1999 Results*, May 2000, available at www.itsdocs.fhwa.dot.gov, as of Feb. 8, 2001.

now implementing Nationwide DGPS to bring the same positioning accuracy to all parts of the continental United States and Alaska.

Railroads are developing positive train control (PTC) systems that will use nationwide DGPS to provide precise positioning information. PTC can prevent overspeed accidents and collisions between trains and between trains and maintenance-of-way crews. PTC can also improve the efficiency of railroad operations by reducing train over-the-road delays and increasing running time reliability, track capacity, and asset utilization. [3].

Sources

1. U.S. Department of Transportation, Federal Aviation Administration, General Aviation and Air Taxi Survey, 1996, available at http://api.hq.faa.gov/ga96/gatoc. htm, as of Dec. 5, 2000, table 7.2.

2. U.S. Department of Transportation, Federal Highway Administration, ITS Joint Program Office, *Tracking the Deployment of the Integrated Metropolitan Transportation Systems Infrastructure in the USA: FY 1999 Results,* May 2000, available at http://www.itsdocs.fhwa.dot.gov, as of Feb. 8, 2001.

3. ____. "What Is Positive Train Control?" available at http://frarnd.volpe.dot.gov, as of Dec. 4, 2000.

Roads

oad building and widening continue to slowly increase the extent of the public road system and the length of lane-miles open to the public. Since 1980, miles of public road increased only about 1.5 percent, although lane-miles increased twice as much (3.2 percent). Paved roadways constituted about 62 percent of all highway mileage in 1999, up from 54 percent in 1980 and 24 percent in 1950. Nearly all of the public roads in urban areas are paved. However, about half of the miles of rural public roads are unpaved, accounting for 97 percent of total unpaved public road miles—much the same ratio as in 1980 (figure 1) [1].

Source

1. U.S. Department of Transportation, Federal Highway Administration, *Highway Statistics* (Washington, DC: Annual editions).

Figure 1
Urban and Rural Roadway Mileage by Surface Type: 1950–1999

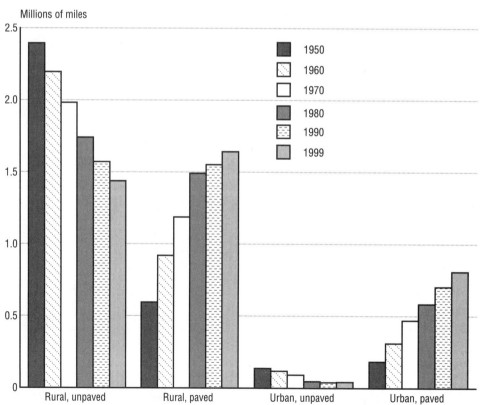

SOURCES: U.S. Department of Transportation, Federal Highway Administration, *Highway Statistics* (Washington, DC: Annual editions), table HM-12.
_____. *Highway Statistics Summary to 1995* (Washington, DC: 1997), table HM-212.

U.S. Vehicle Fleet

Between 1989 and 1999, the most noteworthy development in the U.S. vehicle fleet was the rapid growth in the number of registered light-duty trucks, including minivans, pickups, and sport utility vehicles (figure 1). During this period, the number of these vehicles grew from nearly 46 million to over 75 million, an increase of about 64 percent. This category now accounts for 34 percent of the total U.S. fleet, up from 23 percent in 1989. Fueled by the rapid increase in the number of light-duty trucks, the total U.S. fleet grew to nearly 220 million vehicles in 1999, an 11 percent increase over the 198 million vehicles registered in 1989 [1].

In contrast to the rapid growth of light-duty trucks, the number of other types of vehicles remained relatively steady, while the shares declined in some cases. The number of cars, though still 60 percent of the total fleet at nearly 132 million vehicles in 1999, decreased slightly over the past 10 years, and accounted for nearly 10 percent less of the total fleet in 1999 than in 1989. Over the same period, the number of large trucks and buses increased at roughly the same rate as the total U.S. fleet, while motorcycle registrations declined somewhat [1].

Source

1. U.S. Department of Transportation, Federal Highway Administration, *Highway Statistics 1999* (Washington, DC: 2001).

Figure 1
Highway Vehicle Trends: 1989–1999

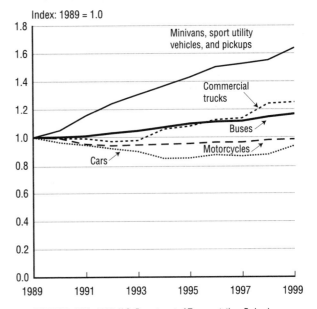

SOURCES: 1991–1995: U.S. Department of Transportation, Federal Highway Administration, *Highway Statistics Summary to 1995* (Washington, DC: 1997), tables MV-201 and VM201a.
1996–1997: ____. *Highway Statistics 1997* (Washington, DC: 1998), table VM-1.
1998–1999: ____. *Highway Statistics 1999* (Washington, DC: 2000), table VM-1.

High-Speed Rail Corridors

In recent years, high-speed rail (HSR) service for intercity passengers has experienced renewed interest). HSR technologies allow trains to travel at top speeds of 90 to 300 miles per hour (the highest speeds can be achieved by trains powered by magnetic levitation). Several parts of the country have HSR plans, and a number of rail corridors are under development.

In May 2000, the U.S. Department of Transportation announced grants totaling $5.3 million to five HSR corridors to eliminate hazards at public and private highway-rail grade crossings [1]. Funds can be used to close crossings, install advanced train control or traffic control systems, and upgrade warning devices, among other things. The five initially designated corridors were the Pacific Northwest Corridor, the Chicago Hub Corridor, the Gulf Coast Corridor, Southeast Corridor, and the Empire Corridor. In October 2000, the program was extended (see map below).

Sources

1. Slater, Rodney, Secretary of Transportation, U.S. Department of Transportation, "Funding for Grade Crossing Hazard Elimination Programs in Designated High-Speed Rail Corridors," May 12, 2000.

2. _____. "U.S. Transportation Secretary Slater Designates Two New High-Speed Rail Corridors, press release, Oct. 11, 2000, available at http://www.dot.gov/affairs/fra2000.htm, as of June 2001.

Designated High-Speed Rail Corridors: 2000

SOURCE: U.S. Department of Transportation, Federal Railroad Administration, 2000.

Urban Transit

Urban transit is a complex mix of heavy, light, and commuter rail; buses and demand responsive vehicles; ferries; and other less prevalent types such as inclined planes, trolley buses, and automated guideways. The capacity of this mode, measured by revenue vehicle-miles of service provided, grew by nearly 30 percent between 1991 and 1999 to over 3 billion miles. The U.S. population grew by 8 percent over this same period. The largest transit modes, bus and heavy rail, showed the slowest growth during this period (about 10 percent), while demand responsive transit grew the fastest (125 percent) (figure 1). Among rail modes, both light rail and commuter rail have seen substantial increases in service provided over this period, 77 percent and 23 percent, respectively [1].

The number of urban transit vehicles in rush hour service increased 26 percent between 1991 and 1999, with the number of buses rising 10 percent from 42,900 to 47,100, and rail vehicles moving up 8 percent from 12,900 to 13,900. The largest percentage gain occurred for commuter rail vehicles—17 percent, compared with 3 percent for heavy rail and 12 percent for light rail. Vehicles used in demand-responsive service soared nearly 90 percent from 8,400 in 1991 to 15,900 in 1999 [2].

The Federal Transit Administration assesses the condition of transit vehicles using a rating scale from 5.0 to 0.0 (excellent to poor condition).[1] Between 1987 and 1997, the average condition of most types of buses remained about the same, although the condition of vans improved (table 1). Most transit rail vehicles

---

[1] These ratings come from the Transit Economic Requirements Model, which uses nonlinear deterioration curves developed from transit asset condition and replacement records.

Figure 1
Revenue Vehicle-Miles by Urban Transit Mode: 1991–1999

Millions of revenue vehicle-miles

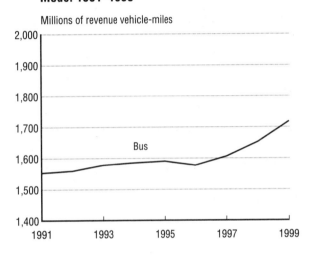

Millions of revenue vehicle-miles

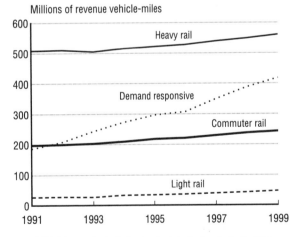

NOTE: Other modes, including ferryboat, trolley bus, and automated guideway, are not shown.

SOURCE: U.S. Department of Transportation, Federal Transit Administration, National Transit Database, Various years.

Table 1
Condition of Transit Vehicles: 1987–1997

Type of vehicle	Rating	
	1987	1997
Articulated buses	3.1	2.7
Full-size buses	3.0	3.0
Mid-size buses	3.0	3.0
Small buses	3.3	3.4
Vans	3.2	3.5
Locomotives	4.5	4.5
Heavy railcars	4.7	3.9
Unpowered commuter railcars	4.2	4.2
Powered commuter railcars	4.8	3.7
Light-rail vehicles	4.5	4.6

Key to ratings: 0.0–1.99 = poor; 2.0–2.99 = substandard; 3.0–3.99 = adequate; 4.0–4.9 = good; 4.9–5.0 = excellent.

SOURCE: U.S. Department of Transportation, Federal Highway Administration and Federal Transit Administration, *1999 Status of the Nation's Surface Transportation System: Condition and Performance* (Washington, DC: 2000).

were in better condition than buses, but heavy railcars and powered commuter railcars showed notable deterioration over this period [1].

Sources

1. U.S. Department of Transportation, Federal Highway Administration and Federal Transit Administration, *1999 Status of the Nation's Surface Transportation System: Condition and Performance* (Washington, DC: 2000).

2. U.S. Department of Transportation, Federal Transit Administration, National Transit Database, various years.

U.S.-Flag Vessels

More than 41,000 U.S.-flag vessels were available for service in U.S. maritime trade as of December 1999 [1], and 80 percent were in use that year. The segments of the U.S.-flag fleet with the highest percentage of operating vessels were dry bulk vessels, dry cargo barges, and tank barges (table 1). Barges operate primarily on the U.S. inland waterways and carry more than 90 percent of that tonnage [2]. Tankers, on the other hand, provide service primarily on the U.S. coastal waterways (table 2).

Vessel owners have been reflagging their ships to foreign registries in order to reduce operating costs (e.g., higher wages of U.S. crews). In addition, major U.S. vessel owners and operators

Table 1
U.S.-Flag Vessels: Available vs. Operating, by Vessel Type: 1999

Vessel type	Vessels available	Vessels operating	Percent operating	Total operating companies
Self-propelled	**8,379**	**4,747**	**57**	**1,001**
Dry cargo (total)	695	448	65	135
Dry bulk	68	57	84	15
Containership	74	49	66	3
General cargo	320	186	58	92
Specialized	233	156	67	41
Passenger	970	599	62	285
Offshore support	1,470	719	49	120
Tanker	142	113	80	41
Towboat	5,098	2,867	56	670
Nonself-propelled	**33,387**	**28,272**	**86**	**467**
Dry cargo (total)	29,414	24,962	87	313
Tank barge (total)	3,973	3,310	84	200

NOTE: Totals are greater than the sum because of unclassified vessels.

SOURCE: U.S. Army Corps of Engineers, Water Resources Support Center, *Waterborne Transportation Lines of the United States, Calendar Year 1999, Volume 1–National Summaries* (New Orleans, LA: Dec. 31, 2000).

Table 2
Selected U.S. Vessels Available to Operate: By Region, as of December 31, 1999

Vessel type	Atlantic, Gulf & Pacific Coasts	Mississippi River System & Gulf Intracoastal Waterway	Great Lakes System
Self-propelled			
Dry cargo	1,314	1,376	220
Tankers	135	3	4
Nonself-propelled (barges)			
Dry cargo	3,095	26,031	257
Tank barge	629	3,324	20

SOURCE: U.S. Army Corps of Engineers, Water Resources Support Center, *Waterborne Transportation Lines of the United States, Calendar Year 1999, Volume 1–National Summaries* (New Orleans, LA: Dec. 31, 2000).

have, in recent years, merged with or were acquired by foreign companies.

About 42 percent of the U.S. fleet is more than 20 years old (table 3). Over the next few years, many vessels in all segments will need to be replaced or rebuilt, potentially increasing activity for U.S. shipyards. In addition, approximately one-third of the self-propelled U.S. domestic fleet is more than 25 years old. While the high cost of building in U.S. shipyards may limit replacement in some segments, there are encouraging prospects in others, such as the increasing use of articulated tug/barge units as an alternative to tankers.

Sources

1. U.S. Army Corps of Engineers, Navigation Data Center, "The U.S. Waterway System—Transportation Facts," December 1999.

2. U.S. Department of Transportation, Bureau of Transportation Statistics, Maritime Administration, and U.S. Coast Guard, *Maritime Trade and Transportation 99*, BTS99-02 (Washington, DC: 1999).

(continued on next page)

Table 3
Age of the U.S.-Flag Vessels: As of December 31, 1999[1]

Vessel type	Number	Age (percentage of total for each vessel type)[2]					
		≤ 5	6–10	11–15	16–20	21–25	> 25
Vessels (total)[3]	**41,766**	**19.1**	**9.4**	**4.2**	**24.3**	**18.0**	**24.6**
Self-propelled (total)	**8,379**	**9.1**	**5.4**	**6.0**	**23.5**	**17.4**	**38.4**
Dry cargo	695	8.6	7.1	14.0	21.0	14.2	35.0
Tanker	142	8.5	2.1	8.5	24.6	21.1	35.2
Towboat	5,098	5.9	2.7	2.9	21.6	18.7	48.0
Passenger[4]	970	14.8	15.1	18.9	12.4	9.8	29.1
Offshore supply	1,470	16.7	7.8	4.1	38.8	19.3	13.0
Barge (total)	**33,387**	**21.6**	**10.5**	**3.8**	**24.4**	**18.2**	**21.1**
Dry covered	13,477	27.4	6.7	0.8	33.7	19.2	12.2
Dry open	9,146	22.5	17.5	7.6	22.2	15.0	15.1
Lash/SEABEE[5]	1,796	0.0	16.0	6.2	2.0	43.9	31.9
Deck	4,842	17.9	8.2	6.3	16.0	11.0	38.0
Other dry cargo[6]	153	7.2	5.2	7.2	24.2	11.1	37.3
Single hull tank	685	3.5	1.9	1.9	19.3	11.4	61.9
Double hull tank	2,621	16.6	10.4	0.8	19.0	21.6	31.7
Other tank[7]	667	16.0	1.8	0.9	16.9	17.2	45.9

[1] Survey date as of December 31, 1998; includes updates through December 2000.
[2] Age (in years) is based on the year the vessel was built or rebuilt, using calendar year 1999 as the base year.
[3] Total is greater than the sum because of 4 unclassified vessels and 168 of unknown age; figures include vessels available for operation.
[4] Includes passenger and excursion/sightseeing.
[5] Lighter aboard ship (barge rides on a mother ship).
[6] Includes dry cargo barges that may be open or covered, railcar, pontoon, roll-on/roll-off, container, or convertible.
[7] Includes tank barges that may be double-sided only, double-bottom only, or not elsewhere classified.

SOURCE: U.S. Army Corps of Engineers, Navigation Data Center, U.S. Waterway System Facts, available at http://www.wrsc.usace.army.mil/ndc/wcsc.htm.

Ports and Cargo-Handling Services

In 1999, world waterborne trade reached 5.23 billion metric tons, the 14th year of consecutive growth [2], spurring global competitiveness among ports worldwide. U.S. ports that engage in foreign trade, and their strategic global partners, evaluate port operations in order to improve productivity. Landside congestion, intermodal connectors, water depth, and direction and concentration of trade can affect productivity.

Landside access to water ports comprises a system of intermodal rail and truck services [5]. Landside congestion, caused by inadequate control of truck traffic into and out of port terminals combined with the lack of adequate on-dock or near-dock rail access, affects the productivity of U.S. ports and the flow of U.S. international trade. Generally, productivity is difficult to measure. Cargo throughput can be used to measure physical productivity, however, it does not take into account the more efficient use of resources gained from capital investment [1].

The U.S. port industry has invested approximately $21 billion since 1946 on improvements in its facilities and infrastructure—about one-third of that total (approximately $6.6 billion) was invested between 1995 and 1999. Types of investment include new construction and modernization/rehabilitation. In 1999, new construction accounted for two-thirds of the total expenditures. Since 1994, the U.S. Pacific regions accounted for more than 50 percent of the annual investments and the majority of this investment was in the South Pacific region [4]. In the 1970s and 1980s, the North Atlantic region ranked highest in the level of total industry investments.

Changes in vessel design impact access to both landside and waterside services. For example, container vessels have increased in size and capacity, which, in turn, drives a need for adequate transshipment hub and feeder ports. Hub ports must have large capacity cranes, deep water, a large amount of backup land, and direct intermodal connections. The top ports in U.S. foreign trade are deep draft (with drafts of at least 40 feet) [3]. The majority of containerships with capacities greater than 5,000 20-foot equivalent units (TEUs) call at ports in the U.S. Pacific region (table 1).

Imports exceed exports in maritime foreign trade, particularly in the container trade. Containers entering the United States are full, but the amount of exported cargo is not enough to fill the containers for a return trip. As a result, empty containers are stacked at port terminals or intermodal transfer facilities in increasing numbers. Moreover, U.S. container trade is increasingly concentrated (see pages 121 to 122 for more discussion of container trade). Today, Long Beach and Los Angeles are the top U.S. container ports. The concentration of port activity in the U.S. container trade has increased since 1998, so that the top 10 ports in the trade handle more than 80 percent of total TEUs (table 2).

Sources

1. Robinson, Dolly, Measures of Port Productivity and Container Terminal Design, *Cargo Systems*, April 1999.
2. United Nations Conference on Trade and Development, *Review of Maritime Transport 2000*, Report by the UNCTAD Secretariat (New York, NY: United Nations, 2000).
3. U.S. Department of Transportation, *The Maritime Transportation System: A Report to Congress* (Washington, DC: 1999).
4. U.S. Department of Transportation, Office of Intermodalism, *The Impacts of Changes in Ship Design on Transportation Infrastructure and Operations* (Washington, DC: February 1998).
5. U.S. Department of Transportation, Maritime Administration, *U.S. Port Development Expenditure Report* (Washington, DC: December 2000).

Table 1
Top 15 U.S. Containership Port Calls, by Vessel Size: Calendar Year 1999
Vessels engaged in U.S. foreign transportation[1]

Port		Capacity of vessel (20-foot equivalent units)				
	All vessels	<2,000	2,001–3,000	3,001–4,000	4,001–5,000	>5,000
New York, NY	1,983	465	710	575	227	6
Charleston, SC	1,458	352	566	298	236	6
Long Beach, CA	1,256	307	246	357	168	178
Los Angeles, CA	1,207	429	208	220	294	56
Oakland, CA	1,110	123	291	405	183	108
Norfolk, VA	1,105	155	411	394	139	6
Miami, FL	745	347	244	154	0	0
Seattle, WA	638	157	180	175	57	69
Houston, TX	623	346	169	58	50	0
Savannah, GA	590	144	156	264	26	0
New Orleans, LA	434	297	119	18	0	0
Port Everglades, FL	412	297	63	0	52	0
Baltimore, MD	396	192	123	30	51	0
Tacoma, WA	376	33	105	83	30	125
San Juan, PR	337	307	30	0	0	0
All other ports	2,016	1,176	569	95	172	4
Total all U.S. ports	**14,686**	**5,127**	**4,190**	**3,126**	**1,685**	**558**
Top 15 as a percentage of total	**86**	**77**	**86**	**97**	**90**	**99**

[1] Containerships 10,000 deadweight tons and above.

SOURCE: U.S. Department of Transportation, Maritime Administration, *U.S. Vessel Movements,* 1999, available at http://www.marad.dot.gov/Marad_statistics/index.html.

Table 2
Top 10 U.S. Container Ports: 2000
(thousands of 20-foot equivalent units)

Port	1992	1993	1994	1995	1996	1997	1998	1999	2000
Los Angeles, CA	1,639	1,627	1,786	1,849	1,873	2,085	2,293	2,552	3,228
Long Beach, CA	1,356	1,543	1,939	2,137	2,357	2,673	2,852	3,048	3,203
New York, NY	1,294	1,306	1,404	1,537	1,533	1,738	1,884	2,027	2,201
Charleston, SC	564	579	655	758	801	955	1,035	1,170	1,246
Oakland, CA	746	772	879	919	803	843	902	915	989
Seattle, WA	743	781	967	993	939	953	977	962	959
Norfolk, VA	519	519	570	647	681	770	793	829	851
Houston, TX	368	392	419	489	538	609	657	714	733
Savannah, GA	387	406	418	445	456	529	558	625	720
Miami, FL	418	469	497	497	505	624	603	618	683
Total top 10 ports	**8,035**	**8,394**	**9,534**	**10,271**	**10,486**	**11,779**	**12,553**	**13,459**	**14,813**
Top 10 as a percentage of total	**76%**	**69%**	**72%**	**77%**	**71%**	**76%**	**81%**	**81%**	**83%**
Total all ports	**10,583**	**12,238**	**13,173**	**13,328**	**14,794**	**15,556**	**15,556**	**16,564**	**17,938**

SOURCE: Journal of Commerce, Port Import/Export Reporting Service (PIERS), various data files.

Airport Runways

In general, U.S. airport runway pavement is in good condition. When it is deteriorated, runway pavement can cause damage to aircraft turbines, propellers, and landing gear, and may result in runway closure. To prevent major problems, runway pavement requires regular maintenance to seal cracks and repair damage as well as a major overhaul every 15 to 20 years [1]. The U.S. Department of Transportation, Federal Aviation Administration (FAA), inspects runways at public-use airports and classifies runway condition as good (all cracks and joints sealed), fair (mild surface cracking, unsealed joints, and slab edge spalling), or poor (large open cracks, surface and edge spalling, vegetation growing through cracks and joints).

Airport runway quality improved from 1986 to 1999 (table 1). At the over 3,000 airports listed in the FAA's National Plan of Integrated Airport Systems (NPIAS), runways in fair or poor condition dropped from 39 percent in 1986 to 28 percent in 1999. Those in good condition rose from 61 percent to 72 percent. At commercial service airports, a subset of the NPIAS, only 2 percent of runways were in poor condition in 1999, but the percentage in poor or fair condition—22 percent—has remained the same since 1986. Overall, however, commercial airport runways remain in better condition than other NPIAS airports.

Source

1. U.S. Department of Transportation, Federal Aviation Administration, *National Plan of Integrated Airport Systems (1998-2002)* (Washington, DC: 1999).

Table 1
U.S. Airport Runway Pavement Conditions: 1986 and 1999

	1986	1999
NPIAS[1] airports, total	**3,243**	**3,344**
Condition (%)		
Good	61	72
Fair	28	23
Poor	11	5
Commercial service airports,[2] total	**550**	**547**
Condition (%)		
Good	78	78
Fair	15	20
Poor	7	2

[1] The Federal Aviation Administration's (FAA) National Plan of Integrated Airport Systems (NPIAS) is composed of all commercial service airports, all reliever airports, and selected general aviation airports. It does not include over 1,000 publicly owned public-use landing areas, privately owned public-use airports, and other civil landing areas not open to the general public. NPIAS airports account for 100% of all enplanements and serve 91.5% of all aircraft (based on an estimated fleet of 200,000 aircraft). In 1997, there were 14,961 non-NPIAS airports.
[2] Commercial service airports are defined as public airports receiving scheduled passenger service and having at least 2,500 enplaned passengers per year.

NOTE: Data are as of January 1 of each year. Runway pavement condition is classified by FAA as follows:
Good: All cracks and joints are sealed.
Fair: Mild surface cracking, unsealed joints, and slab edge spalling.
Poor: Large open cracks, surface and edge spalling, vegetation growing through cracks and joints.

SOURCE: Various sources as cited in U.S. Department of Transportation, Bureau of Transportation Statistics, *National Transportation Statistics 2000* (Washington, DC: 2001).

Highway Conditions

Overall, in 1999, 44 percent of the nation's roads were classified as being in good or very good condition and 17 percent as mediocre or poor; the rest were classified as fair (table 1). The generally poorer condition of urban roads, as compared with rural roads, can be attributed to the higher levels of traffic they carry. Since 1993, the condition of all roadways shows only modest improvement with rural areas outpacing urban areas [1].

In 1999, about 30 percent of urban Interstates were in poor or mediocre condition, as measured using Interstate standards (which are higher than

Figure 1
Urban and Rural Interstates in Poor or Mediocre Condition: 1993–1999

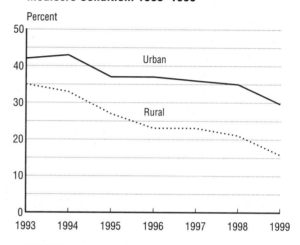

SOURCE: U.S. Department of Transportation, Federal Highway Administration, *Highway Statistics* (Washington, DC: Annual issues).

standards for other types of roads). By contrast, only 16 percent of rural Interstate miles were classified as poor or mediocre. Despite continued growth in vehicle travel, some improvement can be seen in the condition of urban Interstates since 1993, when more than 40 percent were classified as poor or mediocre (figure 1).

Table 1
Condition of Roads: 1993 and 1999
(Percent)

Type of road	Poor and mediocre	Fair	Good and very good
Urban			
1993	25	42	33
1999	24	39	37
Rural			
1993	19	45	36
1999	14	39	47
Total			
1993	21	44	35
1999	17	39	44

NOTE: Rural does not include minor collectors or local.

SOURCE: U.S. Department of Transportation, Federal Highway Administration, *Highway Statistics* (Washington, DC: Annual issues), table HM-63 for rural major collectors, urban minor arterials, and urban collectors; table HM-64 for all other categories.

Source

1. U.S. Department of Transportation, Federal Highway Administration, *Highway Statistics* (Washington, DC: Annual issues).

Bridge Conditions

The condition of bridges nationwide has improved markedly since 1990. Of the nearly 600,000 roadway bridges in 1999, about 29 percent were found to be structurally deficient or functionally obsolete, compared with 42 percent in 1990. About 15 percent of *all* bridges were structurally deficient and 14 percent functionally obsolete in 1999 [1]. Structurally deficient bridges are those that are restricted to light vehicles, require immediate rehabilitation to remain open, or are closed. Functionally obsolete bridges are those with deck geometry (e.g., lane width), load carrying capacity, clearance, or approach roadway alignment that no longer meet the criteria for the system of which the bridge is a part. Overall in the 1990s, there was a greater reduction in the number and share of structurally deficient bridges than those deemed to be functionally obsolete (figure 1).

Overall, bridges in rural areas suffer more from structural deficiencies than functional obsolescence, whereas the reverse is true in urban areas (see map and table 1). Nearly one-quarter of bridges in rural areas that support local roads were structurally deficient and one-fifth of urban Interstate bridges were functionally obsolete in 1999. Nevertheless, a large number of both structurally deficient and functionally obsolete bridges support local roads in rural areas [1].

Figure 1
Deficient Bridges: 1990–1999

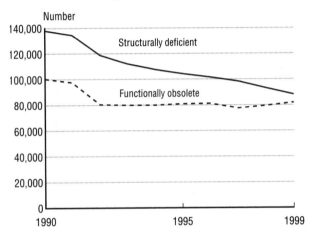

SOURCE: U.S. Department of Transportation, Federal Highway Administration, Office of Engineering, Bridge Division, National Bridge Inventory database, available at http://www.fhwa.dot.gov/bridge/britab.htm, as of Oct. 27, 2000.

Source

1. U.S. Department of Transportation, Federal Highway Administration, Office of Engineering, Bridge Division, National Bridge Inventory database, available at http://www.fhwa.dot.gov/bridge/britab.htm, as of Oct. 27, 2000.

(continued on next page)

Bridge Condition by State: 1999

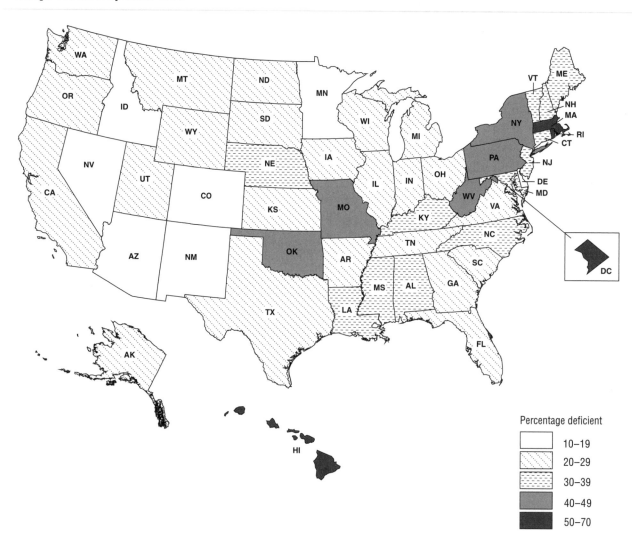

Percentage deficient

	10–19
	20–29
	30–39
	40–49
	50–70

SOURCE: U.S. Department of Transportation, Federal Highway Administration, Office of Engineering, Bridge Division, National Bridge Inventory database, available at http://www.fhwa.dot.gov/bridge/britab.htm, as of Oct. 27, 2000.

Table 1
Bridge Conditions by Functional Class: 1999

Type of roadway	Not deficient Number	Percent	Structurally deficient Number	Percent	Functionally obsolete Number	Percent
Rural						
Interstates	23,021	84	1,098	4	3,395	12
Other principal arterials	29,317	83	2,305	7	3,734	11
Minor arterials	30,656	79	3,581	9	4,612	12
Major collectors	73,354	77	11,979	13	10,315	11
Minor collectors	34,468	72	7,158	15	5,928	12
Local roads	136,099	65	49,332	23	24,851	12
Rural total	**326,915**	**72**	**75,453**	**17**	**52,835**	**12**
Urban						
Interstates	20,233	73	1,692	6	5,805	21
Other freeways and expressways	11,457	73	928	6	3,347	21
Other principal arterials	16,037	67	2,424	10	5,431	23
Minor arterials	14,126	62	2,576	11	5,992	26
Collectors	9,313	62	1,959	13	3,708	25
Local roads	17,141	68	3,388	13	4,782	19
Urban total	**88,307**	**68**	**12,967**	**10**	**29,065**	**22**
Rural and urban total	**415,222**	**71**	**88,420**	**15**	**81,900**	**14**

SOURCE: U.S. Department of Transportation, Federal Highway Administration, Office of Engineering, Bridge Division, National Bridge Inventory database, available at http://www.fhwa.dot.gov/bridge/britab.htm, as of Oct. 27, 2000.

Chapter 3
Transportation Safety

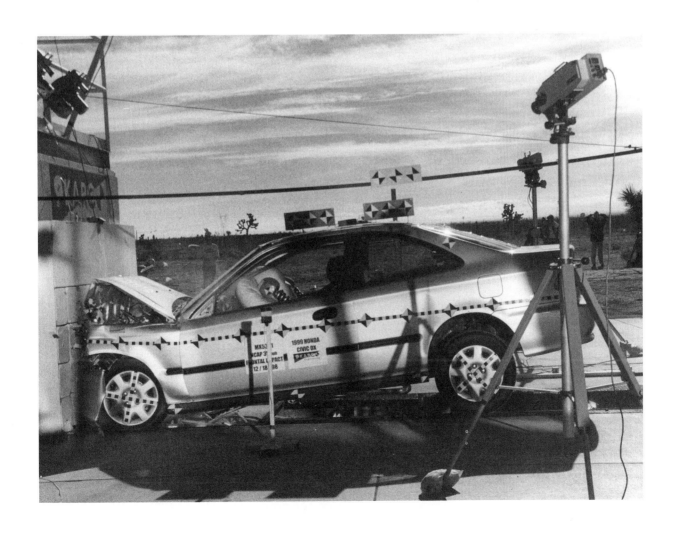

Introduction

The highest priority of the U.S. Department of Transportation (DOT) is to "promote public health and safety by working toward the elimination of transportation-related deaths, injuries, and property damage" [1]. The United States has made much progress in reducing the number of transportation-related deaths, but crashes and incidents involving transportation vehicles, vessels, aircraft, and pipelines still claimed nearly 44,000 lives and injured more than 3 million people in 1999. Transportation accidents are the seventh single leading cause of death in the United States (figure 1). However, motor vehicle crashes are the leading cause of death for people between 6 and 27 years of age.

Figure 1
**Leading Causes of Death of People of
All Ages in the United States: 1998**
(In thousands)

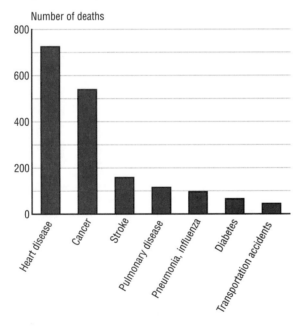

SOURCES: Diseases—U.S. Department of Health and Human Services, Centers for Disease Control and Prevention, National Center for Health Statistics, *National Vital Statistics Reports*, vol. 47, No. 25, October 1999. Transportation accidents—U.S. Department of Transportation, Bureau of Transportation Statistics, *National Transportation Statistics 2000* (Washington, DC: 2001).

Motor vehicle collisions account for about 95 percent of transportation-related deaths and an even higher percentage of transportation injuries. Human behavior—such as alcohol and drug use, reckless operation of vehicles, failure to properly use occupant protection devices, and fatigue—is a major factor in a high proportion of crashes.

DOT has set specific targets for the next few years to improve transportation safety. These include goals to lower the U.S. commercial air carrier fatal crash rate by 80 percent by 2007, reduce highway fatalities by 20 percent by 2008, and reduce commercial truck-related fatalities by 50 percent by 2010. Specific safety initiatives for rail, transit, maritime, and pipelines are also in place.

Source

1. U.S. Department of Transportation, *1999 Strategic Plan* (Washington, DC: September 2000).

Transportation Fatalities: A Modal Picture

Over the last 25 years, fatalities on the nation's roads, rails, and waters and in the skies have declined (figure 1). Despite progress, transportation crashes and incidents claimed 43,873 lives in 1999, of which 41,611 involved highway vehicles. (The National Highway Traffic Safety Administration's early assessment of highway fatalities in 2000 is 41,800.) Occupants of passenger cars and light trucks (i.e., sport utility vehicles, vans and minivans, and pickup trucks) accounted for over 70 percent of the transportation fatalities in 1999; pedestrians, motorcyclists, bicyclists, and others involved in motor vehicle collisions accounted for most of the remaining deaths (table 1).

Of the 2,262 transportation fatalities in 1999 that did not involve highway vehicles, recreational boating and general aviation (e.g., private planes for individual and business use) together claimed the lives of 1,364 people. Commercial carriers (airlines, trains, waterborne vessels, and buses) accounted for slightly under 900 fatalities. Many of these were bystanders and others outside of vehicles.

Figure 1
Total Fatalities by All Modes of Transportation

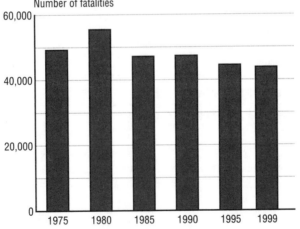

NOTE: For 1975, 1980, and 1985 some double counting may be included. The double counting affects about 1 percent of the data and should not impact the trend shown in the chart.

SOURCE: Various sources as cited in U.S. Department of Transportation, Bureau of Transportation Statistics, *National Transportation Statistics 2000* (Washington, DC: 2001).

Table 1
Distribution of Transportation Fatalities by Mode: 1999

Category	Number	Percent
Passenger car occupants	20,818	47.5
Light-truck occupants	11,243	25.6
Pedestrians struck by motor vehicles	4,906	11.2
Motorcyclists	2,472	5.6
Large-truck occupants	758	1.7
Pedalcyclists struck by motor vehicles	750	1.7
Recreational boating	734	1.7
General aviation	630	1.4
Trespassers on railroad property (excluding grade crossings)	478	1.1
Other and unknown motor vehicle occupants	457	1.0
Other nonoccupants struck by motor vehicles[1]	149	0.3
Heavy-rail transit (subway)	84	0.2
Waterborne transportation (nonvessel-related)	67	0.2
Bus occupants (school, intercity, and transit)	58	0.1
Grade crossings (not involving motor vehicles)	57	0.1
Waterborne transportation (vessel-related)	44	0.1
Railroad employees/contractors	43	0.1
Air taxi	38	0.09
Gas distribution pipelines	20	0.05
Light-rail transit	17	0.04
Air carriers	12	0.03
Commuter air	12	0.03
Transit buses (not related to accidents)[2]	11	0.03
Railroad[3]	9	0.02
Hazardous liquid pipelines	4	0.01
Gas transmission pipelines	2	<0.01
Total[4]	**43,873**	**100.0**
Redundant with above[5]		
Grade crossings, with motor vehicles	345	
Commuter rail (included in railroad)	95	
Transit buses (accident-related)	91	
Passengers on railroad trains	14	
Demand responsive transit (accident-related)	1	

[1] Includes all nonoccupant fatalities, except pedalcyclists and pedestrians.
[2] Includes incidents such as suicides, heart attacks, and shootings.
[3] Includes fatalities outside trains.
[4] Unless otherwise specified, includes fatalities outside the vehicle.
[5] Fatalities at grade crossings with motor vehicles are included under relevant motor vehicle modes. Commuter rail fatalities are counted under railroad. For transit bus and demand responsive transit accidents, occupant fatalities are counted under "bus" and nonoccupant fatalities are counted under "pedestrians," "pedalcyclists," or other motor vehicle categories.

SOURCES:
Air: National Transportation Safety Board, available at http://www.ntsb.gov/aviation, as of April 2000.
Highway: U.S. Department of Transportation, National Highway Traffic Safety Administration, *Traffic Safety Facts 1998* (DOT HS 808 983) (Washington, DC: October 1999), table 4, and personal communication, Oct. 4, 1999.
Railroad: U.S. Department of Transportation, Federal Railroad Administration, *Railroad Safety Statistics, Annual Report 1999* (Washington, DC: August 2000), table 1-1.
Transit: U.S. Department of Transportation, Federal Transit Administration, *Safety Management Information Statistics* (Washington, DC: Annual issues).
Waterborne transportation: U.S. Department of Transportation, U.S. Coast Guard, Office of Investigations and Analysis, Compliance Analysis Division (G-MOA-2), personal communication, Apr. 13, 1999.
Recreational boating: U.S. Department of Transportation, U.S. Coast Guard, Office of Boating Safety, *Boating Statistics* (Washington, DC: Annual issues).
Pipeline: U.S. Department of Transportation, Research and Special Programs Administration, Office of Pipeline Safety, available at http://ops.dot.gov, as of June 28, 2000.

Transportation Fatality Rates

The more people travel, the greater the risk they incur. Thus, using the absolute numbers of fatalities to compare the safety of a given mode over time (table 1) can be misleading, since any change in the fatality numbers might be explained by a change in the amount of transportation activity. A clearer picture can be derived from exposure rates. Exposure rates are calculated by dividing the absolute numbers of fatalities (or other adverse outcome) by an activity measure, such as number of trips, number of miles traveled, or number of hours of vehicle operation.

Figure 1 shows fatality rates for selected modes for a time period of two decades or more. It is clear that safety in most modes has improved over the last 25 years. However, for several of the modes, the greatest improvement in fatality rates tended to occur in the earlier years of the period.

The activity measures used as denominators are not the same for all modes. For highway travel, exposure to risk is approximately proportional to distance traveled, hence the use of vehicle-miles as the denominator. For aviation, the greatest proportion of crashes occurs during takeoff and landing; hence risk is approximately proportional to the number of operations (measured as departures). Data on departures are not available for general aviation for recent years, so hours flown is used instead. For some means of travel, there are no good measures of the risks entailed. For example, while over 4,900 pedestrians were

struck by motor vehicles and died in 1999, exposure measures are lacking because good data are not available for the amount of time, distances, or other circumstances of pedestrian travel.

Highway submodes show considerable improvement in fatality rates since 1975, when the federal government began to collect systematic national data from states. While all highway submodes show improved rates, there is much variation among them. Occupants of passenger cars and light trucks (including pickup trucks, vans, and sport utility vehicles) have much higher fatality rates than occupants of large trucks. Motorcycle riders have the highest fatality rate by far among the highway submodes. A large number of factors influence the difference in fatality rates. For example, the greater size and mass of large trucks serves to protect the occupants of these vehicles in crashes with smaller vehicles or less massive objects.

Many factors may interact to explain the decreasing fatality rates. For highway modes, promotion of safety belt, child safety seat, and motorcycle helmet usage, and measures to discourage drunk driving have all had a beneficial effect. So, too, have improvements in vehicle and highway design and greater separation of traffic. Finally, some of the decrease in transportation fatalities may be a consequence of better and prompter medical attention for victims of transportation crashes and accidents.

Table 1
Fatalities by Transportation Mode

Year	Air carriers[1]	Commuter air[1]	On-demand air taxi[2]	General aviation[2]	Highway[3]	Rail[4]	Transit[5]	Waterborne[6]	Recreational boating	Gas and hazardous liquid pipeline
1975	124	28	69	1,252	44,525	575	N	573	1,466	15
1980	1	37	105	1,239	51,091	584	N	487	1,360	19
1985	526	37	76	956	43,825	454	N	261	1,116	33
1990	39	7	R51	R767	44,599	599	339	186	865	9
1995	168	9	52	734	41,817	567	274	183	829	21
1999	12	12	38	630	41,611	530	299	111	734	26
2000[7]	92	5	71	592	41,800	518	NA	NA	NA	38

[1] Large carriers operating under 14 CFR 121, all scheduled and nonscheduled service.

[2] All scheduled and nonscheduled service operating under 14 CFR 135 and all operations other than those operating under 14 CFR 121 and 14 CFR 135.

[3] Includes occupants of passenger cars, light trucks, large trucks, buses, motorcycles, other or unknown vehicles, nonmotorists, pedestrians, and pedalcyclists. Motor vehicle fatalities at grade crossings are counted here.

[4] Includes fatalities resulting from train accidents, train incidents, and nontrain incidents (e.g., fires in railroad repair sheds). Thus, the data cover many nonpassengers, making comparisons to other modes difficult. Motor vehicle fatalities at grade crossings are counted in the highway column. Figures include Amtrak.

[5] Includes motor bus, commuter rail, heavy rail, light rail, demand responsive, van pool, and automated guideway. Some transit fatalities are also counted in other modes. Reporting criteria and source of data changed between 1989 and 1990. Starting in 1990, fatality figures include those occurring throughout the transit station, including nonpatrons. Fatalities include those arising from incidents involving no moving vehicle (e.g., falls on transit property). Thus, the data cover many nonpassengers, making comparisons to other modes difficult. Prior to 1998, only data from directly operated transit services were reported. Beginning in 1998, fatality data for purchased transit service, such as paratransit services, were included.

[6] Includes fatalities related to vessel and nonvessel casualties (e.g., an individual who falls overboard and drowns).

[7] All 2000 numbers are preliminary.

KEY: N = data are nonexistent; NA = not available; R = revised.

SOURCE: U.S. Department of Transportation, Bureau of Transportation Statistics, *National Transportation Statistics 2000* (Washington, DC: 2001).

Figure 1
Fatality Rates for Selected Modes

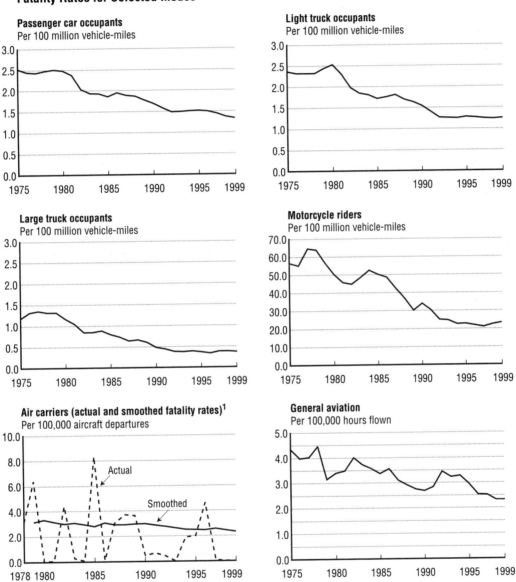

Passenger car occupants
Per 100 million vehicle-miles

Light truck occupants
Per 100 million vehicle-miles

Large truck occupants
Per 100 million vehicle-miles

Motorcycle riders
Per 100 million vehicle-miles

Air carriers (actual and smoothed fatality rates)[1]
Per 100,000 aircraft departures

Actual

Smoothed

General aviation
Per 100,000 hours flown

[1] For air carriers, the data were dampened, or smoothed, to reduce the month-to-month fluctuations. This dampening was performed using an exponential smoothing model, with a weight of 0.95. Departure data, and hence the denominator of the rates, are not strictly comparable between pre- and post-1977 eras.

SOURCE: Various sources, as cited in U.S. Department of Transportation, Bureau of Transportation Statistics, *National Transportation Statistics 2000* (Washington, DC: 2001).

Highway Crash Characteristics

The overwhelming majority of highway fatalities occur as a result of single-vehicle crashes and crashes involving two vehicles. For example, in 1999, 41 percent of traffic crash fatalities were vehicle occupants (including drivers) killed in single-vehicle crashes and 38 percent of fatalities occurred as a result of two-vehicle crashes (table 1). Crashes in which three or more vehicles were involved caused only 7 percent of traffic fatalities in 1999. (Some preliminary highway crash statistics are available from the National Highway Traffic Safety Administration (NHTSA). See box.)

An average of one-third of all motor vehicle crash fatalities nationwide result from single vehicle run-off-the-road (ROR) crashes, and two-thirds of these ROR fatalities occur in rural areas. It has been estimated that 40 to 60 percent of these crashes are due to driver fatigue, drowsiness, or inattention. The Federal Highway Administration recommends the use of rumble strips along the roadway shoulder as an effective way to reduce these incidents. The noise pro-

> **National Highway Traffic Safety Administration Early Assessment 2000 Motor Vehicle Data**
>
> In March 2001, the National Highway Traffic Safety Administration (NHTSA) released its early assessment estimates for motor vehicle traffic crashes in 2000 and the resulting injuries and fatalities. These early assessment numbers, based on NHTSA's Fatality Analysis Reporting System (FARS) and the National Automotive Sampling System General Estimates System (NASS GES), estimate that highway fatalities increased by 0.5 percent from 1999 to 2000, while injuries decreased by about 0.4 percent.
>
> However, NHTSA cautions that its early assessment estimates are based on data that are incomplete or preliminary. For example, both FARS and NASS GES data for the earlier months of 2000 are likely to be more complete than data for later months. Therefore, fatality and injury estimates for the year were obtained by combining the more complete data from earlier months with data for later months that were extrapolated from 1999 data. For FARS, the degree of completion of 2000 data varies by state. NASS GES uses extrapolated data for the final three months of the year. NHTSA also used projected vehicle-miles of travel from the Federal Highway Administration to estimate fatality rates.
>
> Where appropriate, NHTSA early assessment data are presented in sections of this chapter.

Table 1
Total Fatalities in Motor Vehicle Crashes by Type of Crash: 1999

Type of crash	Number
Drivers/occupants killed in single-vehicle crashes	17,052
Drivers/occupants killed in two-vehicle crashes	15,690
Drivers/occupants killed in crashes of three-vehicles or more	3,064
Pedestrians killed in single-vehicle crashes	4,488
Bicyclists killed in single-vehicle crashes	714
Pedestrians/bicyclists killed in multiple-vehicle crashes	454
Others/unknown	149
Total	**41,611**

SOURCE: U.S. Department of Transportation, National Highway Traffic Safety Administration, Fatality Analysis Reporting System 1999, available at http://www-fars.nhtsa.dot.gov, as of Nov. 15, 2000.

duced by vehicle tires on these rumble strips warns drivers that they are leaving the roadway. Studies of the effectiveness of shoulder rumble strips indicate that they can reduce the overall rate of ROR crashes between 15 and 70 percent [1]. In the future, the development of in-vehicle technologies that detect driver drowsiness and inattention and suitably warn the driver may further reduce the incidence of such crashes.

Traffic crashes between light trucks or vans and passenger cars is of increasing concern. Since the early 1980s, the category of light trucks and vans (LTVs) has grown dramatically (figure 1).

Figure 1
Growth in the Number of Passenger Cars and Light Trucks

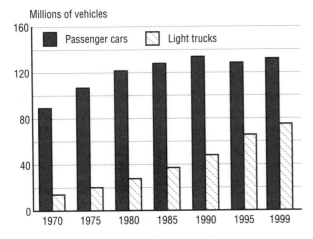

Millions of vehicles

SOURCES: U.S. Department of Transportation, Federal Highway Administration, *Highway Statistics Summary to 1995*, FHWA-PL-97-009 (Washington, DC: July 1997), table MV-201.
____. *Highway Statistics 1999* (Washington, DC: 2000).

LTVs include pickup trucks, vans, minivans, truck-based wagons, and sport utility vehicles (SUVs). Differences in vehicle size, weight, and geometry in multivehicle crashes can put occupants of passenger cars at greater risk in a crash with a light-duty truck than in a crash involving two or more passenger cars. For example, a study done for NHTSA by the University of Michigan Transportation Research Institute shows that when an SUV strikes a passenger car in a frontal crash, occupants of the car are almost twice as likely to have fatal injuries as the occupants of the SUV. In frontal collisions between two cars of similar weight, the ratio of deaths is 1:1. The same study found that, in side impact crashes, SUVs are more injurious as a striking vehicle than are passenger cars. For example, when SUVs strike passenger cars on the left side, the risk of death to the car driver can be 25 times greater than the risk to the SUV occupant. However, in the same type of crash involving two cars, the risk of death to the driver of the car being struck is only 10 times greater than the occupant of the other car [2].

Another issue related to SUVs is their propensity to rollover during certain steering maneuvers. SUVs are constructed with higher ground clearance for occasional offroad use and, thus, have a higher center of gravity. SUV height, along with other factors, contributes to the average rate of 98 rollover fatalities per million registered vehicles compared with 44 such fatalities per million registered vehicles for all other light vehicle types [3]. Also, in fatal crashes SUVs are twice as likely to rollover as compared with passenger cars, increasing the risk of occupant ejection, fatality, or injury [2].

Sources

1. U.S. Department of Transportation, Federal Highway Administration, *Effectiveness of Rumble Strips,* available at http://safety.fhwa.dot.gov, as of Feb. 1, 2001.

2. U.S. Department of Transportation, National Highway Traffic Safety Administration/University of Michigan Transportation Research Institute, *Fatality Risks in Collisions Between Cars and Light Trucks* (Washington, DC: September 1998).

3. U.S. Department of Transportation, Office of the Assistant Secretary of Public Affairs, *News Release: DOT Requires Upgraded Rollover Warning Label for Sport Utility Vehicles,* Mar. 5, 1999, available at http://www.nhtsa.dot.gov/nhtsa/announce/press/1999/1999press.dbm, as of Jan. 31, 2001.

Economic Costs of Motor Vehicle Crashes

According to the National Highway Traffic Safety Administration (NHTSA), motor vehicle crashes cost society $4,800 per second. Deaths, injuries, and property damages due to these crashes are not only a major cause of personal suffering and financial loss to the victims, their families, and friends, but also to society at large. NHTSA estimates that in 1994 the economic cost of motor vehicle crashes was $150.5 billion. Included in this amount are lost productivity, legal and court costs, medical and emergency service costs, insurance administration costs, travel delay, property damage, and workplace losses [1]. (NHTSA expects to have updated economic cost data in mid-2001.)

Motor vehicle crashes affect both the individual crash victims and society as a whole in a number of ways. The cost of medical care, for example, is borne by the individual through payments for expenses not covered by insurance and by society through higher insurance premiums and the diversion of medical resources away from other needs. Considerable costs are also associated with the loss of productivity when an individual's life is claimed at an early age or when a crash results in a disabling injury.

Of the total economic loss of $150.5 billion, medical costs were responsible for $17 billion, property losses for $52.1 billion, lost productivity (both market and household) was $54.7 billion, and other costs were $26.6 billion (figure 1). The largest single cost component is property damage, which accounted for over one-third of total economic costs. The high cost of property damage is primarily a function of the large number of minor crashes in which injury is either insignificant or nonexistent.

Alcohol use is one of the major causes of motor vehicle crashes. Historically, almost half of all fatalities have occurred in crashes where a driver or pedestrian had been drinking. In 1994, alcohol was involved in crashes that accounted for 30 percent of all economic costs, with over 78 percent of these costs involving crashes where a driver or pedestrian was legally intoxicated [1].

Speeding is another prevalent factor contributing to traffic crashes. The economic cost to society of speeding-related crashes is estimated to be $28 billion per year. In 1999, speeding was a contributing factor in 30 percent of all fatal crashes, and 12,628 lives were lost in speeding-related crashes [2].

Sources

1. U.S. Department of Transportation, National Highway Traffic Safety Administration, *The Economic Cost of Motor Vehicle Crashes, 1994,* 1996, available at http://www.nhtsa.dot.gov/people/economic, as of Nov. 27, 2000.

2. ___. *Traffic Safety Facts 1999: Speeding,* available at http://www.nhtsa.dot.gov/people/ncsa, as of Nov. 27, 2000.

Figure 1
**Components of Economic Costs of
Vehicle Crashes: 1994**

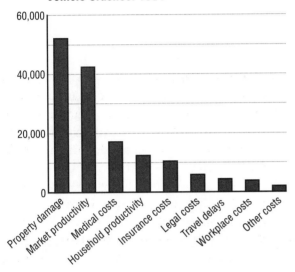

SOURCE: U.S. Department of Transportation, National Highway
Traffic Safety Administration, *The Economic Cost of Motor Vehicle
Crashes, 1994* (Washington, DC: 1996).

Highway Crashes on Rural and Urban Roads

Two- and three-lane rural roads make up the majority of the highway system in the United States. If Interstate highways are excluded, these rural roads represent four times the highway mileage of urban roads in the U.S. highway system [1].

In 1999, approximately 60 percent of fatal highway crashes occurred on rural roads, with almost 79 percent occurring on rural roads and rural Interstates with speed limits of 55 mph or more (table 1). When rural and urban Interstates are excluded, 84 percent of higher speed crashes occurred on rural roads. Regardless of the speed limit, 13 percent of all fatal crashes in rural areas occurred on Interstates; 15 percent were on urban Interstates [2].

Road conditions contribute to the greatest proportion of fatal crashes in rural areas. In particular, two-way traffic on roads posted for high speed limits is a concern. Rural drivers often must deal with challenging road geometry (e.g., width, alignment, and sight distances) and challenging geography (e.g., steep grades and mountain passes). Adverse weather can further affect rural road conditions and sparse and patchy telecommunications infrastructure can slow emergency response time when a crash occurs. On average, emergency response time to highway crashes in rural areas is 1.5 times greater than in urban areas, however, response-time data on a large percentage of crashes are not available (table 2).

Sources

1. Transportation Research Board, National Cooperative Highway Research Program, *Accident Mitigation Guide for Congested Rural Two-Lane Highways,* Report 440 (Washington, DC: 2000).

2. U.S. Department of Transportation, National Highway Traffic Safety Administration, Fatality Analysis Reporting System database, 1999, 2000, available at www.nhtsa.dot.gov/people/ncsa/fars.html, as of January 2001.

Table 1
Fatal Crashes by Speed Limits and Type of Road: 1999

Speed limit	Rural			Urban			Unknown	Total
	Interstate	Principal arterial	Other	Interstate	Principal arterial	Other		
30 mph or less	2	61	987	11	28	2,802	94	**3,985**
35 or 40 mph	15	181	1,899	39	114	4,383	129	**6,760**
45 or 50 mph	35	612	3,085	121	208	3,046	187	**7,294**
55 mph	186	2,510	8,629	684	368	1,308	229	**13,914**
60 mph or higher	2,971	1,846	1,535	1,430	580	197	14	**8,573**
No posted limit	5	14	89	1	0	16	9	**134**
Unknown	22	56	368	61	56	362	26	**951**
Total	**3,236**	**5,280**	**16,592**	**2,347**	**1,354**	**12,114**	**688**	**41,611**

SOURCE: U.S. Department of Transportation, National Highway Traffic Safety Administration, Fatality Analysis Reporting System database, 2000.

Table 2
Average Emergency Medical Service (EMS) Response
Time for Rural and Urban Fatal Crashes: 1998
(In minutes)

Event	Rural	Unknown	Urban	Unknown
Time of crash to EMS notification	6.77	37%	3.62	46%
EMS notification to EMS arrival at crash scene	11.36	35%	6.26	47%
EMS arrival at crash scene to hospital arrival	36.28	67%	26.63	72%
Time of crash to hospital arrival[1]	51.78	68%	35.46	71%

[1] Not a total of the above categories, as separate records are kept for this category.

SOURCE: U.S. Department of Transportation, National Highway Traffic Safety Administration, *Traffic Safety Facts 1998* (Washington, DC: 1999).

Alcohol-Related Highway Crashes

In 1999, 38 percent of the 41,611 highway fatalities were related to alcohol. In 1982, the first year for which data are available, 25,165 people died in alcohol-related motor vehicle crashes—57 percent of all highway fatalities. By 1999, alcohol-related fatalities had dropped to 15,787 (figure 1), and the National Highway Traffic Safety Administration's early assessment for 2000 shows 16,068 such fatalities. The U.S. Department of Transportation has a goal of reducing alcohol-related fatalities to no more than 11,000 by 2005 [3].

Improved state and local education programs, stricter law enforcement, adoption of a 0.08 blood alcohol concentration (BAC) by 18 states, higher minimum drinking ages, more stringent license revocation laws, and reduced tolerance for drinking and driving have all been cited as factors in reducing alcohol-related deaths. Despite improvements, 18 percent of passenger car drivers, 20 percent of light truck drivers, 1 percent of large truck operators, and 31 percent of motorcycle operators involved in fatal crashes in 1998 were legally intoxicated with a BAC of 0.10 or greater [4].

In 1999, the highest intoxication rates in fatal crashes involved drivers between 21 and 24 years of age (figure 2). In addition, the highest arrest rates for drunken driving were also for drivers in this age group [3]. Between 1989 and 1999, intoxication rates decreased for drivers of all age groups involved in fatal crashes. The largest decreases were for those drivers aged 16 to 20 (30 percent) and drivers over 64 (29 percent) [2].

Alcohol-related fatalities declined more quickly in the 1980s than in the 1990s. Between 1994 and 1999, the percentage of highway fatalities attrib-

Figure 1
Alcohol-Related Fatalities in Motor Vehicle Crashes: 1982–1999

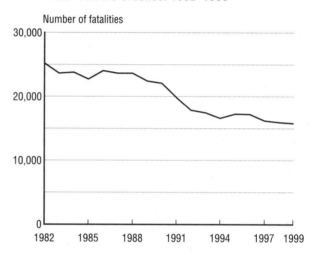

Number of fatalities

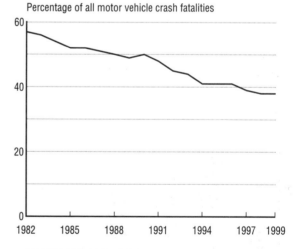

Percentage of all motor vehicle crash fatalities

SOURCES: 1982–1998—U.S. Department of Transportation, National Highway Traffic Safety Administration, *Traffic Safety Facts 1998* (Washington, DC: 1999).
1999—____. Fatality Analysis Reporting System database, 1999, 2000.

uted to alcohol declined by only 3 percent—from 41 percent to 38 percent. Moreover, while alcohol-related fatalities among drivers 16 to 20 years of age decreased, alcohol consumption in this age group increased every year from 1993 to 1999 [3].

Fatality rates vary by state (see map on next page). It is illegal in every state and the District of Columbia to drive a motor vehicle while under the influence of alcohol. In addition, every state except Massachusetts has laws that make it illegal for a person to drive a motor vehicle with a specific amount of alcohol in his or her blood. As of October 2000, 31 states defined intoxicated driving as 0.10 BAC—the level at which a person's blood contains 1/10th of 1 percent of alcohol. Eighteen states and the District of Columbia have enacted 0.08 BAC laws [1].

In 2000, Congress enacted legislation that provides strong encouragement for states to adopt the 0.08 BAC [6]. States have until October 1, 2003, to pass the stricter limit or face the withholding of 2 percent of their federal highway construction funds. After 2003, states that fail to pass the 0.08 BAC will lose an additional 2 percent of their federal funding every year. By October 1, 2006, and each year thereafter, states that still have not adopted 0.08 BAC laws will lose 8 percent of their funding [5].

Highway safety advocates have encouraged states to take a systems approach to reducing drunk driving. Some states have enacted a combination of measures. In addition to 0.08 BAC limits, such measures include stringent license revocation laws (under which a person deemed to be driving under the influence has his or her driving privileges suspended or revoked), comprehensive screening and treatment programs for alcohol offenders, vehicle impoundment, and zero tolerance BAC and other laws for youths [7].

Sources

1. Mothers Against Drunk Driving (MADD), "President Clinton Signs Federal 0.08 BAC Drunk Driving Law," press release, available at http://www.madd.org/media/pressrel, as of Oct. 23, 2000.

2. U.S. Department of Justice, Bureau of Justice Statistics, *More Than 500,000 Drunk Drivers on Probation or Incarcerated* (Washington, DC: 1999), also available at http://www.ojp.usdoj.gov/bjs/pub/press/dwiocs.pr, as of Oct. 27, 2000.

3. U.S. Department of Transportation, *FY 1999 Performance Report/FY 2001 Performance Plan* (Washington, DC: 2000), also available at http://www.dot.gov/ost, as of Oct. 23, 2000.

4. U.S. Department of Transportation, National Highway Traffic Safety Administration, *Traffic Safety Facts 1998* (Washington, DC: 1999), also available at http://www.nhtsa.dot.gov/people/ncsa, as of Oct. 23, 2000.

5. ____. "Congress Agrees to 0.08% Blood Alcohol as the Legal Level for Impaired Driving," *NHTSA Now Newsletter,* Oct. 16, 2000.

6. U.S. Department of Transportation, Office of Public Affairs, "Statement by U.S. Transportation Secretary Rodney Slater Upon Signing of Transportation Appropriations Act by President Clinton," Oct. 23, 2000.

7. U.S. General Accounting Office, Resources, Community, and Economic Development Division, *Highway Safety: Effectiveness of State 0.08 Blood Alcohol Laws* (Washington, DC: June 1999).

Figure 2

Intoxicated Drivers by Age: 1999

(0.10 BAC or greater)

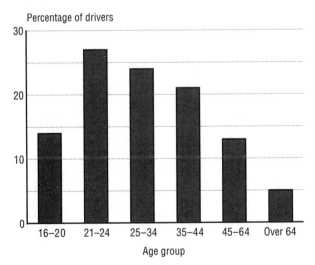

SOURCE: U.S. Department of Transportation, National Highway Traffic Safety Administration, *Traffic Safety Facts 1999* (Washington, DC: 2000).

Alcohol-Related Motor Vehicle Fatality Rates per 100,000 Licensed Drivers: 1999

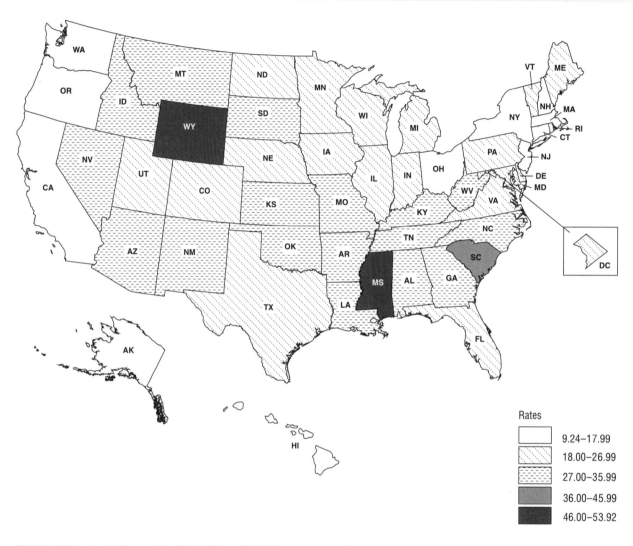

Rates

	9.24–17.99
	18.00–26.99
	27.00–35.99
	36.00–45.99
	46.00–53.92

SOURCE: U.S. Department of Transportation, National Highway Traffic Safety Administration, *Traffic Safety Facts 1999* (Washington, DC: 2000).

Occupant Protection: Safety Belts, Air Bags, and Child Restraints

The National Highway Traffic Safety Administration (NHTSA) estimates that, in 1999, safety belts saved the lives of 11,197 passenger vehicle occupants over 4 years old (figure 1). NHTSA also estimates that 20,750 lives could have been saved that year if all passenger vehicle occupants aged 4 and older wore safety belts [1].

The number of lives saved has increased dramatically since 1984 when states began to enact safety belt laws. A June 2000 NHTSA survey showed that 71 percent of passenger vehicle occupants used safety belts [4]. Usage rates differ noticeably among the states based on how the safety belt laws are enforced (see map on safety belt use rates on page 56). There are three levels of enforcement: primary enforcement allows a police officer to stop and cite someone for not wearing a safety belt; secondary enforcement allows a police officer to cite someone for not wearing a safety belt only if they have been stopped for some other infraction; and no enforcement [1]. Usage in the 17 states with primary enforcement was 77 percent as opposed to 63 percent in the 33 states with secondary enforcement laws (see map on safety belt use laws on page 57). Safety belt usage in New Hampshire, which does not require adults to wear safety belts, was 56 percent.

Beginning in September 1997 (model year 1998), all new passenger vehicles were required to have driver and passenger air bags. The following year, the same requirement was applied to light trucks. NHTSA estimated that, as of 1999, more than 91 million air-bag-equipped passenger vehicles were on the road, including 65 million with dual air bags. In 1999, an estimated 1,263 lives were saved by air bags. From 1987 through 1999, an estimated total of 4,969 lives were saved [1].

According to NHTSA, air bags, combined with safety belts, offer the most effective safety protection available today for passenger vehicle occupants. Air bags are supplemental protection and are designed to deploy in moderate-to-severe frontal crashes. Adults and some children riding in front seats have been injured or killed by air bags inflating in low severity crashes. While far more lives have been saved by air bags than have been lost, since 1990, 168 deaths from injuries caused by air bags have occurred. This includes 99 children riding in the front seat [2]. If children under the age of 13 ride in the back seat of passenger vehicles and are secured by appropriate restraint systems, risk of injuries or death from air bags can be avoided [1].

In 1999, 543 passenger vehicle occupant fatalities were reported among children less than 5 years of age [3]. NHTSA estimated that in 1999, use of child restraint systems saved the lives of

Figure 1
Estimated Number of Lives Saved Each Year by Use of Safety Belts: 1975–1999

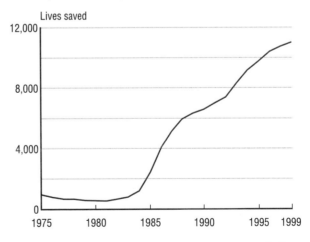

SOURCE: U.S. Department of Transportation, National Highway Traffic Safety Administration.

Safety Belt Use Rates: 1999[1]

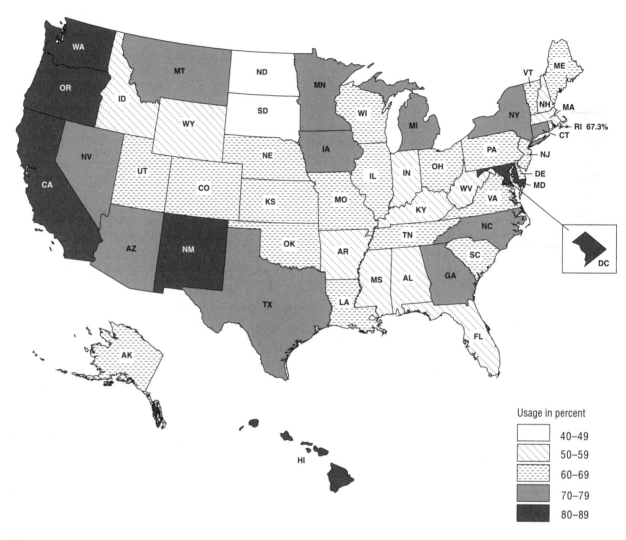

Usage in percent

	40–49
	50–59
	60–69
	70–79
	80–89

[1] Maine, New Hampshire, South Dakota, and Wyoming data are for 1998 from U.S. Department of Transportation, National Highway Traffic Safety Administration, *Traffic Safety Facts 1998* (Washington, DC: 1999).

SOURCE: U.S. Department of Transportation, National Highway Traffic Safety Administration, "Research Note: 1999 State Shoulder Belt Use Survey Results," October 2000.

307 children under the age of 5. An additional 162 lives could have been saved—for a total of 469—if every child under age 5 had been proper- ly restrained in a child safety seat. From 1975 through 1999, an estimated 4,500 lives were saved by child restraints [1].

Type of Safety Belt Use Laws, by State: As of 2000

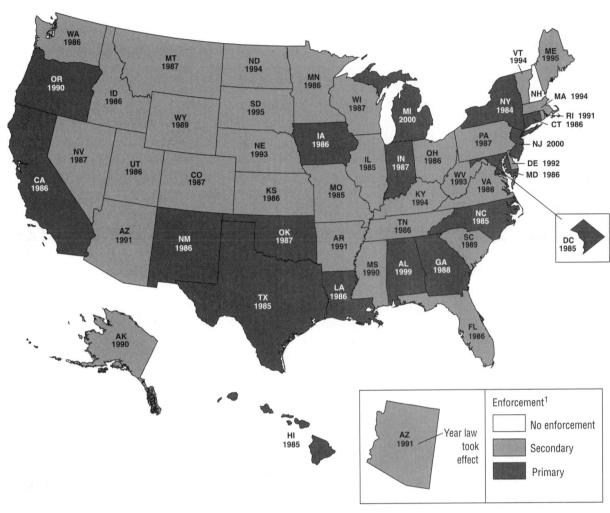

[1] Primary enforcement allows police officers to stop vehicles and write citations whenever they observe violations of safety belt laws. Secondary enforcement permits police officers to write a citation only after a vehicle is stopped for some other traffic violation.

SOURCE: U.S. Department of Transportation, National Highway Traffic Safety Administration, "State Highway Safety Laws: Enforcement Provisions of Safety Belt Use," Aug. 1, 2000.

Sources

1. U.S. Department of Transportation, National Highway Traffic Safety Administration, *Traffic Safety Facts 1999: Occupant Protection* (Washington, DC: 2000).

2. ____. *Air Bag Fatalities and Serious Injury Report* (Washington, DC: 2000), also available at http://www.nhtsa.dot.gov/people/ncsa, as of Oct. 25, 2000.

3. ____. *Early Assessment of 1999 Crashes, Injuries, and Fatalities* (Washington, DC: 2000), also available at http://www.nhtsa.dot.gov/people/ncsa, as of Oct. 25, 2000.

4. ____. "Research Note: Observed Safety Belt Use from December 1999 and June 2000," November 2000.

Tire Recalls

In 2000, several tire manufacturers recalled a total of 14.4 million tires in use in the United States due to a variety of defects. Of these, in August 2000 the Bridgestone/Firestone Corporation recalled all but about 12,500[1] tires prone to tread separation [5]. By December 2000, the tires had been linked to highway crashes resulting in nearly 150 deaths and more than 500 injuries since the early 1990s. Although the tires are found on a variety of vehicles, most of the tires in question were original equipment on Ford vehicles, primarily the Explorer sport utility vehicle. By the end of 1999, the National Highway Traffic Safety Administration (NHTSA) had received 46 reports over 9 years about incidents involving these tires. However, the number of complaints escalated rapidly after news reports dramatized the question of the tires' safety—by December 2000, NHTSA had received over 4,000 complaints [4].

Accidents involving Firestone tires were also reported in the Middle East and Latin America. Ford replaced Firestone tires on Explorers in Saudi Arabia and Venezuela because of tread separation problems [2]. Auto safety advocates and many lawmakers contend that Firestone and Ford should have reported the overseas tire problems to NHTSA even though they were not required to do so [1].

In response to the problems brought to light by the tire recall, Congress enacted legislation in late 2000—the Transportation Recall Enhancement, Accountability and Documentation (TREAD) Act—that gives NHTSA additional authority to require manufacturers to report defects that first appear in vehicles or equipment in foreign countries. The TREAD Act also calls on NHTSA to upgrade tire safety standards and gives the agency greater authority to obtain lawsuit data to help identify trends that might indicate potential defects. The additional authority granted to NHTSA is expected to strengthen the agency's hand in its oversight of the industry by enhancing not only its enforcement capability but also its ability to collect industry data [3].

Sources

1. *Congressional Quarterly Weekly*, "House Panel Spurns Industry Objections, Approves Potential Criminal Penalties For Misleading Regulators on Auto Safety," No. 2279, Sept. 30, 2000.

2. Nasser, Jac, President, Ford Motor Co., testimony before the Committee on Commerce, Science, and Transportation, United States Senate, Sept. 12, 2000.

3. National Highway Traffic Safety Administration, *Now Newsletter*, Dec. 11, 2000, available at http://www.nhtsa.dot.gov, as of Jan. 31, 2001.

4. National Highway Traffic Safety Administration, Associate Administrator for Safety Assurance, Recall Analysis Division, Consumer Advisory, available at http://www.nhtsa.dot.gov/hot/firestone/index.html, as of Jan. 31, 2001.

5. _____. personal communication, Jan. 31, 2001.

[1] Firestone estimated that approximately 6.5 million of the recalled ATX, ATX II, and Wilderness AT tires manufactured at the company's Decatur, Illinois, plant were still on the road.

Large Trucks

In 1999, 5,362 people were killed in crashes involving large trucks. The number of fatalities has varied from a low of 4,462 in 1992 to a high of 6,702 in 1979 (figure 1). (National Highway Traffic Safety Administration early assessment data show 5,307 fatalities in large truck crashes in 2000.) The number of drivers and occupants of large trucks killed in crashes has declined since the late 1970s, when fatalities averaged about 1,200, compared with about 700 in the 1990s. The overwhelming majority of people killed in large truck collisions—86 percent in 1999—were occupants of other vehicles or nonmotorists [1]. In two-vehicle crashes involving a large truck and a passenger vehicle, driver-related crash factors were cited by police officers at the scene for 26 percent of the truck drivers involved and for 82 percent of the passenger vehicle drivers. Table 1 shows the percent of crashes in which either the large-truck driver or the passenger-vehicle driver or both were cited for one or more of the top 10 factors identified as primary causes of crashes.

Large truck safety issues have received increased attention in recent years. In 1999, Congress passed the Motor Carrier Safety Improvement Act, which created the Federal Motor Carrier Safety Administration within the U.S. Department of Transportation. Among other provisions, the legislation calls for increased roadside inspections, compliance reviews and enforcement actions, improvements in safety data, and additional research into crash causes. About 25 percent of the over 2.2 million motor carrier vehicles inspected in 1999 were taken out of service (figures 2 and 3).

Figure 1
Fatalities in Large Truck Crashes: 1975–1999

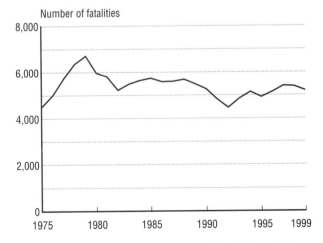

Number of fatalities

SOURCES: U.S. Department of Transportation, National Highway Traffic Safety Administration, *Traffic Safety Facts 1999* (Washington, DC: 2000), table 11.
____. Fatality Analysis Reporting System database, 1999.

Table 1
Driver-Related Factors Cited in Two-Vehicle Fatal Crashes Between Large Trucks and Passenger Vehicles: 1998

Top 10 factors cited	Large trucks	Passenger vehicles
Failure to yield right-of-way	5.3%	20.3%
Ran off road/out of traffic lane	4.8%	27.8%
Driving too fast	3.8%	14.9%
Failure to obey traffic devices	3.0%	12.1%
Inattentive	2.7%	9.8%
Erratic/reckless driving	1.6%	5.1%
Manslaughter, homicide	1.5%	1.3%
Following improperly	1.4%	2.1%
Making improper turn	1.0%	2.6%
Vision obscured by weather	0.9%	1.7%

NOTES: 1998 is the most recent year for which data are available. Number of drivers involved in two-vehicle, large truck/passenger car crashes = 2,740.

SOURCE: U.S. Department of Transportation, Federal Motor Carrier Safety Administration, *Large Truck Crash Profile: The 1998 National Picture* (Washington, DC: January 2000).

Figure 2
Motor Carrier Vehicle Inspections

Millions of inspections

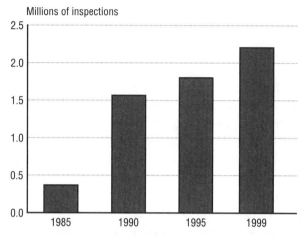

SOURCE: U.S. Department of Transportation, Federal Motor Carrier Safety Administration, Motor Carrier Inspection Database.

Figure 3
Percentage of Vehicle Inspections in which the Vehicle is Taken Out of Service: 1984–1999

Percent

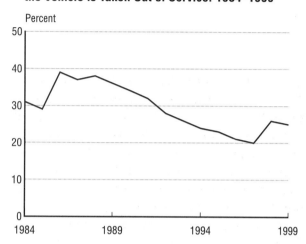

SOURCE: U.S. Department of Transportation, Federal Motor Carrier Safety Administration, Motor Carrier Inspection Database.

Source

1. U.S. Department of Transportation, National Highway Traffic Safety Administration, *Traffic Safety Facts 1999: Large Trucks* (Washington, DC: 1999).

Bicycles

In 1999, 750 bicyclists were killed in crashes with motor vehicles—a 25 percent reduction since 1975 (figure 1). (The National Highway Traffic Safety Administration's early assessment of bicycle fatalities for 2000 is 738.) While bicycle fatalities have declined, the U.S. Department of Transportation's Nationwide Personal Transportation Survey shows that bicycle trips more than doubled—from 1.3 billion to 3.3 billion trips between 1977 and 1995 [2].[1]

Exposure data for bicycling are limited, which makes it difficult to make statements about changes in risk over time or how risk profiles are affected by different behaviors. For example, it is notable that 28 percent of bicyclists killed in traffic

crashes in 1999 were 15 years old or younger, a large decrease compared with the 1975 figure of 68 percent (figure 2). However, this change may be the result of an increase in bicycling by adults, a decrease by children, or a change in their relative safety rates.

In 1999, 64 percent of bicycle fatalities occurred in urban areas, with 70 percent of the fatalities arising at nonintersection locations. About 37 percent of bicycle fatalities occurred between the hours of 5:00 p.m. and 9:00 p.m., and 34 percent happened during the months of July, August, and September. Additionally, males accounted for 88 percent of the bicycle fatalities and 82 percent of those injured.

Alcohol is involved in about one-third of traffic crashes resulting in the death of a bicyclist. The bicyclist was intoxicated in 22 percent of these fatalities [6].

---

[1] 1995 data are the latest available.

Figure 1
Bicycle Fatalities in Motor Vehicle Crashes: 1975–1999

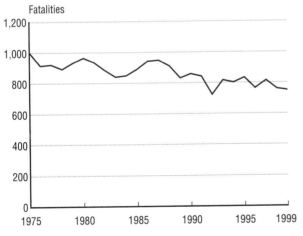

SOURCES: U.S. Department of Transportation, National Highway Traffic Safety Administration, *Traffic Safety Facts 1998* (Washington, DC: 1999). ____. *Traffic Safety Facts 1999: Pedalcyclists* (Washington, DC: 2000). ____. Fatality Analysis Reporting System (FARS) database, 1999.

Figure 2
Bicycle Fatalities by Age of Bicyclist: 1975–1999

SOURCE: U.S. Department of Transportation, National Highway Traffic Safety Administration, Fatality Analysis Reporting System (FARS) database, available at www.nhtsa.dot.gov, as of January 2001.

There were 51,000 bicyclists injured in crashes with motor vehicles in 1999. Although 90 percent of bicycle *fatalities* involve a collision with a motor vehicle, most bicycle *injuries* do not. There are about 500,000 bicycle-related emergency room visits annually [4]. Most bicycle mishaps leading to emergency room visits involve falls and collisions with fixed objects. Collisions with motor vehicles accounted for 15 percent of emergency room visits [3]. Collisions with pedestrians, other bicycles, and animals are prevalent, but states do not generally record these data since they do not involve motor vehicles.

The Bureau of Transportation Statistics' Omnibus Survey of adults 16 years of age or older asked survey respondents to rate their level of concern about specific transportation issues. For bicycle travel, 58 percent indicated they felt "very unsafe" (30 percent) or "unsafe" (28 percent), greatly exceeding the 18 percent who felt "safe" (8 percent) or "very safe" (10 percent). The remaining 24 percent were neutral on this question [5].

Nearly one-third (32 percent) of bicyclists involved in crashes were riding against traffic [1, table 37]. In fact, a study that calculated relative risk based on exposure rates found that bicy-cling against traffic increased the risk of a collision with a motor vehicle by a factor of 3.6 [7].

Sources

1. Hunter, W.W., J.C. Stutts, and W.E. Pein, Bicycle Crash Types: A 1990's *Informational Guide*, FHWA-RD-96-104 (Washington, DC: U.S. Department of Transportation, Federal Highway Administration, 1997).

2. Pickrell, D. and P. Schimek, *Trends in Personal Motor Vehicle Ownership and Use: Evidence from the Nationwide Personal Transportation Survey* (Washington, DC: U.S. Department of Transportation, Federal Highway Administration, 1997).

3. Rivara, F.P., D.C. Thompson, and R.S. Thompson, *Circumstances and Severity of Bicycle Injuries* (Seattle, WA: Snell Memorial Foundation, Harborview Injury Prevention and Research Center, 1996).

4. Tinsworth, D., C. Polen, and S. Cassidy, *Bicycle-Related Injuries: Injury, Hazard, and Risk Patterns*, Technical Report (Washington, DC: U.S. Consumer Product Safety Commission, 1993).

5. U.S. Department of Transportation, Bureau of Transportation Statistics, Omnibus Survey, August 2000.

6. U.S. Department of Transportation, National Highway Traffic Safety Administration, *Traffic Safety Facts 1999: Pedalcyclists* (Washington, DC: 2000).

7. Wachtel, A. and D. Lewiston, "Risk Factors for Bicycle-Motor Vehicle Collisions at Intersections," *ITE Journal*, September 1994, pp. 30–35.

Pedestrians

In 1999, 4,906 pedestrians were killed in crashes involving motor vehicles, compared with 7,516 in 1975 (figure 1). (For 2000, the National Highway Traffic Safety Administration's early assessment of pedestrian fatalities is 4,727.) While pedestrian fatalities have declined, the risk has not necessarily decreased. The U.S. Department of Transportation's Nationwide Personal Transportation Survey shows that walking trips rose from 19.7 billion to 20.3 billion between 1977 and 1995[1] [1]. Table 1 presents factors that can contribute to motor vehicle-related pedestrian fatalities.

Data evaluating exposure risks faced by pedestrians are very limited. State data on pedestrian fatalities per 100,000 population show that, although the levels of fatalities are spread across the country, several states in the southeast, along the Gulf Coast, and in the southwest have higher than median fatality rates (figure 2).

Pedestrians comprised less than 3 percent or 85,000 of the 3,236,000 people injured in motor vehicle crashes in 1999, but almost 12 percent of the fatalities involving motor vehicles. The majority of pedestrian fatalities in 1999 occurred in urban areas (69 percent), at nonintersection locations (78 percent), in normal weather conditions (90 percent), and at night (65 percent). Additionally, males accounted for about 70 percent of the pedestrian fatalities in 1999. An estimated 31 percent of pedestrians killed in traffic

Figure 1
Pedestrian Fatalities in
Motor Vehicle Crashes: 1975–1999

SOURCES: U.S. Department of Transportation, National Highway Traffic Safety Administration, *Traffic Safety Facts 1998* (Washington, DC: 1999). ____. *Traffic Safety Facts 1999: Pedalcyclists* (Washington, DC: 2000). ____. Fatality Analysis Reporting System (FARS) database, 1999.

Table 1
Pedestrian Fatalities, by Related Factors: 1999

Factors	Number	Percent
Total pedestrian fatalities	**4,906**	**100.0**
Improper crossing of roadway or intersection	1,474	30.0
Walking, playing, working, etc., in roadway	1,420	28.9
Failure to yield right-of-way	672	13.7
Darting or running into road	640	13.0
Not visible	395	8.1
Inattentive (talking, eating, etc.)	107	2.2
Physical impairment	80	1.6
Failure to obey traffic signs, signals, or officer	68	1.4
Emotional (e.g., depressed, angry, disturbed)	21	0.4
Nonmotorist pushing vehicle	20	0.4
Mentally challenged	18	0.4
Getting on/off/in/out of vehicle	16	0.3
Ill, blackout	15	0.3
Other factors	106	2.2
None reported	1,241	25.3
Unknown	98	2.0

NOTE: The sum of the numbers and percentages is greater than the total pedestrians killed as more than one factor may be present for the same pedestrian.

SOURCE: U.S. Department of Transportation, National Highway Traffic Safety Administration, *Traffic Safety Facts 1999* (Washington, DC: 2000), table 98.

---

[1] 1995 data are the latest available.

Figure 2
Pedestrian Traffic Fatalities by State: 1999

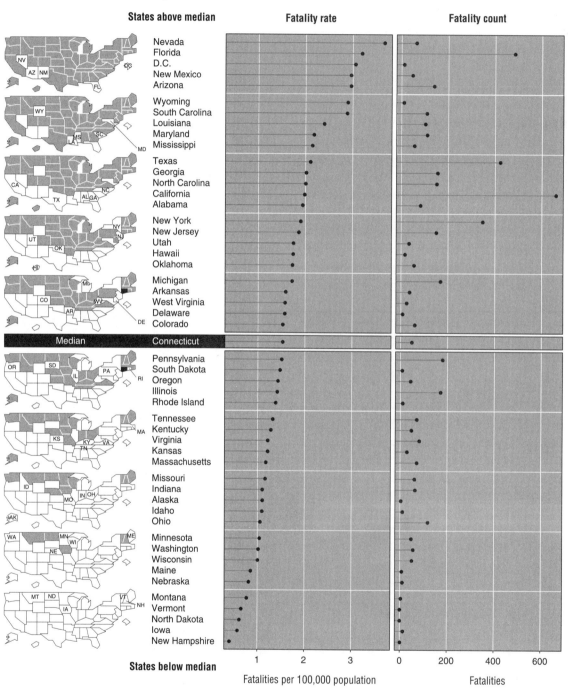

SOURCE: U.S. Department of Transportation, Federal Highway Administration, *Traffic Safety Facts 1999: Pedestrians* (Washington, DC: 2000).

crashes in 1999 were intoxicated (with a BAC of 0.10 or more) as were 12 percent of the drivers in fatal pedestrian crashes [3].

The Bureau of Transportation Statistics Omnibus Survey of adults 16 years of age or older asked survey respondents to rate their level of concern about particular transportation issues. When asked to identify how safe they felt when using specific modes of transportation (e.g., highways, commercial air, intercity train), more respondents felt "safe" or "very safe" than "unsafe" or "very unsafe." However, for pedestrian travel, 43 percent felt "very unsafe" (23 percent) or "unsafe" (20 percent). Only 30 percent

said they felt "safe" (16 percent) or "very safe," (14 percent). About 27 percent were neutral [2].

Sources

1. Pickrell, D. and P. Schimek, *Trends in Personal Motor Vehicle Ownership and Use: Evidence from the Nationwide Personal Transportation Survey* (Washington, DC: U.S. Department of Transportation, Federal Highway Administration, 1997), also available at http://www.cta.ornl.gov/npts/1995/Doc/publications.html.

2. U.S. Department of Transportation, Bureau of Transportation Statistics, Omnibus Survey, August 2000.

3. U.S. Department of Transportation, Federal Highway Administration, *Traffic Safety Facts 1999: Pedestrians* (Washington, DC: 2000).

Commercial Aviation

Overall, aviation is a remarkably safe mode of transportation. Commercial aviation, used by most Americans when they fly, experiences less than 1 fatal crash for every 1 million flights. While commercial air travel in the United States has increased dramatically over the past two decades, the accident rate has remained low [2]. However, differences exist among the various categories of service that make up commercial aviation.[1]

In 2000,[2] 92 fatalities were reported in U.S. air carrier accidents. For the third consecutive year, no fatal accidents were reported for commercial chartered airlines. Overall, 54 U.S. air carrier accidents were reported in 2000 [1].

Historically, air taxis experience a greater number of accidents than air carriers or commuter carriers (figure 1). However, the number of fatalities across the categories varies greatly from year to year, because a single crash of a major airliner can result in a large number of deaths (table 1).

---

[1] For safety reporting and analysis, commercial aviation consists of air carriers (those with aircraft having 10 or more seats), cargo haulers, commuter carriers (those with aircraft having 9 seats or fewer in scheduled service), air taxi service (those carriers with aircraft having 9 seats or fewer in unscheduled service), and helicopter service.

[2] 2000 data are preliminary.

Figure 1
Commercial Aviation Accidents by Type of Operation: 1990–2000

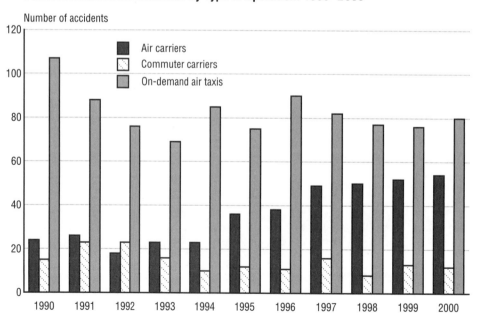

SOURCE: National Transportation Safety Board, *Accidents, Fatalities, and Rates, 1982–2000* (Washington, DC: 2001).

Table 1
Number of Commercial Aviation Fatalities by Type of Operation: 1990–2000

Category	1990	1991	1992	1993	1994	1995	1996	1997	1998	1999	2000
Air carriers	39	62	33	1	239	166	380	8	1	12	92
Commuter carriers	7	99	21	24	25	9	14	46	0	12	5
On-demand air taxis	51	78	68	42	63	52	63	39	48	38	71

SOURCE: National Transportation Safety Board, *Accidents, Fatalities, and Rates, 1982–2000* (Washington, DC: 2001).

The overall accident rate for all three types of commercial aviation operations combined is 0.69 accidents per 100,000 flight hours. However, differences in the accident rates among the three types of operations do exist (figure 2). For example, the accident rate for air carriers has historically been well below that of commuter carriers and air taxis.

Finally, although the overall accident and fatality rates for commercial aviation remain low, the continued growth forecast for U.S. aviation in the coming decade raises concern. The Federal Aviation Administration (FAA) estimates that commercial aviation aircraft (excluding air taxis) will fly more than 24 million hours in 2007, a 37 percent increase over 1999. Commercial aviation (excluding air taxis) experienced an average of 6 fatal accidents a year in the United States between 1994 and 1996. If the projected growth in flight hours occurs and the fatal accident rate is not reduced, aviation experts estimate that the number of fatal commercial aviation accidents could rise to 9 per year by 2007. To address this potential danger, FAA's "Safer Skies" program has a goal of reducing the number of fatal commercial accidents per million flight hours by 80 percent by 2007 [3].

Figure 2
Commercial Carrier Accident Rates: 1990–2000
(Per 100,000 flight hours)

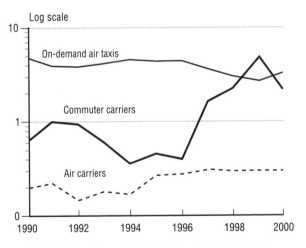

SOURCE: National Transportation Safety Board, *Accidents, Fatalities, and Rates, 1982–2000* (Washington, DC: 2001).

Sources

1. National Transportation Safety Board, *Accidents, Fatalities, and Rates, 1982–2000* (Washington, DC: 2001), also available at http://www.ntsb.gov/aviation/htm, as of Apr. 17, 2001.

2. U.S. Department of Transportation, *The Changing Face of Transportation* (Washington, DC: 2000).

3. U.S. Department of Transportation, Federal Aviation Administration, *Safer Skies: A Focused Agenda*, 2000, available at http://www/faa.gov/apa/safer_skies/saftoc.htm, as of Sept. 20, 2000.

General Aviation

Most aviation accidents involve general aviation (GA) aircraft[1] (table 1); however, GA fatalities and fatality rates have decreased over the last quarter century (figure 1). In 1975, general aviation experienced 1,252 fatalities—over twice as many as the 592 reported in 2000 (preliminary data). Moreover, the fatality rate (expressed as fatalities per 100,000 hours flown) declined from 4.35 to 1.92 over the same period [2].

The major causes of fatal general aviation accidents are weather, pilot loss of control or other maneuvering errors made during flight, and accidents on approach to the airport [5]. In fact, 32 percent of the GA accidents from 1983 to 1994 occurred in weather conditions requiring pilots to have instrument ratings [3]. Furthermore, the number of fatalities also varies a great deal by month, with fewer fatalities generally occurring in the winter months because of fewer flights (figure 2).

Another area of concern is the growing number of runway incursions[2] involving GA aircraft. In 1999, GA pilot error caused 139 (76 percent) of the 183 runway incursions [1].

Changes in flight hours can also affect accident rates. The Federal Aviation Administration (FAA) estimates that GA flight hours will increase to about 36 million hours by 2007—nearly 19 percent higher than 1999. Although general aviation accidents and fatalities have been trending

---

[1] General aviation includes a wide variety of aircraft, ranging from corporate jets to small piston-engine aircraft used for recreational purposes, as well as helicopters, gliders, and aircraft used in operations such as firefighting and agricultural spraying.

[2] A *runway incursion* is any occurrence on a runway involving an aircraft, vehicle, or pedestrian that creates a collision hazard for aircraft taking off, intending to take off, landing, or intending to land.

Table 1
Fatal Accidents and Deaths by Type of Aviation Operation: 1988–1997

Type of operation	Fatal accidents		Deaths	
	Number	**Percent**	**Number**	**Percent**
General aviation	4,386	98	8,046	82
Commercial aviation	85	2	1,756	18
Total	**4,471**	**100**	**9,802**	**100**

SOURCE: U.S. General Accounting Office, *Aviation Safety: Safer Skies Initiative has Taken Initial Steps to Reduce Accident Rates by 2007* (Washington, DC: 2000).

Figure 1
General Aviation Fatality Rates: 1975–2000

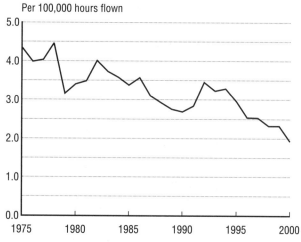

Per 100,000 hours flown

NOTE: 2000 data are preliminary.

SOURCES: National Transportation Safety Board, *Accidents, Fatalities, and Rates, 1982–1999* (Washington, DC: 2000), also available at http://www.ntsb.gov/aviation/htm, as of Apr. 17, 2001; and U.S. Department of Transportation, Bureau of Transportation Statistics, *National Transportation Statistics Historical Compendium: 1960–1992* (Washington, DC: 1993).

downward for 25 years, aviation experts believe these numbers will rise over the next decade with the projected increase in flight hours. Because of the potential safety implications associated with rapid growth in both commercial and GA flight hours, FAA initiated the "Safer Skies" program in 1998 with the goal of reducing aviation accident rates. FAA's goal for GA is to reduce the number of fatal accidents to 350 by 2007—a 20 percent reduction from the 1996–1998 baseline [4].

Sources

1. Deyoe, Robin, Runway Safety Program Office, Federal Aviation Administration, U.S. Department of Transportation, personal communication, Sept. 13, 2000.

2. National Transportation Safety Board, *Accidents, Fatalities, and Rates, 1982-2000* (Washington, DC: 2001), also available at http://www.ntsb.gov/aviation/htm, as of Apr. 17, 2001.

3. U.S. Department of Transportation, Federal Aviation Administration, *General Aviation Accidents, 1983–1994: Identification of Factors Related to Controlled-Flight-Into-Terrain (CFIT) Accidents* (Washington, DC: July 1997).

4. ____. *Safer Skies: A Focused Agenda,* 2000, available at http://www.faa.gov/apa/safer_skies/saftoc.htm, as of Sept. 20, 2000.

5. U.S. General Accounting Office, Resources, Community, and Economic Development Division, *Aviation Safety: Safer Skies Initiative Has Taken Initial Steps to Reduce Accident Rates by 2007* (Washington, DC: June 2000).

Figure 2
General Aviation Fatalities: 1990–2000
(Monthly data)

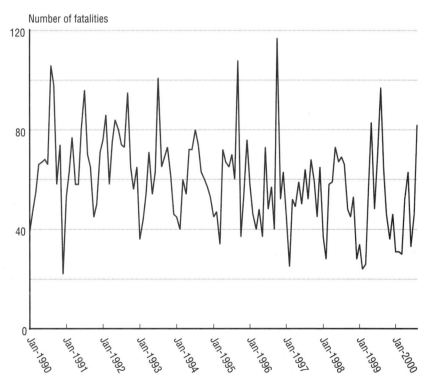

SOURCE: National Transportation Safety Board, Office of Aviation Safety, available at http://www.ntsb.gov/aviation.

Commercial Maritime Vessel Incidents

About 50,000 commercial vessels carrying freight and passengers call at U.S. ports every year. In 2000, there were almost 7,000 verified U.S. and foreign vessel incidents[1] in U.S. waters. Over the last six years, the number of commercial vessel incidents in U.S. waters has declined (table 1). Approximately 90 percent of these incidents occurred among 10 vessel types, and this concentration has been increasing since 1997.

Towboats and tugboats have ranked as the number one vessel type involved in incidents since 1994. Prior to 1994, fishing vessels ranked number one; they now rank second. However, the number of incidents involving both of these vessel types has been declining in recent years

---

[1] Incidents are defined as collisions, groundings, and "allisions" (when two vessels sideswipe each other).

[5]. Towboats and tugboats primarily push and pull barges on U.S. inland waterways and provide tug assist services in ports and along coastal areas. Towboats and tugboats, which can handle as many as 35 barges at a time, have limited maneuverability, especially when the crew is involved in maneuvering barges [4]. People falling overboard account for the majority of the fatalities in the inland towing industry [2].

A study of U.S. maritime incident data revealed that in 2000 the highest proportion (42 percent) of all maritime fatalities occurred among commercial fishing vessels. The next highest proportion of fatalities were among towboats and barges (11 percent), freight ships (10 percent), and passenger vessels (10 percent) [1]. The U.S. Coast Guard, which estimates that there are between 100,000 to 120,000 vessels in the U.S. commercial

Table 1
Number of Commercial Vessel Incidents by Type of Vessel—Top 10 Vessel Types: 1992–2000

Vessel type	1992	1993	1994	1995	1996	1997	1998	1999	2000
Towboat/tugboat	1,508	1,690	2,355	2,633	2,429	2,211	2,180	2,049	1,802
Fishing boat	1,984	1,991	1,959	1,546	1,296	1,284	1,154	1,232	1,125
Passenger ship	684	789	932	982	977	903	944	936	908
Freight barge	723	795	909	983	964	792	747	771	640
Tank barge	818	861	1,066	949	799	778	729	647	619
Freight ship	915	955	1,037	937	746	701	689	668	510
Recreational boat	489	639	718	277	189	325	411	437	480
Tank ship	542	545	628	467	355	358	348	286	230
Oversized vessel	210	242	184	135	136	146	179	138	131
Unclassified vessel	146	132	175	153	397	393	223	166	115
Total, top 10	**8,019**	**8,639**	**9,963**	**9,062**	**8,288**	**7,891**	**7,604**	**7,330**	**6,560**
Total, all vessels	**8,734**	**9,457**	**10,852**	**9,806**	**9,191**	**8,915**	**8,479**	**7,862**	**6,903**
Percentage of total, top 10	91.8%	91.4%	91.8%	92.4%	90.2%	88.5%	89.7%	93.2%	95.0%

SOURCE: U.S. Department of Transportation, U.S. Coast Guard, Resources Management Directorate, Data Administration Division, personal communication, February 2001.

Figure 1
Worker Fatalities on Fishing Vessels: 1995–1999

Number of fatalities

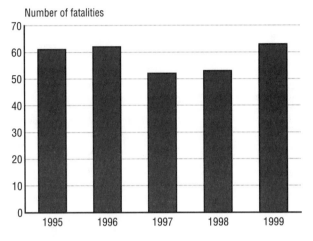

SOURCE: U.S. Department of Transportation, U.S. Coast Guard, *U.S. Coast Guard Marine Safety and Environmental Protection Business Plan FY 2001–2005,* available at http://www.uscg.mil, as of February 2001.

Figure 2
Commercial Vessel Incidents Involving Recreational Boats: 1992–2000

Number of incidents

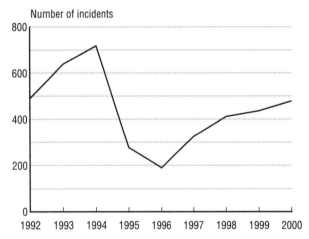

SOURCE: U.S. Department of Transportation, U.S. Coast Guard, Resources Management Directorate, Data Administration Division, personal communication, February 2001.

fishing fleet, believes the industry to be one of the most hazardous in the nation [3]. The number of fishing vessel worker fatalities appears to be climbing after a drop in 1997 (see figure 1). This may be due to increased economic pressure and competition in the commercial fishing industry, which encourages risk taking [3].

The number of recreational boats involved in commercial vessel incidents has been climbing since 1996 (figure 2). The safety of these boaters can be dependent on their ability to recognize commercial vessels, particularly tugboats and towboats, and accurately assess their movements [2].

Sources

1. Ungs, Timothy J. and Michael L. Adess, U.S. Department of Transportation, U.S. Coast Guard, *Water Transportation and the Maritime Industry,* available at http://www.uscg.mil, as of February 2001.

2. U.S. Department of Transportation, U.S. Coast Guard, "Epilogue," *American Waterways Operators,* available at http://www.uscg.mil, as of February 2001.

3. ____. *U.S. Coast Guard Marine Safety and Environmental Protection Business Plan FY 2001–2005,* available at http://www.uscg.mil, as of February 2001.

4. U.S. Department of Transportation, U.S. Coast Guard, Marine Safety Office, Providence, RI, available at http://www.uscg.mil, as of Feb. 24, 2001.

5. U.S. Department of Transportation, U.S. Coast Guard, Resources Management Directorate, Data Administration Division, personal communication, February 2001.

Recreational Boating

Most fatalities, injuries, and accidents on the water involve recreational boating. In 1999, the U.S. Coast Guard (USCG) reported a total of 7,931 recreational boating accidents and 4,315 injuries (figure 1). Personal watercraft and open motorboats account for the highest number of these accidents. Although fatalities remain high, the number has declined from 865 in 1990 to 734 in 1999. In 1999, 34 percent of recreational boating accidents involved collisions with other vessels (table 1). Substantially more drownings were related to the use of open motorboats than for any other type of recreational craft (table 2).

The majority of recreational boating accidents occurred during vessel operation and were caused

Table 1
Types of Recreational Boating Accidents: 1999

Accident type	Accidents	Injuries	Fatalities
Collision with vessel	2,729	1,406	93
Collision with fixed object	881	460	44
Falls overboard	624	439	200
Capsizing	549	269	223
Grounding	507	190	13
Flooding/swamping	460	91	43
Skier mishap	450	444	14
Fall in boat	352	362	3
Fire/explosion (fuel)	222	125	2
Sinking	220	53	29
Collision with floating object	172	63	5
Struck submerged object	161	42	6
Fire/explosion (other than fuel)	141	18	2
Struck by boat	132	112	5
Struck by motor/propeller	99	98	9
Other and unknown	232	143	43
Totals	**7,931**	**4,315**	**734**

SOURCE: U.S. Department of Transportation, U.S. Coast Guard Office of Boating Safety, personal communication, February 2001.

by operator error, such as recklessness, inattention, and speed (table 3). Alcohol involvement accounted for 6.3 percent of accidents due to operator error in 1999. USCG found that 49 percent of all boating fatalities occurred on boats where the operator lacked safe boating education [2].

Regardless of the cause of the accident or the type of boat involved, boaters can improve their chances of survival by wearing life jackets or using other personal flotation devices (PFDs). Eight out of 10 fatal boating accident victims were not wearing a PFD. USCG estimates that the use of life jackets could have saved the lives of 509 drowning victims in 1998 [1].

Figure 1
Recreational Boating Accidents, Injuries, and Fatalities: 1988–1999

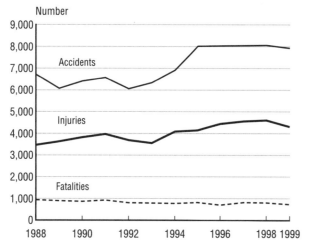

SOURCES: Injuries and accidents, 1988–1998—U.S. Department of Transportation,U.S. Coast Guard, *Boating Statistics – 1998*, COMDTPUB P16754.12 (Washington, DC: Dec. 30, 1999). Fatalities, 1988–1998—U.S. Department of Transportation, Bureau of Transportation Statistics, *National Transportation Statistics 2000* (Washington, DC: 2001), table 3-1. All 1999 data—U.S. Department of Transportation, U.S. Coast Guard, Office of Boating Safety, personal communication, February 2001.

Table 2
Number of Fatalities by Type of Vessel: 1999

Boat type	Total	Drownings	Other deaths
Open motorboat	**408**	294	114
Canoe/kayak	**84**	80	4
Personal watercraft	**66**	15	51
Rowboat	**50**	43	7
Cabin motorboat	**46**	25	21
Pontoon	**20**	12	8
Auxiliary sail	**14**	11	3
Houseboat	**14**	9	5
Inflatable	**14**	13	1
Sail (only)	**5**	5	0
Jet boat	**1**	0	1
Other and unknown	**12**	10	2
Total	**734**	**517**	**217**

SOURCE: U.S. Department of Transportation, U.S. Coast Guard, Office of Boating Safety, personal communication, February 2001.

Table 3
Recreational Boating Accidents Due to Operator Error: 1999

Cause	Accidents
Operator inattention	983
Operator inexperience	947
Careless/reckless operation	830
Excessive speed	676
No proper lookout	588
Alcohol use	337
Passenger/skier behavior	333
Restricted vision	118
Rules of the road infraction	93
Sharp turn	86
Improper loading	68
Overloading	56
Improper anchoring	48
Off throttle steering-jet	42
Standing/sitting on gunwale, bow, or transom	30
Lack of or improper boat lights	21
Failure to vent	15
Drug use	3
Starting in gear	2
Number of accidents	**5,276**

SOURCE: U.S. Department of Transportation, U.S. Coast Guard Office of Boating Safety, personal communication, February 2001.

Sources

1. U.S. Department of Transportation, U.S. Coast Guard, *United States Coast Guard 1999 Annual Report* (Washington, DC: 2000).

2. U.S. Department of Transportation, U.S. Coast Guard, Office of Boating Safety, personal communication, February 2001.

Rail

Most railroad fatalities occur on railroad rights-of-way and at highway-rail grade crossings, not on trains. (Railroad fatalities include people killed and injured in train and nontrain incidents and accidents on railroad-operated property.) Of the 932 people killed in accidents and incidents involving railroads in 1999, only 14 were train passengers. As major train accidents are relatively infrequent, the number of fatalities fluctuates from year to year (table 1). The fatality rate per million train-miles changed little between 1978 and 1993, but since that time has dropped by about 40 percent (figure 1).

Although far fewer people die in highway-rail grade-crossing accidents than in the past, the toll is still large (figure 2). Of the 402 lives lost in 1999 in this type of accident, only 11 were passengers on trains; most were in motor vehicles or on foot [1].

Trespassers not at grade crossings (people on railroad property without permission) accounted for 478 (about 51 percent) of the railroad deaths in 1999. Better understanding of trespassing and its motivations could be essential to addressing this high toll.

Source

1. U.S. Department of Transportation, Bureau of Transportation Statistics, *National Transportation Statistics 2000* (Washington, DC: In press).

Table 1
Train Accidents and Fatalities: 1978–1999
(Excludes highway-rail crossings)

Year	Accidents	Fatalities
1978	10,991	61
1980	8,205	29
1985	3,275	8
1990	2,879	10
1995	2,459	14
1999	2,768	9

SOURCE: U.S. Department of Transportation, Federal Railroad Administration, *Accident/Incident Overview* (Washington, DC: Various years).

Figure 1
Rail-Related Fatality Rate: 1978–1999
(Including highway-rail grade crossings)

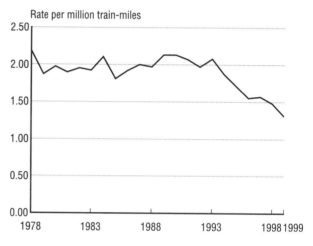

SOURCE: U.S. Department of Transportation, Federal Railroad Administration, *Accident/Incident Overview* (Washington, DC: Various years).

Figure 2
Highway-Rail Grade-Crossing Fatalities: 1993–1999

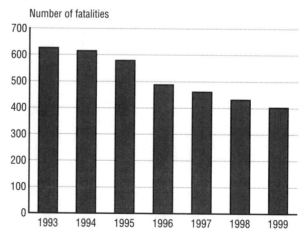

SOURCE: U.S. Department of Transportation, Federal Railroad Administration, *Railroad Safety Statistics Annual Report 1999* (Washington, DC: August 2000), also available at http://www.fra.dot.gov, as of Nov. 8, 2000.

Pipelines

Pipelines carry vast quantities of natural gas, petroleum products, and other materials to fuel the nation's commercial and consumer demands. Pipelines are a relatively safe way to transport energy resources and other products, but they are subject to forces of nature, human actions, and material defects that can cause potentially catastrophic accidents [4].

Major causes of pipeline accidents include excavation, material failure, and corrosion. The U.S. Department of Transportation issues regulations covering pipeline design, construction, operation, and maintenance for both natural gas and interstate hazardous liquid pipelines. The number of fatalities related to pipeline incidents varies from year to year, reflecting the high consequences associated with a limited number of failures (figures 1 and 2). In fact, the 38 pipeline fatalities in 2000 were more than twice the number recorded in 1975 [1].

Many of the hazardous liquid and natural gas transmission pipelines in the United States are 30 to 50 years old. Pipeline age may have been a contributing factor in the violent rupture of a 30-inch natural gas pipeline near the Pecos River in Carlsbad, New Mexico, on August 19, 2000, in which 12 people were killed—the deadliest pipeline accident in the continental United States in almost 25 years. Preliminary examination of the pipeline section that failed in Carlsbad revealed considerable internal corrosion and pipe wall loss greater than 50 percent. This section of pipe was almost 50 years old. Although age alone does not indicate that a pipeline may be unsafe, determining the integrity of pipelines becomes increasingly important as the nation's pipeline systems age [2].

Excavation and other outside force damage are the leading cause of pipeline failures, averaging 39 percent of the total, followed by corrosion with an

Figure 1
Fatalities in Pipeline Incidents

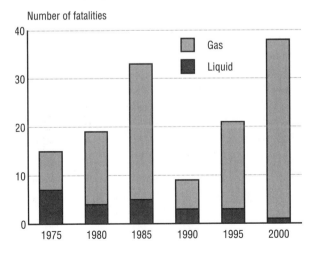

SOURCE: U.S. Department of Transportation, Research and Special Programs Administration, Office of Pipeline Safety.

Figure 2
Pipeline Incidents/Accidents: 1995–2000

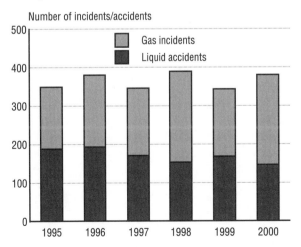

SOURCE: U.S. Department of Transportation, Research and Special Programs Administration, Office of Pipeline Safety.

average of 20 percent [3]. Other causes of failure are incorrect operation, construction, or material defects; equipment malfunction; and failed pipe. To reduce the problem of excavation damage, one-call notification centers have been established in 48 states and the District of Columbia [1].

Major advances in the materials used for pipes and welding, inspections, and the installation process over the past 25 years have reduced the number of leaks and made those that take place less severe. New corrosion coatings and new application processes have produced dramatically longer lives for pipes.

Sources

1. National Transportation Safety Board, *We Are All Safer*, SR-98-01, 2nd ed. (Washington, DC: July 1998), also available at http://www.ntsb.gov/Publictn/1998/ SR9801.pdf, as of Oct. 26, 2000.

2. ___. "NTSB To Hold Pipeline Safety Hearing in November," press release, Sept. 22, 2000, available at http://www.ntsb.gov/Pressrel/2000/000922.htm, as of Oct. 25, 2000.

3. U.S. Department of Transportation, Research and Special Programs Administration, Office of Investigations and Analysis, Compliance Analysis Division, personal communication, June 20, 2000.

4. U.S. Department of Transportation, Research and Special Programs Administration, Office of Pipeline Safety, *Pipeline Statistics* (Washington, DC: 2000), also available at http://ops.dot.gov/stats.htm, as of Apr. 19, 2001.

Hazardous Materials Transportation Accidents and Incidents

Like all modes of transportation, the movement of hazardous materials comes with the risk of accidents and incidents, including the threat of explosion, fire, or contamination of the environment. The safe transportation of hazardous materials has long been an area of governmental concern and oversight. The U.S. Department of Transportation (DOT), together with the Nuclear Regulatory Commission (for radioactive materials), are responsible for developing safety regulations for the transportation of hazardous materials, including training and packaging requirements, emergency response measures, enforcement, and data collection.

In 1999, more than 17,000 incidents were reported to DOT's Hazardous Materials Information System (HMIS), the primary source of national data on hazardous materials transportation safety. These incidents resulted in 7 deaths and 252 injuries directly attributable to the materials being transported [1]. As shown in table 1, a vast majority (85 percent) of reported incidents occurred on the nation's highways. Although the number of incidents has increased in years, much of the increase can be attributed to improved reporting, an expansion of reporting requirements, and the occurrence of high-consequence, low-probability events.[1] [2]

Two types of data are needed to establish and evaluate the risk of transporting hazardous materials: incident/accident data and flow/exposure data. Through DOT's HMIS database, detailed data are available on hazardous materials transportation incidents and accidents. The release of the 1997 Commodity Flow Survey provided a

Table 1
Hazardous Materials Transportation Fatalities, Injuries, and Incidents: 1990–1999

Fatalities					
Year	Air	Highway	Rail	Water	Total
1990	0	8	0	0	8
1991	0	10	0	0	10
1992	0	16	0	0	16
1993	0	15	0	0	15
1994	0	11	0	0	11
1995	0	7	0	0	7
1996	110	8	2	0	120
1997	0	12	0	0	12
1998	0	13	0	0	13
1999	0	7	0	0	7
Total	**110**	**107**	**2**	**0**	**219**

Injured persons					
Year	Air	Highway	Rail	Water	Total
1990	39	311	73	0	423
1991	31	333	75	0	439
1992	23	465	116	0	604
1993	50	511	66	0	627
1994	57	425	95	0	577
1995	33	296	71	0	400
1996	33	216	926	0	1,175
1997	24	156	45	0	225
1998	20	153	22	2	197
1999	12	205	35	0	252
Total	**322**	**3,071**	**1,524**	**2**	**4,919**

Incidents					
Year	Air	Highway	Rail	Water	Total
1990	297	7,297	1,279	7	8,880
1991	299	7,644	1,155	12	9,110
1992	413	7,760	1,130	8	9,311
1993	622	11,080	1,120	8	12,830
1994	929	13,995	1,157	6	16,087
1995	814	12,764	1,153	12	14,743
1996	916	11,917	1,112	6	13,951
1997	1,028	11,863	1,103	5	13,999
1998	1,380	12,971	990	11	15,352
1999	1,576	14,443	1,061	8	17,088
Total	**8,274**	**111,734**	**11,260**	**83**	**131,351**

SOURCE: U.S. Department of Transportation, Hazardous Materials Information System database, 2000, available at http://hazmat.dot.gov.

---

[1] A high-consequence, low-probability event is an incident or most often an accident that might statistically occur very infrequently, but results in a catastrophic and tragic outcome.

major expansion in the availability of flow/exposure data. Improvements in highway and air data were particularly noteworthy. Table 2 shows average miles per shipment for the nine classes of hazardous materials. These data are useful for risk analysis, which can provide the basis for informed decisionmaking regarding the safe transportation of hazardous materials.

Sources

1. U.S. Department of Transportation, Hazardous Materials Information System database, 2000, available at http://hazmat.dot.gov, as of Mar. 12, 2001.

2. U.S. Department of Transportation, Research and Special Programs Administration, *Biennial Report on Hazardous Material Transportation Calendar Years 1992–1993* (Washington, DC: 1995).

Table 2
Hazardous Materials Shipments by Class and Miles Shipped: 1997

Class	Average miles per shipment
Flammable solids	838
Explosives	549
Radioactive materials	445
Toxics (poison)	402
Corrosive materials	201
Oxidizers/organic peroxides	193
Flammable liquids	73
Gases	66
Miscellaneous dangerous goods	323
Weighted average	**113**

SOURCE: U.S. Department of Commerce, Census Bureau, *1997 Economic Census—1997 Commodity Flow Survey, Hazardous Materials* (Washington, DC: December 1999), table 2.

Transportation Workers

Occupational risk from transportation incidents is often overlooked in safety analyses. The U.S. Department of Labor, Bureau of Labor Statistics collects data using the Census of Fatal Occupational Injuries. These data classify occupational deaths by event or type of exposure, one of which is "transportation incidents." Transportation incidents are further classified into three additional levels of detail (e.g., highway incident/noncollision/jackknifed vehicle).

For all workers, occupational fatalities in the United States fell slightly from 6,217 in 1992 to 6,026 in 1998. Transportation incidents, the largest single cause of occupational fatalities, however, increased from 2,484 to 2,630 (table 1). Consequently, transportation's share in the total rose from 40 percent in 1992 to 44 percent in 1998. Highway incidents accounted for over half of the transportation-related deaths in 1998. Truck drivers alone made up 14.6 percent of all occupational fatalities, with 879 killed, 721 of them in transportation incidents (table 2). Occupational deaths caused by highway incidents increased by almost 24 percent between 1992 and 1998, while deaths in aircraft incidents decreased by 37 percent during the same period [1].

The risk of being killed while working in a transportation occupation was more than five times the average for all occupations. Among transportation occupations, airplane pilots and navigators and taxicab drivers were at highest risk. Bus drivers had the lowest risk of being killed on the job. Measured by work-related fatalities per 1,000 employees (resulting from all accidents), the risk for all occupations, on average, was 0.047 in 1998 (i.e., 47 workers were killed on duty for every million employees) (table 3). In contrast, the risk for transportation occupations was 0.259.

Table 1
Transportation-Related Occupational Fatalities: 1992 and 1998

	1992	1998
Total occupational fatalities (all causes)	**6,217**	**6,026**
Total transportation-related fatalities	**2,484**	**2,630**
Highway	1,158	1,431
Off-highway road (farm, industrial, premises)	436	384
Air transportation	353	223
Worker struck by vehicle, mobile equipment	346	413
Water transportation	109	112
Railroad transportation	66	60
Other, not elsewhere classified	16	7

SOURCE: U.S. Department of Labor, Bureau of Labor Statistics, *Census of Fatal Occupational Injuries,* 1992 and 1998.

Between 1993 (the first year for which data are available) and 1998, the national average risk, in terms of work-related fatalities per 1,000 employees, decreased 15 percent. For transportation occupations as a whole, however, it decreased only 3 percent, though the risk for taxicab drivers, rail transportation occupations, and water transportation occupations decreased appreciably. In 1993, the risk for taxicab drivers was 1.66 fatalities per 1,000 employees, the highest among all transportation occupations. By 1998, it fell to 0.96, lower than that for airplane pilots and navigators. In terms of percentage change, the decreases in risk for rail transportation and water transportation occupations were even larger—62 percent for rail and 51 percent for water.

Source

1. U.S. Department of Labor, Bureau of Labor Statistics, *Census of Fatal Occupational Injuries,* 1992 and 1998.

Table 2
Occupational Fatalities in Transportation Occupations: 1998

	Total fatalities	Transportation incidents	Assaults and violent acts	Contact with objects and equipment	Falls	Exposure to harmful substance or environment	Fires and explosions
All occupations	6,026	2,630	958	940	699	572	205
Transportation occupations	1,257	926	96	138	34	39	23
Truck drivers	879	721	30	76	22	21	7
Drivers (sales workers)	36	27	6	–	–	–	–
Bus drivers	13	10	–	–	–	–	–
Taxicab drivers and chauffeurs	82	32	50	–	–	–	–
Airplane pilots and navigators	91	91	–	–	–	–	–
Rail transportation occupations	15	13	–	–	–	–	–
Water transportation occupations	25	18	–	–	–	3	–
Other transportation occupations[1]	116	15	–	–	–	–	–

[1] Includes other vehicle operators, couriers, and material moving labor, etc.

KEY: – = no data reported or data that do not meet publication criteria.

SOURCE: U.S. Department of Labor, Bureau of Labor Statistics, *Census of Fatal Occupational Injuries*, 1998.

Table 3
**Occupational Fatality Rates of
Transportation Occupations: 1993–1998**
Per thousand employees

	1993	1998
All occupations	0.056	0.047
Transportation occupations	0.267	0.259
Truck drivers	0.328	0.325
Drivers (sales workers)	0.133	0.124
Bus drivers	0.028	0.021
Taxicab drivers and chauffeurs	1.658	0.959
Airplane pilots and navigators	1.188	0.993
Rail transportation occupations	0.464	0.177
Water transportation occupations	0.967	0.476
Other transportation occupations[1]	–	0.126

[1] Includes other vehicle operators, couriers, and material moving labor, etc.

KEY: – = no data reported or data that do not meet publication criteria.

SOURCE: U.S. Department of Labor, Bureau of Labor Statistics, *Census of Fatal Occupational Injuries*, 1998.

Chapter 4
Mobility and Access to Transportation

Introduction

Transportation exists to help people and businesses overcome the distance between places (e.g., work and home, factory and store, store and home). Two concepts, mobility and accessibility, are most often used to measure the success of the transportation system. Mobility measurements focus on how far people and goods travel. Accessibility is a measure of the relative ease with which people and businesses can reach a variety of locations. Mobility and access are often positively related, but not always. For instance, less travel (lower mobility) might be the result of better access in cases where opportunities are located nearby. Many factors affect mobility and access, including the availability and cost of transportation and the infrastructure in place to facilitate it, population growth and economic fluctuations, and the knowledge of and ability to apply logistical options (particularly for businesses).

Both passenger travel and goods movement continue to increase in the United States, despite some signs of strain in the transportation system. About 4.6 trillion passenger-miles of travel were supported by the system in 1999, an annual increase of 2.2 percent since 1990. In addition, there were over 3.8 trillion ton-miles of domestic freight shipped in 1999, representing an annual growth rate of 2.0 percent since 1990.

Increases in population, numbers of workers, vehicle availability, and disposable personal income are among the factors that contribute to passenger travel growth. This growth can also be seen in international travel. Between 1989 and 1999 the number of U.S. residents traveling out of the country rose 44 percent. Growth is also evident when measured by mode, with increases in enplanements at large air traffic hubs, capacity in the North American cruise industry, and fast-ferry traffic.

Highway passenger travel continues to grow, with travel in light trucks posting the largest increases. The light truck share of passenger-miles of travel grew from 14 percent in 1975 to 31 percent in 1999. Despite some gains for the transit mode, the number of people driving to work alone continued its upward trend along with the distance traveled. Accessibility measures show growth, as well: the number of household vehicles, for instance, has risen to equal the number of licensed drivers. Nevertheless, there were 8 million households without a car in 1995. Access to intercity public transportation is also very high, with about 95 percent of the U.S. population now living within a reasonable distance of commercial air service, intercity bus, or Amtrak.

Congestion on the highways and in the skies slows traffic and creates a drag on the nation's economic productivity. On the highways, hours of delay per driver almost tripled between 1982 and 1997, with drivers in the largest metropolitan areas suffering from the worst congestion. Each driver in the largest metropolitan areas lost an average of 54 hours in 1997. Flight delays tend to vary from year to year making comparisons difficult; in 2000, one in four flights by major U.S. air carriers were delayed, canceled, or diverted. Causes of congestion in the air and on the highways show some similarities: system capacity that is not keeping pace with increasing volumes and delays caused by inclement weather. Because data are not regularly collected for waterborne transportation, measures of the extent of congestion for this mode are not available.

Economic activity is a key factor affecting freight movement. So, too, are changes in business logistics, such as the location of distribution centers at greater distances from consumers and the wide use of just-in-time manufacturing. Air carrier and intercity trucking ton-miles are increasing at a faster rate than the other modes, while water ton-miles have decreased since 1980, due to a decline in Alaskan crude oil shipments. The value of air freight stood at $229 billion in 1997, up from $151 billion in 1993 (in 1997 dollars). Compared with other freight modes, air was used more often to move higher value commodities over longer distances. Despite the rapid growth of goods movement by air, however, most freight (measured in tons) was moved by trucks.

The heavier commodities—coal, gravel and crushed stones, gasoline, limestone and chalk, and fuel oils—accounted for the most tonnage shipped domestically in 1997. Measured by value, the top commodities shipped were motor vehicle parts and accessories, miscellaneous manufactured products, computer equipment, mixed freight, and pharmaceutical products. The U.S. transportation system also moved—mostly by truck— more than 1.5 billion tons of hazardous materials in 1997.

U.S. international waterborne container trade increased throughout the 1990s. In general, however, demand for U.S. exports has not kept pace with consumer demands for imports. This imbalance increases shipping costs because of the need to reposition empty containers or store them indefinitely on U.S. port facility property.

Passenger Travel

All modes of transportation continue to show growth in passenger-miles of travel (pmt). Light trucks (pickups, minivans, and sport utility vehicles) posted the biggest gains, increasing its share of pmt from 14 percent to 31 percent over the 1975 to 1999 period. In absolute terms, passenger travel in light trucks grew from 363 million miles in 1975 to 1.4 trillion miles in 1999. The passenger car share of pmt declined from 76 percent in 1975 to 54 percent in 1999. Air travel also increased its share from 5 percent to 11 percent. Overall, pmt, excluding miles traveled in heavy trucks, grew from about 2.6 trillion in 1975 to 4.6 trillion in 1999 (figure 1). On a per capita basis, people traveled 16,900 miles in 1999 compared with 11,900 in 1975 [3].

Several factors contribute to the continued growth in pmt (figure 2). The resident population, for example, increased by nearly 57 million people, a rise of 27 percent between 1975 and 1999. Moreover, the number of people in the civilian labor force, most of whom commute to work, grew twice as fast as the population over the same period. People also have more money to spend on transportation, particularly for automobiles and air travel. Disposable personal income per capita rose from $14,393 in 1975 to $23,244 in 1999 (in chained 1996 dollars) [2].

An increasing number of people can now afford to buy vehicles and travel services, especially since the cost of the most widely used kinds of transportation—travel in cars and planes—fell in real terms. For example, the inflation-adjusted average airfare for domestic scheduled service declined from $174 in 1975 to $110 in 1995, and has stayed at that level through 1998 (measured in chained 1996 dollars) [3]. Despite recent

Figure 1
Passenger-Miles of Travel

Trillions

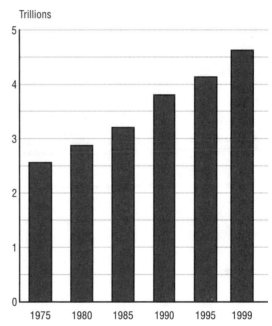

SOURCE: 1975–1995—various sources as cited in U.S. Department of Transportation, Bureau of Transportation Statistics, *National Transportation Statistics 2000* (Washington, DC: 2001); 1999 data—various sources as compiled by the Bureau of Transportation Statistics.

Estimating Passenger-Miles of Travel

Passenger-miles of travel are estimated on a yearly basis by adding together estimates for each mode, which are derived from separate sources. Passenger-miles of travel for large air carriers and intercity trains are estimated from tickets and are very accurate. A variety of methods are used to estimate travel in other modes, each with different strengths and weaknesses. For more information see the Accuracy Profiles in BTS's *National Transportation Statistics 2000*.

Figure 2
Increases in Passenger-Miles of Travel (PMT) and Factors Affecting Travel Demand: 1975–1999

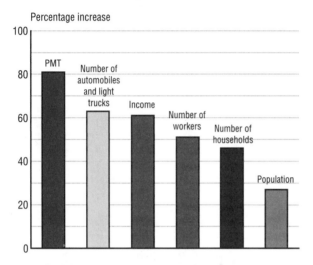

SOURCES: U.S. Department of Commerce, Census Bureau, *Statistical Abstract of the United States: 2000* (Washington, DC: 2000); various sources as cited in U.S. Department of Transportation, Bureau of Transportation Statistics, *National Transportation Statistics 2000* (Washington, DC: 2001); and various sources as compiled by Bureau of Transportation Statistics.

increases, gasoline prices, too, have been at historically low levels for much of the past 15 years [1]. However, intercity rail fares decreased only slightly between 1975 and 1995 and intercity bus fares actually increased more than inflation during this period. Rising bus fares tend to affect individuals with lower incomes more than people at higher income levels.

Sources

1. American Petroleum Institute. "How Much We Pay for Gasoline: 1999–April 2000 Review," May 2000, available at http://www.api.org/pasp/biggas.pdf, as of Sept. 9, 2000.

2. U.S. Department of Commerce, Census Bureau, *Statistical Abstract of the United States, 2000, 120th Edition* (Washington, DC: 2001), table 722.

3. U.S. Department of Transportation, Bureau of Transportation Statistics, *National Transportation Statistics 2000* (Washington, DC: 2001).

Vehicle-Miles of Travel

With increases in both population and individual travel, highway usage has risen substantially. Annual vehicle-miles of travel (vmt) in the United States rose by nearly 30 percent to almost 2.7 trillion miles between 1989 and 1999, an annual increase of 2.5 percent. Vmt per capita rose by just over 16 percent during the same period, an annual increase of 1.5 percent. The most heavily populated states, California, Texas, Florida, and New York, are the most heavily traveled. Wyoming, the least populated state, had the highest vmt per capita in 1999 at 16,200, followed by New Mexico, Alabama, Georgia, and Oklahoma at over 12,600. The District of Columbia, Hawaii, and New York had the lowest vmt per capita at just under 7,000. Overall, the percentage change in vmt per capita between 1989 and 1999 ranged from a 42 percent increase in Mississippi to a 3 percent decline in Hawaii, with 13 states showing an increase of at least 25 percent over the 10-year period (see map on the next page).

In recent years, the makeup of the U.S. vehicle fleet changed as well, altering the share of vmt by vehicle type (figure 1). While the share of total vmt by buses and single-unit and combination trucks has remained relatively constant, the increasing popularity of sport utility vehicles and other light trucks in recent years has resulted in a shift in the percentage of total vmt from automobiles to light trucks. Although still the dominant vehicle type in terms of vmt, the share of automobile vmt declined from 67 percent of total vmt to 58 percent between 1989 and 1999. Over the same period, the percentage of total vmt by light trucks (a classification including vans, pickup trucks, and sport utility vehicles) rose to 33 percent of total vmt [1].

Source

1. U.S. Department of Transportation, Federal Highway Administration, *Highway Statistics* (Washington, DC: Annual issues).

The Highway Performance Monitoring System

The Federal Highway Administration analyzes and presents vehicle-miles of travel data in their annual report, *Highway Statistics*, using the Highway Performance Monitoring System (HPMS). The HPMS compiles state-provided data into a national-level database, combining "sample data on the condition, use, performance and physical characteristics of facilities functionally classified as arterials and collectors (except rural minor collectors) and system-type data for all public road facilities within each State." States report data annually. However, in some years, estimates may be made for states with incomplete data.

Source

U.S. Department of Transportation, Federal Highway Administration, *Highway Statistics 1998* (Washington, DC: 1999), p. V-1.

Figure 1
Changes in Vehicle-Miles of Travel by Vehicle Type: 1989–1999

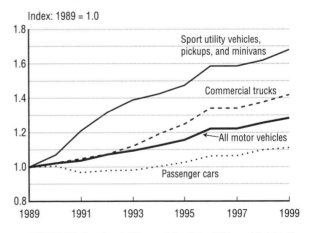

SOURCE: U.S. Department of Transportation, Federal Highway Administration, *Highway Statistics* (Washington, DC: Annual issues).

Percentage Change in Vehicle-Miles of Travel: 1989–1999

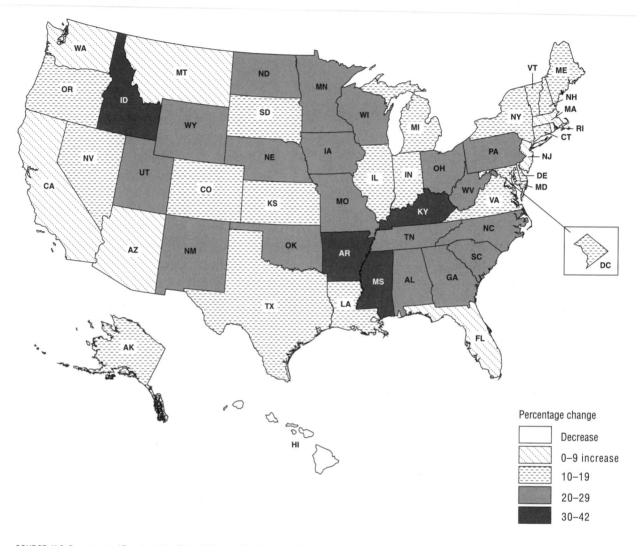

Percentage change

- Decrease
- 0–9 increase
- 10–19
- 20–29
- 30–42

SOURCE: U.S. Department of Transportation, Federal Highway Administration, *Highway Statistics* (Washington, DC: Annual issues).

International Travel To and From the United States

Overnight travel between the United States and foreign countries for both business and pleasure shows continual growth overall during the past decade (figures 1 and 2). Although it does not take into account people staying for less than one night (see box), this growth has implications for the infrastructure at America's borders (including airports and land border crossings) and the demand on transportation infrastructure by foreign nationals while they are in the country. There are also economic implications related to travel spending.

Factors that have contributed to growth include the globalization of the production of goods and services, lower priced air transportation, economic growth, and rising incomes in many parts of the world. According to the U.S. Department of Commerce's Tourism Industries Office of the International Trade Administration, the United States had a 7 percent share of worldwide tourist arrivals and 16 percent of worldwide tourist receipts in 1999 [1].

In 1999, a record 48 million international visitors traveled to the United States. Nearly three-

Figure 1
International Visitors to the United States: 1989–1999

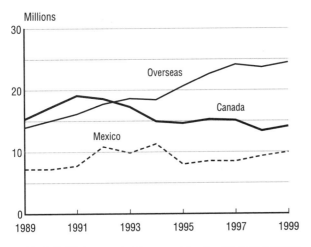

SOURCES: U.S. Department of Commerce, International Trade Administration, Office of Tourism Industries, *International Visitors (Inbound) and U.S. Residents (Outbound) (1989–1998)* (Washington, DC: 2000).
____. *Arrivals to the U.S. 1999 & 1998 (All Countries by Residency)* (Washington, DC: 2000).

Data on International Travel To and From the United States

The data here are limited to people staying one or more nights at their international destination and, therefore, do not include all cross-border movements between the United States, Canada, and Mexico. The data for international arrivals reported in this section come mainly from the Visitors Arrivals Program (Form I-94) administered by the U.S. Department of Justice's Immigration and Naturalization Service (INS) in cooperation with the U.S. Department of Commerce's Office of Tourism Industries.

The Visitors Arrivals Program includes overseas visitors staying for one or more nights for a period of less than 12 months whether for business, pleasure, or study. It does not include people transiting the United States en route to another country. Mexican tourist arrival estimates derived from the I-94 program are limited to those visiting the U.S. interior, beyond the 40 kilometer (25 mile) U.S. border zone, and those traveling by air. These data are supplemented by data from Banco de Mexico to report total Mexican arrivals on an annual basis for people staying one or more nights.

For Canadians, the Office of Tourism Industries relies on Statistics Canada's International Visitor Survey to provide monthly inbound visitors (again, for one or more nights) from Canada to the United States.

Data for U.S. residents traveling internationally are derived from the U.S. International Air Travel Statistics (Form I-92) program, also a joint effort between the INS and the Office of Tourism Industries. Data are collected from airlines for all international arriving and departing flights with the exception of those to and from Canada. U.S. resident travel to Canada for one or more nights is provided by Statistics Canada's International Visitor Survey. Estimates of U.S. resident travel to Mexico by means of transportation other than air is provided by Banco de Mexico.

Figure 2

International Trips by U.S. Residents: 1989–1999

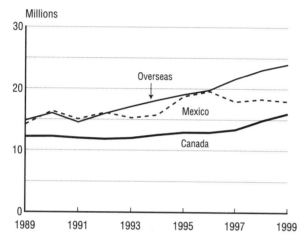

SOURCE: U.S. Department of Commerce, International Trade Administration, Office of Tourism Industries, *International Visitors (Inbound) and U.S. Residents (Outbound) (1989–1999)* (Washington, DC: 2000).

quarters of them were from five countries: Canada, Mexico, Japan, the United Kingdom, and Germany (table 1). The number of visitors from overseas (all countries except Canada and Mexico) has risen in the past few years, while the number of visitors from Canada has declined (figure 1). Canadian travel to the United States was 10 percent lower in 1999 than in 1989.

In 1999, U.S. residents made more than 58 million international trips. Major destinations were Mexico, Canada, and the United Kingdom (table 2). International travel by U.S. residents between 1989 and 1999 grew by more than 40 percent, with travel overseas growing the fastest (figure 2).

Source

1. U.S. Department of Commerce, International Trade Administration, Office of Tourism Industries, "June 2000, International Travel and Forecast for the U.S.," 2000, available at http://tinet.ita.doc.gov, as of Oct. 6, 2000.

Table 1

Top 15 Countries of Origin of International Visitors: 1999

Ranking	Country	Number (thousands)	Percent
1	Canada	14,110	29
2	Mexico	9,915	20
3	Japan	4,826	10
4	United Kingdom	4,252	9
5	Germany	1,985	4
6	France	1,059	2
7	Brazil	665	1
8	Italy	626	1
9	Venezuela	552	1
10	Netherlands	527	1
11	Argentina	502	1
12	South Korea	499	1
13	Australia	483	1
14	Taiwan	453	1
15	Colombia	416	1
	Top 15 total	**40,870**	**84**
	Total, all countries	48,491	100

NOTE: Percentages do not add due to rounding.

SOURCE: U.S. Department of Commerce, International Trade Administration, Office of Tourism Industries, "Top 55 Overseas Markets for International Visitor Arrivals to the United States: 1999 and 1998," available at http://tinet.ita.doc.gov, as of Sept. 11, 2000.

Table 2

Top 15 Countries Visited by U.S. Residents: 1999

Ranking	Country	Number (thousands)	Percent
1	Mexico	17,743	30
2	Canada	16,036	27
3	United Kingdom	4,129	7
4	France	2,728	5
5	Germany	1,966	3
6	Italy	1,893	3
7	Jamaica	1,499	3
8	Japan	1,254	2
9	Bahamas	1,254	2
10	Netherlands	1,032	2
11	Spain	909	2
12	Switzerland	787	1
13	Hong Kong	787	1
14	Republic of Korea	688	1
15	Republic of China (Taiwan)	590	1
15	Australia	590	1
	Top 15 total	**53,295**	**91**
	Total, all countries	58,358	100

SOURCES: U.S. Department of Commerce, International Trade Administration, Office of Tourism Industries, "U.S. Resident Travel to Overseas Countries, Historical Visitation: Outbound, 1988–1998," and "Select Destinations Visited by U.S. Resident Travelers: 1999–1998," available at http://tinet.ita.doc.gov, as of Sept. 11, 2000.

Top Passenger Border Crossings

Over 290 million people entered the United States at crossing points on the U.S.-Mexico border in 1999, triple the 90 million entering on the U.S.-Canada border (table 1). Most people traveled across the border in personal vehicles, although a large number of people entered the United States from Mexico on foot. El Paso, Texas, and San Ysidro, California (near San Diego), were the top vehicle crossing points. On the Canadian border, the top crossing points were Detroit, Michigan, and Buffalo-Niagara Falls, New York (table 2).

Table 1
Land Gateways on the Canadian and Mexican Borders: 1999

	Entering the U.S. from	
	Canada (thousands)	Mexico (thousands)
All personal vehicles	34,519	89,639
All buses	182	295
All personal vehicle passengers	87,691	242,613
All bus passengers	4,805	3,495
All train passengers	184	17
All pedestrians	587	48,186
Total passengers and pedestrians	**93,267**	**294,311**

SOURCE: U.S. Department of Transportation, Bureau of Transportation Statistics, special tabulation, August 2000, based on U.S. Department of Treasury, U.S. Customs Service, Office of Field Operations, Operations Management Database, 1999.

Table 2
Top 5 Gateways for Passengers in Personal Vehicles Entering the United States: 1999

Canada	Number (thousands)
Detroit, MI	19,382
Buffalo-Niagara Falls, NY	16,532
Blaine, WA	8,443
Sault Ste. Marie, MI	5,766
Port Huron, MI	4,309
Mexico	
El Paso, TX	46,397
San Ysidro, CA	33,593
Hildago, TX	29,119
Calexico, CA	20,372
Brownsville, TX	18,948

SOURCE: U.S. Department of Transportation, Bureau of Transportation Statistics, special tabulation, August 2000, based on U.S. Department of Treasury, U.S. Customs Service, Office of Field Operations, Operations Management Database, 1999.

Enplanements at Major U.S. Airports

Although more than 794 airports in the United States provided some form of air passenger service in 1999, most enplanements (i.e., passenger boardings) occur at a relatively small number of airports. In 1999, over 75 percent of all U.S. air passengers enplaned at only 69 airports located in 29 metropolitan areas identified by the U.S. Department of Transportation, Federal Aviation Administration as large air traffic hubs [2]. The top five air traffic hubs (Chicago, Atlanta, Dallas/Fort Worth, Los Angeles, and San Francisco) alone accounted for over 25 percent of all 1999 enplanements (see map on the next page).

Passenger enplanements at large air traffic hubs have grown at about the same rate as for the nation as a whole. Between 1975 and 1999, air passenger enplanements, nationwide, grew from 197 million to 611 million—a 210 percent increase. Over the same period, enplanements at large air traffic hubs grew from 144 million to 459 million—a 219 percent increase [1, 2].

Air traffic hubs located in major vacation areas (e.g., Orlando and Las Vegas), and those airports that became a hub for a commercial airline (e.g., Charlotte and Phoenix), experienced the greatest growth in enplanements (see the box for the difference between an air traffic hub and a commercial airline hub). Air traffic hubs located in the northeast and midwest, while still experiencing substantial net growth in enplanements, saw their *share* of total enplanements decrease. For example, New York's (John F. Kennedy and LaGuardia) share of total enplanements dropped from a little under 7 percent in 1975 to 3 percent in 1999, and it went from being the second largest air traffic hub to the sixth largest. Three cities identified as large hubs

> **What Is a Hub?**
>
> *Air traffic hubs* are not airports; they are geographical areas providing aviation services. An air traffic hub may be served by more than one commercial service airport (e.g., the Washington, DC, hub is served by Reagan National and Dulles International Airports). A large air traffic hub is an area with 1 percent or more of the total annual enplanements by all U.S. certificated air carriers. Medium hubs have between 0.25 and 0.99 percent of enplanements; small hubs have between 0.05 and 0.24 percent; and nonhubs have less than 0.05 percent of enplanements. This definition should not be confused with airline hub, defined below.
>
> A *commercial airline hub* is not the same thing as an air traffic hub. It refers to an airport that serves as a major transfer point in a commercial air carrier's route system. This practice of routing flights through a hub airport was adopted by most major air carriers following airline deregulation as a way to increase passenger loads to and from airports serving smaller markets.

in 1975 (Cleveland, Kansas City, and New Orleans), had less than 1 percent of enplanements in 1999 and are now classified as medium hubs. However, six cities identified as medium hubs in 1975 (Baltimore, Charlotte, Cincinnati, Orlando, Portland (Oregon), and San Diego), increased their share of enplanements to over 1 percent and are now classified as large hubs [1, 2].

Sources

1. Civil Aeronautics Board, *Airport Activity Statistics: Twelve Months Ending December 31, 1975* (Washington, DC: 1976).

2. U.S. Department of Transportation, Bureau of Transportation Statistics, Office of Airline Information, *Airport Activity Statistics of Certificated Air Carriers: Summary Tables, Twelve Months Ending December 31, 1999* (Washington, DC: 2001).

Enplanements at Large Air Traffic Hubs: 1975 and 1999

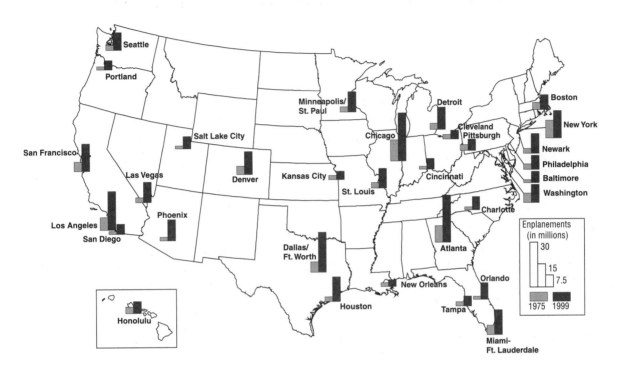

NOTE: These data include hubs that were classified as large hubs in either 1975 or 1999 or in both years. A large hub is a geographic area that enplanes 1 percent or more of nationally enplaned passengers. A hub may include more than one airport.

SOURCES: Civil Aeronautics Board, *Airport Activity Statistics: Twelve Months Ending December 31, 1975* (Washington, DC: 1976); U.S. Department of Transportation, Bureau of Transportation Statistics, Office of Airline Information, *Airport Activity Statistics of Certificated Air Carriers, Summary Tables, Twelve Months Ending December 31, 1999* (Washington, DC: 2001).

Cruise Ship Vacations

In 1999, a record 9 million passengers took cruise vacations. A total of 6.9 million of these cruised from North American ports, up 16 percent from a year earlier. Table 1 shows the top five North American ports by passenger traffic. The top four North American cruise lines (Carnival, Royal Caribbean, P&O/Princess, and Star) control 82 percent of North American cruise capacity and 75 percent of the world market [1].

Passenger capacity in the North American cruise industry has experienced an average growth rate of 8 percent per year since 1989 [2]. Several factors contributed to this growth including: a strong U.S. economy; the availability of new ships with the latest technologies, rich amenities, and services; and aggressive marketing by cruise lines. North American cruise industry growth is expected to continue, but the level of growth may be affected by negative publicity due to a series of shipboard incidents including fires and groundings. Overcapacity is also a potential concern because of the number of ship deliveries expected over the next few years. World shipyards have a record number of cruise ships on order and under construction [1].

Table 1

Top 5 North American Cruise Passenger Ports: 1990 and 1999

(Millions of passengers handled)

Port	1990	1999
Miami	2.7	3.1
Canaveral	0.8	2.8
Everglades	2.2	2.4
San Juan	0.9	1.1
Los Angeles	0.6	1.0

NOTE: Passengers are counted twice, upon embarkation and debarkation. Includes one-day cruises.

SOURCE: Oivind Mathisen, ed., *Cruise Industry News Annual 2000, Thirteenth Edition* (New York, NY: Cruise Industry News, 2000).

Source

1. Mathisen, Oivind, ed., *Cruise Industry News Annual: Industry Status 2000* (New York, NY: Cruise Industry News, 2000).

2. The McGraw-Hill Companies and U.S. Department of Commerce, International Trade Administration, *U.S. Industry and Trade Outlook 2000, Water Transportation* (New York, NY: The McGraw-Hill Companies, Inc., 2000), p. 52-9.

Passenger Ferries

Ferries carried approximately 90 million passengers in 1999 for work trips, leisure travel, and other purposes. Ferry vessels provide fixed-route service across a body of water and carry passengers, freight, and vehicles. According to a U.S. Department of Transportation, Federal Highway Administration (FHWA) survey, there are 578 ferry terminals, 487 ferry route segments, and 677 ferry vessels operating in the United States and its possessions (table 1). Nearly 82 percent of operating ferry vessels carry passengers; 50 percent of them carry passengers only [4].

Ferries were once used more extensively than they are today. At the end of the 19th century, for example, ferries in New York City carried 200 million passengers a year [1]. However, as more tunnels and bridges were built, ferry operations diminished in importance in many areas. In recent years, the ferry has been reestablished in some communities as a means of travel to and from work, often to ease congestion on crowded highways and bridges. About 30,000 passengers a day (about 8 million per year) now use ferry services between New York City and adjacent points in New Jersey. In San Francisco, about 5,500 passengers per weekday avoid crossing the Golden Gate Bridge by using a combination of ferries and feeder buses. Toll revenues collected on the bridge are used to partially subsidize ferry services in the San Francisco area [2].

Fast ferries—those vessels capable of attaining speeds of at least 25 knots—are becoming more popular. FHWA has identified 65 high-speed ferry route segments, of which all but 1 are passenger-only routes. These routes now account for 13 percent of the total U.S. ferry traffic. Passenger fast-ferry traffic increased at an average annual rate of 12.4 percent between 1993 and 1998. This growth rate is expected to continue through 2004 [3].

Table 1
Top 10 States Ranked by Number of Ferry Terminals: 1999

State	Number of ferry terminals	Number of ferry routes
New York	51	56
Washington	46	55
Alaska	41	65
California	38	39
Maine	33	25
Michigan	31	25
Louisiana	30	15
Massachusetts	27	37
North Carolina	27	16
Virginia	20	14
Total top 10	**344**	**347**
Top 10% of total	**59.5%**	**71.3%**
Overall total	578	487

SOURCE: U.S. Department of Transportation, Office of Intermodal and Statewide Programs, National Ferry Study database, October 2000.

Sources

1. Gorman, Bob, "Clearing the Fog about Ferries: National Study to Shed New Light," *TR News*, No. 209, July–August 2000, p. 12.

2. Kupersmith, Celia, General Manager, Golden Gate Highway and Transportation District, "Making Ferries Work," remarks presented at the conference on U.S. Ferry Transportation Service in the 21st Century, Seattle, WA, June 8–9, 2000, available at http://www.marad.dot.gov/ferry/index.html, as of Sept. 1, 2000.

3. The McGraw-Hill Companies and U.S. Department of Commerce, International Trade Association, "Water Transportation," *U.S. Industry and Trade Outlook 2000* (New York, NY: The McGraw-Hill Companies, 2000), p. 52-9.

4. U.S. Department of Transportation, Federal Highway Administration, National Ferry Database, datafile, as of Sept. 1, 2000.

Access to Intercity Public Transportation Services

Access to intercity public transportation services, such as commercial air carriers, passenger rail service, and scheduled intercity buses, is an important indicator of the nation's mobility. For example, over 95 percent of the U.S. population lives within a reasonable access distance[1] of intercity public transportation services [1]. People living in larger urban areas enjoy the greatest levels of accessibility. Every community with a population of 50,000 or more has access to least one intercity transportation mode—an airport, Amtrak rail station, or inter-

Figure 1
Communities with Access to Intercity Public Transportation by Mode

% of communities with access

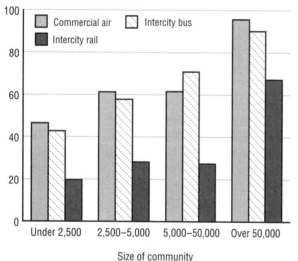

SOURCE: B.D. Spear and R.W. Weil, "Access to Intercity Transportation Services from Small Communities: A Geospatial Analysis," *Transportation Research Record 1666* (Washington, DC: Transportation Research Board, 1999).

---

[1] *Reasonable access distance* is defined as within 75 miles of a large or medium hub airport, 25 miles of a small or nonhub airport, 25 miles of an Amtrak rail station, or 10 miles of an Amtrak or intercity bus stop.

Figure 2
Communities with Access to Intercity Public Transportation by Number of Modes

% of communities with access

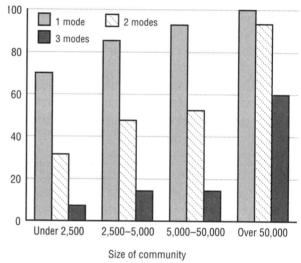

SOURCE: B.D. Spear and R.W. Weil, "Access to Intercity Transportation Services from Small Communities: A Geospatial Analysis," *Transportation Research Record 1666* (Washington, DC: Transportation Research Board, 1999).

city bus terminal—and over 95 percent of these communities have access to two or more modes (figures 1 and 2).

People in small urban communities also have reasonable access to intercity public transportation. Nearly 90 percent of the 4,046 communities with populations between 2,500 and 50,000 located outside of larger urban areas have access to at least one intercity transportation mode. Of the 443 communities located beyond a reasonable access distance, 25 percent are located within the Appalachian or Mississippi Delta Regions, and another 15 percent are concentrated in and around the state of Iowa [1].

Not surprisingly, only 70 percent of rural communities with populations of less than

Access to Transportation Services

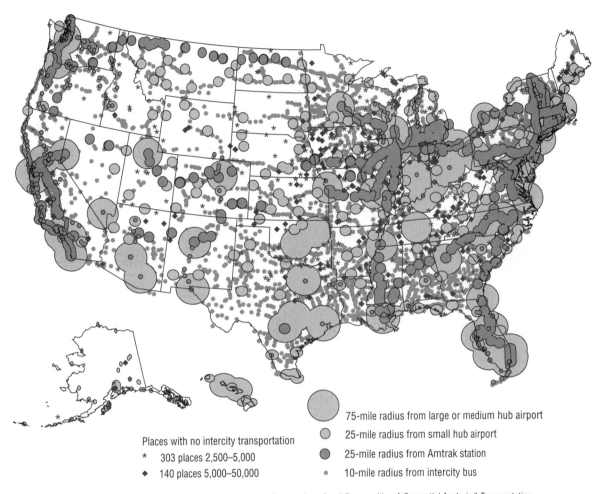

Places with no intercity transportation
* 303 places 2,500–5,000
♦ 140 places 5,000–50,000

75-mile radius from large or medium hub airport
25-mile radius from small hub airport
25-mile radius from Amtrak station
10-mile radius from intercity bus

SOURCE: B. D. Spear and R.W. Weil, "Access to Intercity Transportation Services from Small Communities: A Geospatial Analysis," *Transportation Research Record 1666* (Washington, DC: Transportation Research Board, 1999).

2,500 have accessible intercity public transportation services; however, they represent only 1 percent of the total U.S. population. A majority of these communities are located in the Central Great Plains states (i.e., Kansas, Nebraska, Iowa, and North and South Dakota), and in the Appalachian and Mississippi Delta Regions (see map). Some states and communities in these areas have established bus services to help residents get to public transportation modes.

A recent analysis compared the demographic characteristics of people living in communities with and without access to intercity public transportation service. The analysis showed that people living in communities with no accessible service, on average, have lower incomes, are less likely to have a college education, and are more likely to be white and over 65 years old. [1].

Source

1. Spear, B.D. and R.W. Weil, "Access to Intercity Transportation Services from Small Communities: A Geospatial Analysis," *Transportation Research Record 1666* (Washington, DC: Transportation Research Board, 1999).

Commuting to Work

Between 1985 and 1999, the percentage of people driving to work alone grew, while the percentage of workers carpooling declined. Transit's share of commuters changed little over this period (table 1 and figure 1).

Distances traveled to work increased over this period. In 1999, the median commute to work was 10 miles, up from 8 miles in 1985. About 1 in 3 workers traveled less than 5 miles to work (excluding those that either work at home or have no fixed place of work), while another half traveled between 5 and 20 miles. A very small percentage (about 2 percent) traveled 50 miles or more to work. The remainder reported no fixed place of work or worked at home [1].

The median commute time rose from 19 minutes in 1985 to 21 minutes in 1999. For those individuals reporting a commute, almost three-quarters spent less than half an hour each day getting to work in 1999. About 5 percent spent an hour or more commuting. Workers with incomes below the poverty level are more likely to live closer to work (a median of 7 miles compared with 10 miles for all workers), and spend less time getting to work (a median of 19 minutes compared with 21 minutes for all workers) [1].

Almost half of all workers leave for work between 7:00 a.m. and 9:00 a.m., the traditional

Table 1
Mode of Travel to Work: 1999

Mode	Percent
Drives self	78.2
Carpool	9.4
Mass transportation	4.9
Walks only	3.1
Bicycle or motorcycle	0.6
Taxicab	0.1
Other means	0.8
Works at home	2.8

SOURCE: U.S. Department of Housing and Urban Development and U.S. Department of Commerce, U.S. Bureau of the Census, *American Housing Survey for the United States: 1999*, H150/99 (Washington, DC: 2000).

morning rush period. The largest number leave between 7:00 a.m. and 8:00 a.m.; another 20 percent leave home between 6:00 a.m. and 7:00 a.m. Between 1985 and 1999, only minor changes have occurred in the times people leave for work (figure 2) [1].

Source

1. U.S. Department of Housing and Urban Development and U.S. Department of Commerce, U.S. Bureau of the Census, *American Housing Survey for the United States: 1999*, H150/99 (Washington, DC: 2000).

Figure 1
How People Get to Work: 1985–1999

Percentage of workers

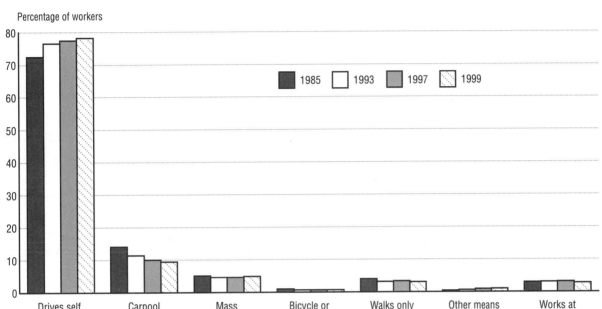

SOURCE: U.S. Department of Housing and Urban Development, American Housing Survey, various years.

Journey-to-Work Data

Three national sources of data provide information on the journey to work:

1. The Census Bureau administers the **decennial census "long form,"** which contains several questions on the journey to work, to approximately 1 in 6 households (about 15 million in 1990). The census provides the most detailed demographic and geographic information on commuting behavior. The decennial census includes the Census Transportation Planning Package, a set of special tabulations on commuting for state, county, county subdivision, places over 2,500, and traffic analysis zones.

2. The **American Housing Survey** (AHS) contains many of the same commuting questions as the decennial census. Every odd year, the Census Bureau conducts the AHS for the Department of Housing and Urban Development with a sample of about 53,000 households nationwide.

3. The Federal Highway Administration conducts the **Nationwide Personal Transportation Survey** (NPTS) approximately every 5 years. (The NPTS is now part of the National Household Travel Survey.) In 1995, the NPTS surveyed a national sample of about 42,000 households. Respondents recorded all trips, including work trips, made on a single day in a trip diary. The diary provided data on work trips (if the respondents went to work on that day) and their relationship to other activities and trips that day. Demographic and geographic data were collected for all respondents.

Figure 2
When People Leave Home to Go to Work: 1985 and 1999

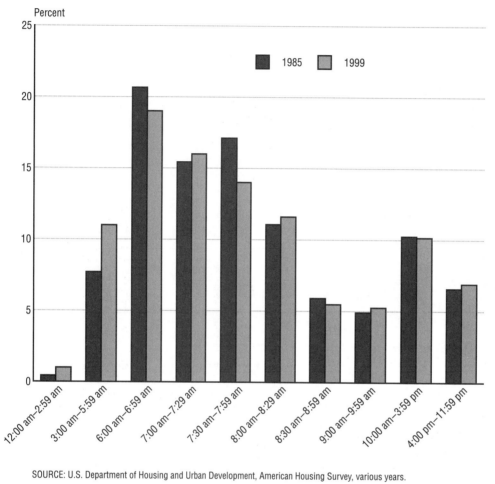

SOURCE: U.S. Department of Housing and Urban Development, American Housing Survey, various years.

Trip Chaining

People often link local trips together in what is known as trip chaining (e.g., dropping a child off at school before traveling to work). In an analysis of trip chaining involving home-to-work and work-to-home trips using data from the latest Nationwide Personal Transportation Survey, researchers found that people are more likely to stop on their way home from work than on their way to work, and women are more likely to trip chain than men [1] (figure 1). Common reasons for trip chaining include shopping, conducting family and personal business, socializing, and to pick up or drop off a passenger.

Trip chaining is thought to be increasing because of rising incomes, the entry of women into the workforce, and the increasing use of automobiles [1]. Many household-sustaining goods and services are now often bought rather than provided in the home (e.g., child care and meals), because more time is spent at work and less time is available for family-oriented needs. As a result, people are making extra trips, and these trips are very often chained with the work commute to save time. In addition, the ability to link trips is enhanced by the flexibility provided by the automobile. Linking nonwork-related trips with the work commute has been posited as one reason for increased congestion problems at rush hour [2].

Sources

1. McGuckin, N. and E. Murakami, "Examining Trip-Chaining Behavior: A Comparison of Travel by Men and Women," 1999, available at http://www-cta.ornl.gov/npts/1995/Doc/publications.shtml.

2. Strathman, J.G. and K.J. Dueker, *Understanding Trip Chaining, Special Report on Trip and Vehicle Attributes,* 1990 NPTS Report Series (Washington, DC: U.S. Department of Transportation, Federal Highway Administration, 1995).

Figure 1

Trip Chaining Involving Work Trips, by Men and Women: 1995

Percentage making one or more stops

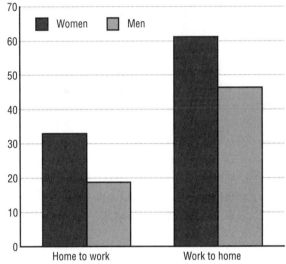

SOURCE: N. McGuckin and E. Murakami, "Examining Trip-Chaining Behavior: A Comparison of Travel by Men and Women," 1999, available at www-cta.ornl.gov/npts/1995/Doc/publications.shtml.

Transit Ridership

Transit ridership has grown steadily since 1995 to top 9 billion (unlinked) trips in 1999 [1]. Preliminary data from the American Public Transportation Association show that another 320 million rides were added in 2000, bringing the growth since 1995 to 20 percent [2]. This ridership level is the highest in more than 40 years. Rail transit ridership posted particularly strong growth (figure 1). Between 1989 and 1999, light rail grew 77 percent, followed by commuter rail at 19 percent, and heavy rail at 6 percent. By comparison, bus ridership fell by nearly 5 percent over this period, although it too has rebounded since 1995. Moreover, most transit trips are still taken by bus [3].

Sources

1. American Public Transportation Association, "APTA Transit Ridership Report," available at http://www.apta.com/stats/ridershp/history.pdf, as of Mar. 8, 2001.

2. _____. "Public Transportation Scored Another Record Year in 2000," press release, Jan. 10, 2001.

3. _____. *Transit Factbook 2000* (Washington, DC: 2000).

Figure 1
Transit Ridership by Mode: 1989–1999

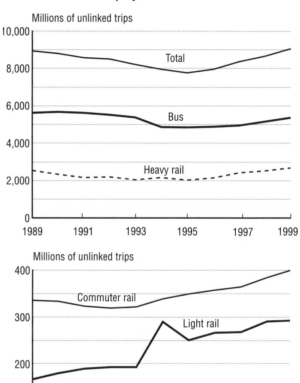

NOTE: Total includes other modes not shown, such as ferry boats, inclined planes, and trolley buses.

SOURCE: American Public Transportation Association, *Transit Fact Book 2000* (Washington, DC: 2000).

Welfare to Work

Changes in our nation's welfare system since 1996 have resulted in a rapidly shrinking number of welfare recipients. About 6 million Americans left the welfare rolls between August 1996, when a sweeping welfare overhaul was signed into law, and June 2000. There were 53 percent fewer individuals and 50 percent fewer families on welfare in June 2000 than in August 1996. Welfare rolls dropped in every state over this period, in some cases, by 90 percent [2].

Because of these changes, communities are becoming increasingly aware that providing adequate and reliable transportation is one of the keys to moving people from welfare to work and helping them keep jobs. A 1997 U.S. Conference of Mayors survey of municipal officials found that 84 percent of respondents identified transportation as one of the most serious barriers for welfare recipients [1]. Moreover, a nationwide sample survey of welfare households found that 10 percent lived outside a metropolitan area had no car [4]. Other obstacles, however, were cited by more respondents and included poor health, lack of work experience, poor education, childcare problems, and lack of English language skills (figure 1).

In metropolitan areas, "spatial mismatch" often occurs when the greatest concentration and growth of job opportunities, particularly entry-level jobs,

Figure 1
Obstacles to Working Reported by
Temporary Assistance for Needy Families (TANF)
Recipients: 1997

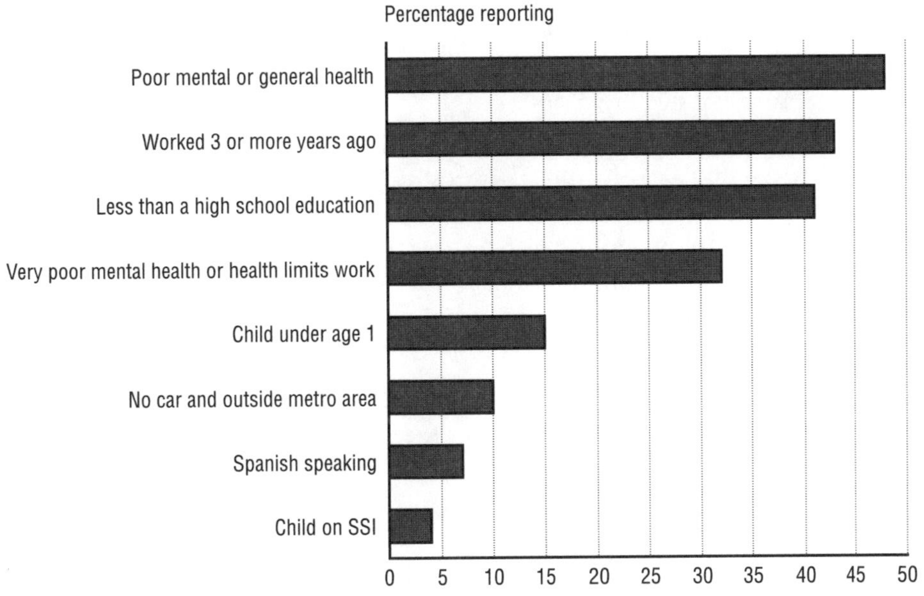

KEY: SSI = Supplemental Security Income.

SOURCE: S.R. Zedlewski, *Work Activity and Obstacles to Work Among TANF Recipients* (Washington, DC: The Urban Institute, 1999).

is in the suburbs, and the greatest concentration of welfare and former welfare recipients is in the central cities. The challenge is, thus, making public transportation available so that it is reasonably possible for these individuals to get to work (figure 2). A Boston area study found that 98 percent of welfare recipients lived within one-quarter mile of a bus or transit station, but only 32 percent of potential employers were that close [3]. Even with transit access, trips often take too long or require several transfers. Furthermore, many entry-level jobs, especially in the service and retail sectors, require employees to work late hours and weekends, times that are often not well served by transit service geared to the standard "8-to-5" workday.

The federal Job Access and Reverse Commute grant program, which is administered by the U.S. Department of Transportation, Federal Transit Administration, was created to respond to these problems. As part of the Transportation Equity Act for the 21st Century, the program assists states and localities in developing new or expanded transportation services that connect welfare recipients and other low-income persons to jobs and other employment-related services. Job Access projects are targeted at developing new and expanding existing transportation services, such as shuttles, vanpools, bus routes, connector services to mass transit, and guaranteed-ride-home programs for welfare recipients and low-income persons. Reverse Commute projects provide transportation services to suburban employment centers from urban, rural, and other suburban locations for all populations.

Figure 2
Metropolitan Job Decentralization: 1993–1996

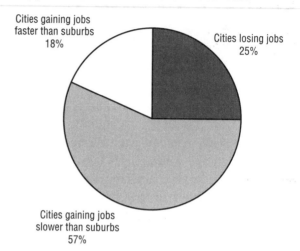

Cities gaining jobs faster than suburbs 18%

Cities losing jobs 25%

Cities gaining jobs slower than suburbs 57%

SOURCE: J. Brennan and E. W. Hill, *Where Are the Jobs? Cities Suburbs, and the Competition for Employment* (Washington, DC: The Brookings Institution Center on Urban & Metropolitan Policy, 1999).

Sources

1. U.S. Conference of Mayors, *Implementing Welfare Reform in America's Cities: A 34-City Survey* (Washington, DC: 1997).

2. U.S. Department of Health and Human Services, *Change in TANF Caseloads Since Enactment of New Welfare Law*, 2000, available at http://www.acf.dhhs.gov/news/stats/aug-dec.htm, as of Sept. 29, 2000.

3. Lacombe, Annalynn, *Welfare Reform and Access to Jobs in Boston*, BTS98-A-02 (Washington, DC: U.S. Department of Transportation, Bureau of Transportation Statistics, 1998).

4. Zedlewski, S.R., *Work Activity and Obstacles to Work Among TANF Recipients* (Washington, DC: The Urban Institute, 1999).

Growth in the Number of Vehicles per Household

Despite shrinking household size, the number of private motor vehicles per household has grown appreciably since the mid-1970s. In 1977, for example, a large percentage of families owned one vehicle. Now, most families own two or more vehicles, and nearly one-fifth of households own three or more vehicles (figure 1 and table 1). Several factors account for this growth, including a rise in household income, greater availability of used vehicles because of increased longevity, and the greater need for a vehicle because of suburban development, among other things [1].

Nevertheless, in the 1990s, growth in the number of household vehicles slowed to the growth in the number of eligible drivers (population 16 years of age or older). Both the number of household vehicles per person 16 years of age or older and the licensing rate remained at about 0.9 between 1990 and 1995 (table 2). Thus, it appears that the number of vehicles per household has reached a plateau equaling the number of licensed drivers per household [1].

Figure 1
Percentage of Households by Number of Vehicles: 1977–1995

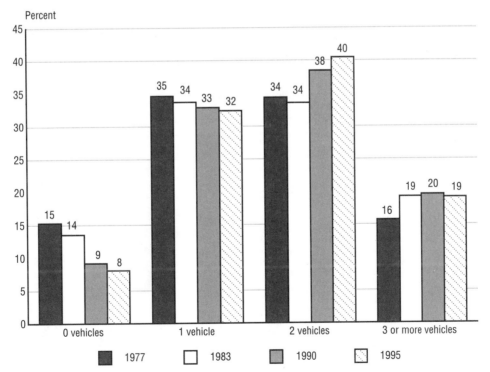

SOURCE: U.S. Department of Transportation, Federal Highway Administration, *Summary of Travel Trends: 1995 Nationwide Personal Transportation Survey* (Washington, DC: 2000).

Table 1

Comparison of Household Size and Number of Household Vehicles: 1977–1995

Year	Household vehicles (thousands)	Vehicles per household	Persons per household
1977	120,098	1.59	2.86
1983	143,714	1.68	2.73
1990	165,221	1.77	2.63
1995	176,067	1.78	2.65

SOURCES: U.S. Department of Transportation, Federal Highway Administration, *Summary of Travel Trends: 1995 Nationwide Personal Transportation Survey* (Washington, DC: 2000); and U.S. Department of Commerce, U.S. Census Bureau, "Households by Size: 1960 to Present," 2000, available at http://www.census.gov/population/socdemo/hh-fam/htabHH-4.txt, as of Aug. 31, 2000.

Table 2

Household Vehicles and Licensed Drivers: 1977–1995

Year	Vehicles per person 16 or older	Licenses per person 16 or older
1977	0.76	0.81
1983	0.82	0.84
1990	0.90	0.89
1995	0.89	0.89

SOURCE: U.S. Department of Transportation, Federal Highway Administration, *Summary of Travel Trends: 1995 Nationwide Personal Transportation Survey* (Washington, DC: 2000).

Source

1. U.S. Department of Transportation, Federal Highway Administration, *Summary of Travel Trends: 1995 Nationwide Personal Transportation Survey* (Washington, DC: 2000).

Households Without Vehicles

Because of improvements in vehicle reliability and longevity and rising incomes, many more people now own a vehicle than in the mid-1970s. In 1995, the number of vehicleless households had declined to about 8 percent of all households, which is about half the share reported 20 years earlier.

About four out of every five households without a vehicle had an annual income of less than $25,000 (among households that reported their income) (figure 1). Half of vehicleless households are in cities. Rural, suburban, and small town households account for about 10 percent each (figure 2). The remaining one-fifth of vehicleless households live in second cities, places that are near an urban center but have a density greater than the typical suburb. Partly because of income and location, African-American households are much more likely to be without a vehicle than other racial and ethnic groups (figure 3).

Figure 2
Vehicleless Households by Location: 1995

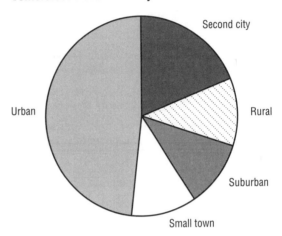

NOTE: Second cities are areas near an urban center, but with a density greater than the typical suburb.

SOURCE: U.S. Department of Transportation, Federal Highway Administration, *1995 Nationwide Personal Transportation Survey,* Microdata Files CD-ROM (Washington, DC: 1997).

Figure 1
Vehicleless Households by Income: 1995

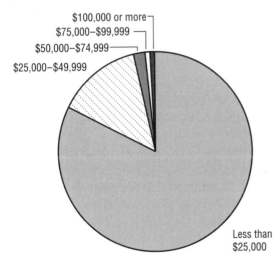

SOURCE: U.S. Department of Transportation, Federal Highway Administration, *1995 Nationwide Personal Transportation Survey,* Microdata Files CD-ROM (Washington, DC: 1997).

Figure 3
Households by Number of Vehicles and Race/Ethnicity: 1995

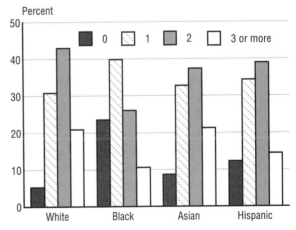

SOURCE: U.S. Department of Transportation, Federal Highway Administration, *1995 Nationwide Personal Transportation Survey,* Microdata Files CD-ROM (Washington, DC: 1997).

Disabilities and Health Factors That Affect Travel

A recent Bureau of Transportation Statistics survey found that 15 percent of adults in the United States have a disability or a health problem that makes travel difficult. Using a random sample of 1,000 adults, the survey also found that about one-third of those reporting difficulties were 65 years of age or older [2].

Data from the National Health Interview Survey on Disability 1994–1995 (NHIS-D) showed that about 72 percent of people with a disability drive a car (an estimated 30 million people), with 24 million driving every day or nearly every day and 6 million driving occasionally or seldom (see box). However, an estimated 5.5 million people do not drive because of an impairment or health problem—nearly half of the disabled adults who do not drive—and more than 40 percent of these individuals live in the suburbs (table 1).

The NHIS-D asked people about their use of standard public transportation in the 12 months prior to being interviewed. About two-thirds of disabled adults, an estimated 27.8 million, lived in areas where regular public transportation is available, but only 6.4 million people had used it during the period in question. This was, however, about three times the number who had used demand responsive services. Overall, about 12 percent of people with disabilities (700,000) who had used public transportation in the past year said they had difficulty using the system, a proportion somewhat higher in the central city than elsewhere. The most common problems were difficulty walking, followed by the need for assistance, and mental cognitive problems. Inadequate hours, cost, and fear were infrequently

---

National Health Interview Survey on Disability (NHIS-D)

The NHIS-D was conducted by the National Center for Health Statistics as a supplement to the National Health Interview Survey, a nationally representative sample survey. The NHIS-D 1994–1995 was conducted in two phases. Phase 1 included a sample of approximately 203,000 individuals who were interviewed in 1994 and 1995. About 34,000 adults and children (20,000 in 1994 and 14,000 in 1995) indicated some form of disability, yielding a nationally representative estimate of about 42 million disabled adults in the household population (excluding people in long-term care facilities and prisons).

In phase 2, adults and children who indicated they had a disability in phase 1 were reinterviewed over a period stretching from 1994 to 1997 using two different questionnaires. Adults were asked for more detailed information on a range of subjects including 12 transportation questions in one section. Some questions in other sections of the interview also included transportation components. Data are based on a sample and subject to sampling variability.

---

mentioned by users and non-users (table 2). Of people with cognitive/mental problems (e.g., remembering where to go/knowing how to avoid trouble) only about 6 percent (49,000 people) said they would use public transportation if they were given mobility training (e.g., what stop to get off, how to transfer, how to pay the fare) [1].

Of the 21.4 million who had not used transit in an area where it is available, about 15 percent said it was because of an impairment. The main reasons given were the same as for disabled users. Nearly 600,000 non-users have wheelchair access problems. Another 80,000 people with disabilities who had used public transportation in the past 12 months also have wheelchair access problems [1].

Table 1
Drivers with Disabilities and Nondrivers

	Total		MSA, central city		MSA, not central city		Non-MSA	
	Number	Percent	Number	Percent	Number	Percent	Number	Percent
Drive	30,078,020	72	8,210,746	64	13,906,868	76	7,960,406	74
Every day or nearly everyday	24,112,493		6,394,213		11,416,503		6,301,777	
Occasionally or seldom	5,965,527		1,816,533		2,490,365		1,658,629	
Never drive	11,616,198	28	4,548,167	36	4,328,966	24	2,739,065	26
Because of an impairment or health problem	5,474,326		1,785,747		2,252,446		1,436,133	
Total	41,694,218	100	12,758,913	100	18,235,834	100	10,699,471	100

KEY: MSA = metropolitan statistical area.

SOURCE: U.S. Department of Health and Human Services, Centers for Disease Control and Prevention, National Center for Health Statistics, *1994–1995 National Health Interview Survey, Phase II* (Hyattsville, MD: July 1998).

Table 2
Types of Difficulties Cited by Users and Non-Users of Public Transportation

	Total		Used public transport but has difficulties		Has not used public transport because of difficulties	
	Number of adults (thousands)	Percent	Number of adults (thousands)	Percent	Number of adults (thousands)	Percent
Total respondents	3,870	100	747	100	3,124	100
Difficulties cited						
Difficulty walking/cannot walk	2,530	65	426	57	2,104	67
Need help from another person	1,158	30	126	17	1,032	33
Other reasons not specified	762	20	210	28	551	18
Cognitive mental problems	757	20	96	13	661	21
Wheelchair/scooter access problems	665	17	83	11	583	19
Vision	622	16	75	10	547	18
Fear	424	11	79	9	354	11
Hearing	240	6	27	4	213	7
Problems with other medical/assistive device	235	6	29	4	207	7
Weather	222	6	51	7	171	5
Cost	74	2	24	3	50	2
Hours inadequate	58	2	22	3	36	1

NOTE: Difficulties cited do not add to total as more than one difficulty was recorded for many respondents.

SOURCE: U.S. Department of Health and Human Services, Centers for Disease Control and Prevention, National Center for Health Statistics, *1994–1995 National Health Interview Survey, Phase II* (Hyattsville, MD: July 1998).

Although being able to drive is an important source of mobility for many people, including people with a disability, car crashes can also cause disability. The NHIS-D found that about 1.1 million people have a problem with at least one of the activities of daily living (e.g., bathing, dressing, eating, or moving inside the home) because of a motor vehicle crash [1].

Sources

1. U.S. Department of Health and Human Services, Centers for Disease Control and Prevention, National Center for Health Statistics, *1994–1995 National Health Interview Survey on Disability, Phase I and II* (Hyattsville, MD: July 1998).

2. U.S. Department of Transportation, Bureau of Transportation Statistics, "Omnibus Survey: Household Survey Results," August 2000.

Highway Congestion in Metropolitan Areas

Being stuck in traffic is a source of frustration for many travelers, particularly commuters, but its impacts go far beyond those individuals immediately affected. By wasting people's time, increasing the time it takes to transport goods, and causing missed meetings and appointments, highway congestion is a drag on economic productivity. Congestion is also an environmental concern. Extra fuel is consumed by cars traveling under these conditions because of increased acceleration, deceleration, and idling. Greater fuel consumption leads to higher emissions of greenhouse gases and may raise the level of other air pollutants.

The Texas Transportation Institute (TTI) studied 68 metropolitan areas in order to estimate congestion and some of its impacts in the United

States. TTI found that between 1982 and 1997 congestion measured by average annual delay per eligible driver increased in all areas (see the map on the next page). Overall in the study areas, average annual delay per driver has almost tripled during the 15-year period, rising from 16 hours per driver in 1982 to 45 hours in 1997 (table 1). (More recent data from TTI show congestion continued to increase between 1997 and 1999.) Furthermore, drivers in the largest metropolitan areas (with a population of over 3 million) experienced the worst congestion (54 hours per driver on average in 1997), and those in small metropolitan areas (population of 500,000 or less) the least (10 hours a year per driver) (figure 1).

Table 1
Congestion Measures in 68 Metropolitan Areas: 1982–1997

Year	Annual delay per eligible driver (person-hours)	Wasted fuel per eligible driver (gallons)	Annual fuel wasted per urban area (million gallons)
1982	16	23	39
1986	27	32	54
1990	34	39	68
1992	39	44	76
1995	40	51	84
1996	43	54	91
1997	45	69	97

SOURCE: D. Shrank and T. Lomax, *The 1999 Annual Mobility Report: Information for Urban America* (College Station, TX: Texas Transportation Institute, 1999).

Figure 1
Annual Hours of Congestion Delay Per Driver by Metropolitan Area Size

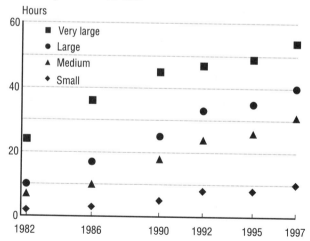

KEY: Very large = over 3 million; Large = over 1 million–3 million; Medium = over 500,000–1 million; Small = 500,000 or less.

SOURCE: D. Shrank and T. Lomax, *The 1999 Annual Mobility Report: Information for Urban America* (College Station, TX: Texas Transportation Institute, 1999).

Annual Person-Hours of Delay per Eligible Driver: 1982 and 1997

(a) Cities with population under 1 million

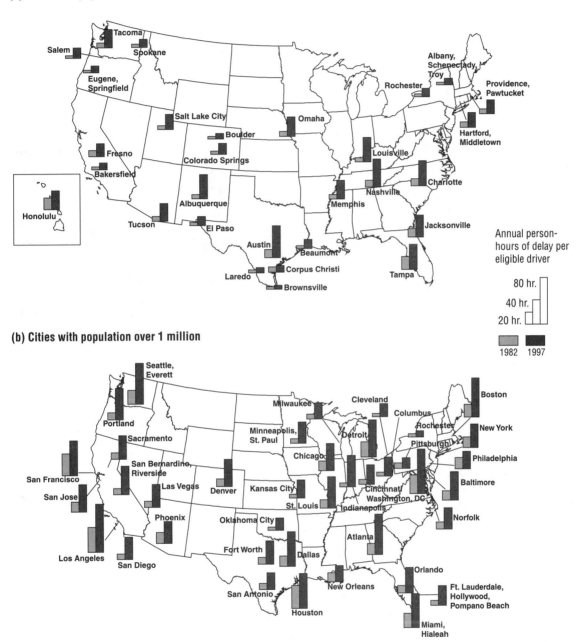

Annual person-hours of delay per eligible driver

80 hr.
40 hr.
20 hr.

1982 1997

(b) Cities with population over 1 million

NOTES: An eligible driver is someone 16 years and older who is eligible for a driver's license. The cities shown represent the 50 largest metropolitan areas, as well as others chosen by the states sponsoring the study. For a detailed explanation of the formulas used, see the source document.

SOURCE: Texas Transportation Institute, *Urban Roadway Congestion Annual Report* (College Station, TX: 1998).

U.S. Airline Delays

Delayed or canceled commercial airline flights cost consumers in many unmeasured ways, including lost personal time, missed meetings, and increased anxiety and stress. Delay also costs the airlines. The Federal Aviation Administration (FAA) estimates that commercial aviation delays cost airlines over $3 billion annually and projects that delays throughout the system will continue to increase as the demand for air travel rises [1]. Both FAA and the airlines consider that improvements in air traffic control should mitigate some flight delay problems. In addition, FAA and the industry are investigating ways to reduce delays attributable to weather, increasing flight volume, and limited system capacity [2].

Both the Bureau of Transportation Statistics (BTS) and FAA track airline delays. According to BTS, a flight is counted as an "on-time departure" if the aircraft leaves the airport gate within 15 minutes of its scheduled departure time, regardless of the time the aircraft actually lifts off from the runway. Also, BTS counts an arriving flight as "on time" if it arrives within 15 minutes of its scheduled gate arrival time [2].

Unlike BTS, which tracks air carrier performance, FAA tracks delays in terms of how well the air traffic control system performs [2]. Tracking begins once a flight is under FAA air traffic control (i.e., after the pilot's request to taxi out to the runway). As such, an aircraft could wait an hour or more at the gate before requesting clearance to taxi. Once under air traffic control, as long as the aircraft took off within 15 minutes of the airport's standard taxi-out time, FAA considers the flight departed on time. [1].

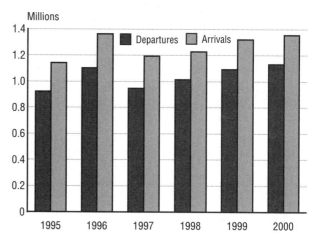

Figure 1
Total Number of Arrival and Departure Flight Delays: 1995–2000

SOURCE: U.S. Department of Transportation, Bureau of Transportation Statistics, Office of Airline Information.

Flight delays have increased since 1995, with the greatest number of total delays occurring in 2000 (figure 1). According to BTS data, 1 in 4 flights by major U.S. air carriers were delayed, canceled, or diverted, affecting approximately 163 million passengers in 2000, with delays averaging over 50 minutes per flight. There were nearly 18 percent more BTS-reported arrival delays in 2000 than in 1999 [2].

Most delays take place while the plane is on the ground, although the actual cause of the delay may occur elsewhere. Poor weather is the most common cause for delays (figure 2). The growth in flight volume is also a major contributor to delays and cancellations. Between 1995 and 1999, the total number of operations at the nation's airports

Figure 2
**FAA-Cited Causes of Departure and
En Route Delays: 1999**
(After pushing back from the gate)

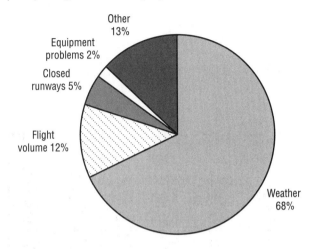

SOURCE: U.S. Department of Transportation, Federal Aviation Administration, Operations Network (OPSNET) database.

increased over 8 percent, from approximately 115.6 million to 125.3 million[1] [1].

There is much debate about the role of airline scheduling in causing delays. The "hub and spoke" systems used by the major airlines concentrate flights into the hub airports. The worst delays tend to be at peak travel times during the day and at certain times of the year (e.g., holidays and the summer months) when travel volume is heavier. When heavy volumes are combined with bad weather between a hub airport and its spokes, the ripple effect can cause delays at dozens of other airports [1]. (Table 1 lists the top 10 airports in terms of delays and cancellations.)

In August 2000, the U.S. Department of Transportation created a task force comprising a cross-section of aviation stakeholders, including representatives from airlines, consumer groups, labor unions, and airport operators, to examine the reasons for flight delays and develop recommendations on how to modify airline on-time reporting. Currently, the on-time information that the 10 largest U.S. passenger carriers are required to submit to BTS[2] identifies only the frequency and duration of flight delays and cancellations, not the cause [3]. The Task Force is considering what further steps, including any necessary rulemaking, may be required to collect data on the causes of flight delays [2].

Sources

1. Mead, Kenneth M., Inspector General, U.S. Department of Transportation, "Flight Delays and Cancellations," statement before the Committee on Commerce, Science, and Transportation, United States Senate, Sept. 14, 2000.

2. U.S. Department of Transportation, Bureau of Transportation Statistics, Office of Airline Information, personal communications, November 2000–April 2001.

3. U.S. Department of Transportation, Office of Public Affairs, press release, Nov. 29, 2000.

---

[1] Flight operations, as reported by FAA, include takeoffs and landings by all types of aircraft (commercial and general aviation) at approximately 3,400 domestic airports.

[2] In addition to the 10 largest carriers, Aloha Airlines and American Eagle have recently begun voluntarily reporting on-time information to BTS.

Table 1
Top 10 Airports for Percentage of Flights Delayed, Canceled, and Diverted: 2000

Ranking	Airport	Scheduled flights	Actual late departures	Actual late arrivals	Flights diverted away from airport	Canceled	% delayed arrivals	% delayed arrivals, cancellations, and diversions
1	New York-La Guardia	104,177	30,139	44,713	869	7,591	35.1	43.0
2	San Francisco International	135,032	40,481	52,963	393	7,177	33.5	39.2
3	Chicago-O'Hare	296,771	98,362	109,178	830	19,318	29.6	36.8
4	Boston-Logan	113,056	28,595	38,967	237	7,689	27.6	34.5
5	Los Angeles International	212,118	58,937	70,953	359	8,120	29.4	33.4
6	Philadelphia International	121,151	34,791	40,313	681	6,442	27.8	33.3
7	Seattle Tacoma International	104,910	26,907	33,895	219	3,264	29.0	32.3
8	Denver International	137,302	39,659	43,655	186	4,251	28.4	31.8
9	Newark	124,496	29,348	38,292	390	6,330	25.4	30.8
10	Washington-Dulles	65,462	16,744	19,788	193	3,678	24.4	30.2

NOTE: A delay is defined as an aircraft departing from or arriving at a gate more than 15 minutes after its scheduled departure or arrival time.

SOURCE: U.S. Department of Transportation, Bureau of Transportation Statistics, Office of Airline Information, 2001.

Domestic Freight Shipments

Freight movements grew significantly over the past quarter century despite a general trend in the economy toward services and high-value, low-weight products. Between 1975 and 1999, domestic freight ton-miles increased 67 percent, from 2.3 trillion to over 3.8 trillion, with air carriers and intercity trucking growing faster than the other modes (figure 1). Despite the decline in the maritime mode since 1980, attributable to the decline in Alaskan crude oil shipments, water transportation still accounted for 656 billion ton-miles in 1999.

Population growth and economic activity remain the key factors that determine freight demand; increases in both mean a greater volume of goods produced and consumed and thus more freight moved (figure 2). Between 1975 and 1999, the resident population rose by 57 million, an increase of 26 percent, while the gross domes-

tic product more than doubled from $4 trillion to $8.9 trillion (in inflation-adjusted chained 1996 dollars). The growth in freight ton-miles was slower than the growth in economic activity during this period but outpaced the increase in population.

As economic activity expanded, particularly in the 1990s, changes in what, where, and how goods were produced affected freight demand and contributed to the increase in total ton-miles. The composition of goods produced also changed as the economy shifted toward more services and high-value, low-weight products. This shift can be measured by the ratio of ton-miles per dollar of

Figure 1
Growth in Domestic Freight Ton-Miles

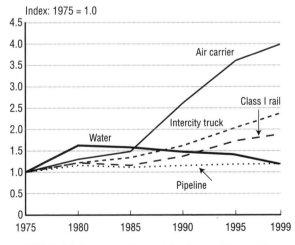

SOURCE: U.S. Department of Transportation, Bureau of Transportation Statistics, *National Transportation Statistics 2000* (Washington, DC: 2001).

Figure 2
Domestic Ton-Miles, Gross Domestic Product, and Resident Population

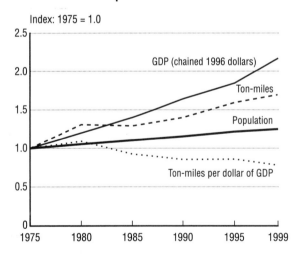

KEY: GDP = Gross Domestic Product.

SOURCE: GDP data—U.S. Department of Commerce, Bureau of Economic Analysis, available at www.bea.doc.gov/bea/dn/gdplev.htm, as of Apr. 20, 2001. Ton-miles data—U.S. Department of Transportation, Bureau of Transportation Statistics, *National Transportation Statistics 2000* (Washington, DC: 2001). Population data—U.S. Department of Commerce, U.S. Census Bureau, available at www.census.gov/population/estimates/nation/popclockest.txt, as of Apr. 20, 2001.

Gross Domestic Product (GDP), which has declined since 1975. This decline suggests that, as the economy becomes more service-based, fewer ton-miles of freight are used to produce a dollar of GDP, making the economy less freight-intensive. It takes more freight ton-miles to produce $1,000 worth of steel than it does to produce $1,000 worth of cellular phones. Today, even traditional products like automobiles are made from lighter, but often more expensive, materials such as engineered plastics.

As economic growth has accelerated, disposable personal income per capita has increased and individual purchasing power risen. Businesses have responded by shipping more freight per resident population. Freight ton-miles per capita rose more than 30 percent, from about 10,600 in 1975 to 14,000 in 1999.

The manufacture, assembly, and distribution of goods continue to change as components of products are produced in facilities located thousands of miles apart, some halfway around the globe. Today, many businesses manage worldwide production and distribution systems, increasing global trade in goods and the demand for freight transportation. Changes in where goods are produced can directly increase total ton-miles and change the average length of haul of shipments. Such changes also affect freight mode choice, with more commodities being shipped by multiple modes as distances increase. This worldwide spatial distribution of production activities and trade impacts transportation requirements in the United States. For example, expanding trade with the Pacific Rim continues to make West Coast container ports more dominant than East Coast ports and poses challenging landside and intermodal access demands.

Air Carrier Freight

Domestic air freight grew much faster than the other transportation modes between 1993 and 1997, whether measured by value, tons, or ton-miles. The value increased 52 percent during this period, from $151 billion to $229 billion in 1997 dollars (table 1), tons carried rose 43 percent, and ton-miles grew by 56 percent. Some shipments using parcel, postal, and courier services are transported via air. Between 1993 and 1997, this type of service, employing multiple modes, grew 40 percent from $613 billion in 1993 to $856 billion in 1997, making it the second fastest growing freight service when measured by value. These Commodity Flow Survey (CFS) estimates cover the most recent years for which comprehensive freight flow data are available.

Air carriers and courier services provide businesses the means to move high-value goods to markets and consumers fast and effectively over long distances. In 1997, the value of goods moved by air carriers averaged over $51,000 per ton, up slightly from $48,000 a ton in 1993 (both in 1997 dollars). Goods moved by parcel, postal, and courier services averaged $36,000 per ton, up from $32,000 per ton in 1993. For other freight modes, the value-to-weight ratio was less than $1,000 per ton in 1993 and 1997 [1].

Categories of commodities[1] of freight shipments can be ranked by value, value per ton, and average miles per ton. Aircraft, spacecraft, and parts ranked the highest in value and value per ton for shipments by air carriers (table 2). Dairy products ranked highest in miles per ton. Similarly, electronic components and parts ranked sec-

Table 1

Value of Commodities Shipped in the United States by Mode of Transportation: 1993 and 1997

(Commodity Flow Survey data only)

Mode	1993 (billions of 1997 dollars)	1997 (billions of 1997 dollars)	1993–1997 % change
All modes	**6,335**	**6,944**	**10**
Air (includes truck and air)	151	229	52
Parcel, postal, and courier	610	856	40
Rail	268	320	19
Pipeline	97	114	17
Water	67	76	14
Truck	4,772	4,982	4
Truck and rail	90	76	−16
Truck and water	10	8	−19
Rail and water	4	2	−54
Other and unknown modes	266	283	6

SOURCE: U.S. Department of Transportation, Bureau of Transportation Statistics and U.S. Department of Commerce, U.S. Census Bureau, 1993 and 1997 Commodity Flow Surveys.

ond in value and value per ton, while footwear was the second in miles per ton. For commodities moved by parcel, postal and courier services, the highest ranked by value was miscellaneous manufactured products (table 3). Electronic components and parts ranked first in value and fresh-cut flowers ranked first in miles per ton.

In 1997, air carriers moved high-value commodities over longer distances than the other freight modes. On average, the top 10 commodities shipped by air, measured by value per ton, were moved over 1,200 miles per ton. Air carriers also moved other commodities over great distances. For example, the three commodities ranked highest by average miles per ton were: dairy products (3,000 miles); footwear (2,500

---

[1] The commodities are based on the three-digit Standard Classification of Transported Goods (SCTG) coding system. The three-digit SCTG commodity data are not available for 1993 to allow comparison.

Table 2
U.S. Freight Shipments by Air Carriers: 1997

(Including truck and air)

SCTG code	Ranking	Measure
	Value	**Value ($millions)**
	All commodities by air carriers	*229,062*
372	Aircraft and spacecraft	55,394
358	Electronic components and parts	32,704
355	Computer and office equipment	27,021
409	Miscellaneous manufactured products	14,962
359	Other electronic and electrical equipment	11,726
210	Pharmaceutical products	10,524
384	Medical instruments, apparatus, and appliances	7,846
353	Line telephone or telegraph apparatus	6,923
357	Transmission apparatus for radio and television	5,603
349	Other machinery	5,213
	Value per ton	**Dollars per ton**
	All commodities by air carriers	*51,187*
372	Aircraft and spacecraft	728,868
358	Electronic components and parts	480,941
342	Turbines, boilers, nuclear reactors, and nonelectric engines	327,077
384	Medieval instruments, apparatus, and appliances	245,188
357	Transmission apparatus for radio and television	233,458
385	Meters and other instruments and apparatus	153,970
210	Pharmaceutical products	148,225
355	Computer and office equipment	120,629
381	Optical elements, instruments, and apparatus	116,267
409	Miscellaneous manufactured products	108,420
	Average miles per ton	**Miles per ton**
	All commodities by air carriers	*1,393*
071	Dairy products, except beverages	3,200
304	Footwear	2,500
264	Windows, doors, frames, and builders joinery	2,333
241	Plastics and rubber in primary forms and sheets	1,889
239	Other chemical products and preparations	1,857
243	Rubber articles	1,750
385	Meters and other instruments and apparatus	1,727
302	Textile clothing and accessories, and headgear	1,701
357	Transmission apparatus for radio or television	1,667
324	Nonferrous metal, except precious	1,643

KEY: SCTG = Standard Classification of Transported Goods.

SOURCE: U.S. Department of Transportation, Bureau of Transportation Statistics and U.S. Department of Commerce, U.S. Census Bureau, 1997 Commodity Flow Survey.

Table 3
U.S. Freight Shipments by Parcel, Postal, and Courier Services: 1997

SCTG code	Ranking	Measure
	Value	**Value ($millions)**
	All commodities by parcel, postal, courier services	*855,897*
409	Miscellaneous manufactured products	91,403
355	Computer and office equipment	74,539
210	Pharmaceutical products	73,149
358	Electronic components and parts	65,525
359	Other electronic and electrical equipment	47,226
302	Textile clothing and accessories, and headgear	41,310
291	Printed books, brochures, and similar printed products	35,429
349	Other machinery	35,237
384	Medical instruments, apparatus, and appliances	31,519
333	Handtools, cutlery, and machine tools	26,156
	Value per ton	**Dollars per ton**
	All commodities by parcel, postal, courier services	*36,131*
358	Electronic components and parts	275,315
372	Aircraft and spacecraft	269,094
357	Transmission apparatus for radio or television	194,627
381	Optical elements, instruments, and apparatus	151,886
385	Meters and other instruments and apparatus	145,898
342	Turbines, boilers, nuclear reactors, and nonelectric engines	127,000
383	Surveying and navigational instruments and appliances	121,500
384	Medical instruments, apparatus, and appliances	118,492
356	Prepared unrecorded or prerecorded media	93,727
355	Computer and office equipment	91,684
	Average miles per ton	**Miles per ton**
	All commodities by parcel, postal, courier services	*760*
039	Fresh-cut flowers, plants, and parts of plants	1,458
293	Advertising material, commercial and trade catalogues	1,164
304	Footwear	1,144
033	Fresh, chilled, or dried edible fruit and nuts	1,133
372	Aircraft and spacecraft	1,132
402	Toys, games, and sporting equipment	1,096
383	Surveying and navigational instruments and appliances	1,083
354	Electronic entertainment products, except parts	1,080
090	Tobacco products	1,042
192	Refined petroleum oils and bituminous minerals oils	1,000

KEY: SCTG = Standard Classification of Transported Goods.

SOURCE: U.S. Department of Transportation, Bureau of Transportation Statistics and U.S. Department of Commerce, U.S. Census Bureau, 1997 Commodity Flow Survey.

miles); and windows, doors, frames, and builders joinery products (2,300 miles) [1].

In the miles per ton category, the top 10 commodities shipped by parcel, postal, and courier services were moved over 900 miles per ton. The three commodities that traveled the longest distance and ranked the highest by average miles per ton were fresh-cut flowers and plants (1,460 miles); advertising materials, commercial and trade catalogues (1,160 miles); and footwear (1.140 miles) [1].

Source

1. U.S. Department of Transportation, Bureau of Transportation Statistics and U.S. Department of Commerce, U.S. Census Bureau, 1993 and 1997 Commodity Flow Surveys.

U.S. Container Trade

World container trade increased overall throughout the 1990s, despite the Asian economic crisis in 1998. In 1999, world container trade grew approximately 9 percent above the 1998 level (table 1). The United States ranked first in world container traffic until 1998, when China moved to the number one position [1].

In general, demand for U.S. exports has not kept pace with U.S. consumer demand for imports. Accordingly, the balance of international container trade (i.e., the volume of U.S. containerized exports compared with containerized imports) has shifted in favor of U.S. imports, particularly in recent years. Between 1993 and 1997, the balance of U.S. international container trade was less than 1 million 20-foot equivalent units (TEUs) per year (figure 1). By 1999, this gap had widened to a difference of 4 million TEUs. At the Port of New York and New Jersey, for example, containerized imports rose 12.9 percent in 1999 while exports fell 4.5 percent, resulting in 402,000 excess TEUs [4]. U.S. imports from Asia are twice the volume of U.S. exports to that region [2].

A major component of operating costs for this segment of the shipping industry is the positioning of containers at strategic points along trade lanes. Containers cost to move whether empty or full. If an outbound trade lane is strong and the inbound side is not as robust, full containers are exported but cargo may be nonexistent for a profitable return trip. In some trade lanes, such as the Transpacific, carriers may be able to add repositioning charges to shipping rates. In other,

Table 1
U.S. and World Container Traffic: 1994–1999
(Millions of TEUs)

Year	World	United States	U.S. rank
1994	128.3	18.4	1
1995	137.2	19.1	1
1996	150.8	21.8	1
1997	160.7	21.8	1
1998	169.6	24.2	2
1999	184.6	26.1	2

KEY: TEUs = 20-foot equivalent units.

NOTE: Numbers have been revised for each annual publication.

SOURCE: Jane Degerlund et al., *Containerisation International Yearbook* (London, England: Informa Group, Inc., Various years, 1997–2001).

less competitive trade lanes, carriers may not have this option. To offset repositioning costs, containers are stacked up at ports or intermodal and other facilities.

The repositioning or storage of millions of containers in the United States could increase the operating costs of the maritime industry and the intermodal transportation industry, as a whole. Although some ports, such as Los Angeles and Long Beach, have been able to secure additional container terminal space, other ports are finding that they have to stack containers higher and higher [3]. This is particularly true for import-intensive ports. In some areas, extensive storage of used containers can become not only a local land-use issue, but may also eventually lead to environmental problems.

(continued on next page)

Figure 1
Balance of U.S. International Container Trade—Net Imports: 1993–1999

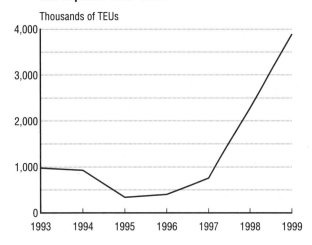

Thousands of TEUs

KEY: TEUs = 20-foot equivalent container units.

SOURCE: *The Journal of Commerce*, Port Import/Export Reporting Service (PIERS) data, various years.

Sources

1. Degerlund, Jane et al., *Containerisation International 2001* (London, England: Informa Group, Inc., 2001), p. 8.

2. Journal of Commerce, "Special Report: Container Shipping, Sacrificing Export Rates," *JOC Week*, vol. 1, No. 28, Dec. 11–17, 2000, p. 28.

3. ____. "Ports Forced to Stack Containers," *Special Report: Intermodal Expo*, Apr. 11, 2000.

4. Port Authority of New York and New Jersey, "Cargo Continues Strong Gains in Port of NY/NJ," press release, Oct. 17, 2000.

U.S. Commercial Freight Activity

The U.S. transportation system moved 3.9 trillion ton-miles of commercial freight in 1997, weighing 15 billion tons and valued at $8.6 trillion (table 1). On an average day, approximately 41 million tons of commodities valued at over $23 billion moved nearly 11,000 miles on the nation's transportation system. This represents an average daily freight flow of 310 pounds moving 40 miles per U.S. resident.

These recently revised Bureau of Transportation Statistics (BTS) total estimates are based on 1997 Commodity Flow Survey (CFS) data (see box) and supplemental estimates prepared for BTS by Oak Ridge National Laboratory. The 1997 CFS covered about 81 percent of the value, 75 percent of the tonnage, and nearly 70 percent of the ton-miles of all the commercial freight moved within the United States. The supplemental estimates cover shipments that were out-of-scope of the CFS and include farm-to-processing plant shipments, surface transportation imports from Canada and Mexico, air cargo imports and exports, and maritime imports and exports.

There are significant differences between the CFS and the supplemental data, especially in how the commodity mix, modal combinations,

> **The Commodity Flow Survey**
>
> Most of the national estimates of freight movement presented in this report are based on results from the 1997 Commodity Flow Survey (CFS), conducted by the Bureau of Transportation Statistics (BTS) and the Census Bureau, and additional estimates of freight shipments that are not fully measured in the CFS. Conducted for the first time in 1993 and again in 1997, the CFS is the nation's primary and most comprehensive data source on domestic freight movement. It surveys a sample of shipments by domestic establishments engaged in manufacturing, mining, wholesale trade, and some selected retail trade services. The CFS collects information about what modes these establishments used to ship their products and materials, the types of commodities they shipped, and the value, weight, distance, origin, and destination of the shipments. The survey collects information on freight moved by each mode of transportation and on freight moved by intermodal combinations (e.g., truck and train).

and average shipment distances are presented. For example, CFS shipments were valued at $626 per ton compared with $437 per ton for supplemental freight flow data, which better covers crude oil and petroleum products. Because imports and exports usually move longer distances than domestic shipments, the average

Table 1
U.S. Commercial Freight Shipment Totals: 1997

Source	Value (1997 $billion)	Tons (millions)	Ton-miles (billions)	Percent			Value per ton (dollars)	Miles per ton
				Value	Tons	Ton-miles		
Commodity Flow Survey	6,944	11,090	2,661	81.1	74.9	69.1	626	240
Supplemental estimates[1]	1,623	3,710	1,190	18.9	25.1	30.9	437	321
Total	**8,567**	**14,800**	**3,851**	**100.0**	**100.0**	**100.0**	**579**	**260**

[1] Based on additional estimates prepared for the Bureau of Transportation Statistics by Oak Ridge National Laboratory. The estimates cover out-of-scope farm-based truck shipments, truck imports from Canada and Mexico, rail imports from Canada and Mexico, air cargo imports and exports, and water imports and exports. The estimates exclude noncommercial freight shipments such as government shipments and municipal solid waste.

SOURCES: U.S. Department of Transportation, Bureau of Transportation Statistics and U.S. Department of Commerce, U.S. Census Bureau, *1997 Commodity Flow Survey, United States,* EC97TCF-US (Washington, DC: 1999); and Oak Ridge National Laboratory data.

ton-miles per ton was higher for the supplemental flows (321 miles per ton) than for the CFS flows (240 miles per ton).

Modal shares of freight shipments have also been estimated using the combined 1997 CFS and supplemental data. When measured by value of shipments or by tons, trucks moved the majority of total U.S. commercial freight (table 2 and figure 1). In 1997, trucking (both for-hire and private) transported about 62 percent of the value and nearly 60 percent of the tonnage. When shipments are measured by ton-miles, rail slightly edged out trucking. Intermodal combinations[1] moved 11 percent of the shipments by value and accounted for over 5 percent of the ton-miles.

---

[1] Intermodal combinations include parcel, postal, and courier services; truck and rail, truck and water; and rail and water. Truck and air are excluded, but have been added to air transportation.

Table 2
U.S. Commercial Freight Shipments by Value, Tons, and Ton-Miles: 1997

Mode	Value (1997 $billions)	Tons (millions)	Ton-miles (billions)
Truck (private and for-hire)	5,336	8,836	1,109
Parcel, postal, and courier	856	34	18
Water	762	2,220	726
Air (including truck and air)	653	10	6
Rail (including truck and rail)	436	1,676	1,132
Pipeline	231	1,448	656
Other and unknown	293	576	204
Total	**8,567**	**14,800**	**3,851**

SOURCES: U.S. Department of Transportation, Bureau of Transportation Statistics and U.S. Department of Commerce, U.S. Census Bureau, *1997 Commodity Flow Survey, United States,* EC97TCF-US (Washington, DC: 1999); and Oak Ridge National Laboratory data.

Figure 1
Modal Shares of U.S. Commercial Freight Shipments by Value, Tons, and Ton-Miles: 1997

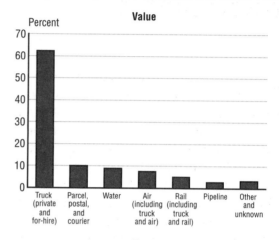

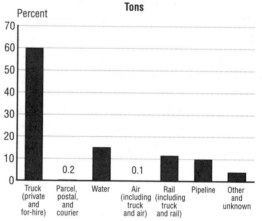

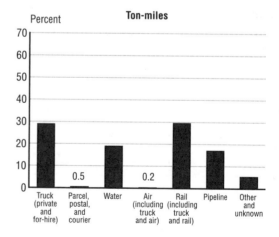

SOURCES: U.S. Department of Transportation, Bureau of Transportation Statistics and U.S. Department of Commerce, U.S. Census Bureau, *1997 Commodity Flow Survey, United States,* EC97TCF-US (Washington, DC: 1999); and Oak Ridge National Laboratory data.

Major Commodity Shipments in the United States

Over 800,000 businesses shipped nearly $7 trillion worth of products via the nation's highways, railroads, waterways, pipelines, and aviation system in 1997. This reflects about a 10 percent increase from 1993 (in real terms)[1] [1].

Motor vehicle parts and accessories[2] accounted for the highest dollar value ($272 billion) of the shipments, followed by miscellaneous manufactured products, computer equipment, mixed freight, and pharmaceutical products (table 1). All of the 10 major commodities measured by value are high value per weight, except gasoline. They accounted for 30 percent of the total value of shipments but only 10 percent of the ton-miles. Reflecting in part the importance of high technology, information, and communications, businesses shipped $536 billion worth of computer equipment, electrical and office equipment, and electronic parts. This represents almost 8 percent of the $6,944 billion worth of shipments made in 1997.

As can be expected, high-weight bulk products topped the list of shipments measured in tons. The top commodity was bituminous coal, at 1.1 billion tons or 10 percent of the total tons shipped. Coal was followed by gravel and crushed stones, gasoline, limestone and chalk, and fuel oils. The 10 major commodities measured by tonnage have an enormous impact on the nation's transportation system, accounting for just over half (51 percent) of the total 11 billion tons and nearly 38 percent of the 2,661 billion ton-miles moved in 1997. Bulk commodity shipments impact both local and long-haul transportation. Five out of the 10 major commodities were shipped between 106 miles and 484 miles per ton [1].

When measured by ton-miles, the 10 major commodities accounted for over 41 percent of the total. Bituminous coal, by far the most dominant U.S. bulk commodity and often shipped long distances and nationwide, accounted for the largest share (20 percent) and generated 540 billion ton-miles. Ranked after coal were corn (except sweet corn), gasoline, limestone, and fuel oils, but these four commodities totaled only 12.9 percent of the ton-miles. In 1997, each ton of bituminous coal was moved, on average, 484 miles. Iron ores and concentrates, at only 41 billion ton-miles, are moved an average of 617 miles per ton [1].

Source

1. U.S. Department of Transportation, Bureau of Transportation Statistics and U.S. Department of Commerce, U.S. Census Bureau, 1993 and 1997 Commodity Flow Surveys.

---

[1] These data, from the Commodity Flow Survey, cover about 75 percent of the total tonnage of domestic freight shipments but do not cover all shipments of commodities such as crude petroleum.

[2] Based on the four-digit Standard Classification of Transported Goods coding system.

Table 1

Major Commodities Shipped in the United States: 1997

(Commodity Flow Survey data only)

SCTG code	Four-digit commodity groups	Value ($billions)	Tons (millions)	Ton-miles (billions)	Value per ton	Miles per ton
	All commodities	**6,944**	**11,090**	**2,661**	**626**	**240**
	Ranked by value					
3640	Parts and accessories for motor vehicles, except motorcycles	272	55	22	4,937	393
4099	Miscellaneous manufactured products, n.e.c.	267	97	33	2,765	338
3551	Computer equipment	233	4	3	63,149	895
4399	Mixed freight	230	110	17	2,090	156
2100	Pharmaceutical products	224	10	6	22,678	564
1710	Gasoline	204	858	110	237	128
3610	Motor vehicles for the transport of less than 10 people, except motorcycles	193	24	15	8,005	623
3020	Textile clothing and accessories, and headgear	186	10	6	19,091	640
3599	Electrical, electronic, and office equipment	158	14	7	11,519	546
3581	Electronic parts	145	1	1	150,640	926
	Ranked by tons					
1510	Nonagglomerated bituminous coal	24	1,114	540	21	484
1202	Gravel and crushed stone, except dolomite, slate, and limestone	7	994	41	7	41
1710	Gasoline	204	858	110	237	128
1201	Limestone and chalk (calcium carbonate)	5	821	52	6	64
1800	Fuel oils	94	482	51	196	106
1101	Silica sands and quartz sands, for construction use	2	332	14	6	44
3194	Nonrefractory mortars and concretes	11	318	7	34	22
0220	Corn, except sweet	31	305	130	103	426
3195	Articles of cement, concrete, or artificial stone	17	281	16	60	56
3220	Flat-rolled products of iron or steel	92	181	48	510	264
	Ranked by ton-miles					
1510	Nonagglomerated bituminous coal	24	1,114	540	21	484
0220	Corn, except sweet	31	305	130	103	426
1710	Gasoline	204	858	110	237	128
1201	Limestone and chalk (calcium carbonate)	5	821	52	6	64
1800	Fuel oils	94	482	51	196	106
3220	Flat-rolled products of iron or steel	92	181	48	510	264
0210	Wheat	17	124	45	134	360
2050	Organic chemicals, n.e.c.	84	85	44	996	514
0340	Soya beans	28	111	43	250	383
1410	Iron ores and concentrates	2	66	41	34	617

KEY: n.e.c. = not elsewhere classified; SCTG = Standard Classification of Transported Goods.

SOURCE: U.S. Department of Transportation, Bureau of Transportation Statistics and U.S. Department of Commerce, U.S. Census Bureau, 1997 Commodity Flow Survey.

Classes of Hazardous Materials Shipped

Shipment of hazardous materials, such as gasoline, fuel oil and other petroleum products, chemicals, and corrosives, are ubiquitous on our nation's highways, rail network, waterways, and by pipelines. The latest Commodity Flow Survey (CFS), conducted by the Bureau of Transportation Statistics and the Census Bureau, shows that hazardous materials account for about 14 percent of the tonnage moved. Flammable liquids exceed all other hazard classes in exposure on the U.S. transportation system, accounting for more than 80 percent of total tons (table 1). The highway, pipeline, and water modes move the largest volume of flammable liquids. Unfortunately, the CFS was unable to capture pipeline ton-miles data because shippers cannot assess the distance material moves once it enters the pipeline network and becomes interchangeable with products already being transported.

The U.S. transportation system moved more than 1.5 billion tons of hazardous materials in 1997, valued at $466 billion [1, 2]. In terms of tons, trucks moved the greatest percentage of hazardous materials, followed by the pipeline, water, rail, and other modes, which include air, parcel, postal, and multiple modes (figure 1).

Table 1
Hazardous Materials Shipments by Class and Tonnage: 1997

Class	Total tonnage (thousands)
Flammable liquids	1,264,281
Gases	115,021
Corrosive materials	91,564
Flammable solids	11,804
Oxidizers/organic peroxides	9,239
Poisons	6,366
Explosives	1,517
Radioactive materials	87
Miscellaneous dangerous goods	65,317
Total	**1,565,196**

SOURCES: U.S. Department of Transportation, Bureau of Transportation Statistics; and U.S. Department of Commerce, Census Bureau, *1997 Economic Census, Transportation—Commodity Flow Survey* (Washington, DC: Apr. 20, 2000), table 6a.

Sources

1. U.S. Department of Commerce, Census Bureau, *1997 Economic Census—Transportation, 1997 Commodity Flow Survey* (Washington, DC: December 1999).

2. U.S. Department of Transportation, Bureau of Transportation Statistics, 2000.

Figure 1
Hazardous Materials Shipments by Mode of Transportation: 1997

Value

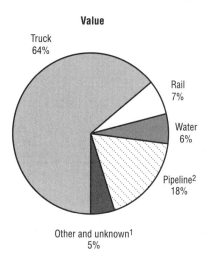

Truck 64%
Rail 7%
Water 6%
Pipeline[2] 18%
Other and unknown[1] 5%

Ton-miles[3]

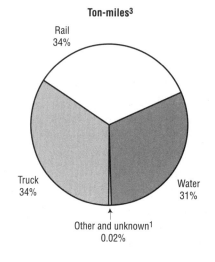

Rail 34%
Truck 34%
Water 31%
Other and unknown[1] 0.02%

Tons

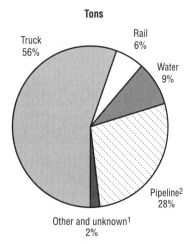

Truck 56%
Rail 6%
Water 9%
Pipeline[2] 28%
Other and unknown[1] 2%

[1] Includes air, parcel, postal, courier, other, and unknown.
[2] Excludes most shipments of crude oil.
[3] Pipeline data are not published because of high sampling variability or other reasons.

NOTE: Percentages may not add to 100 due to rounding

SOURCE: U.S. Department of Commerce, Census Bureau, *1997 Economic Census—1997 Commodity Flow Survey, Hazardous Materials* (Washington, DC: December 1999), table 1.

Intermodal Freight Shipments

The U.S. transportation system, responding to domestic economic growth, global competition, technological advances in information and production technologies, and changing supply chain requirements, has become increasingly intermodal.[1] The ability to shift goods between multiple modes in a timely, cost-effective, reliable manner (primarily through containers) is now essential for a high performing system and plays a key role in U.S. shippers' choice of mode or modes. Growth in the global market for high-value, time-sensitive goods has increased the demand for intermodal freight shipments.

Intermodal freight is increasing at a faster rate than freight moved by single modes.[2] In 1997, intermodal shipments accounted for 2 percent of the tonnage, 8 percent of the ton-miles, and about 17 percent of the value of commercial freight shipments in the United States. The value of intermodal freight, measured by the Commodity Flow Survey, rose from $872 billion in 1993 to $1,175 billion in 1997 (both in 1997 dollars), a 35 percent increase. In comparison, the value of single-mode freight shipments increased from $5,376 billion to $5,720 billion, an increase of 6.4 percent.

The magnitude of intermodal shipments varies by state. Many factors affect the size of intermodal freight transported in each state, including the size of the state's economy and population, its transportation infrastructure, and whether it is a gateway for international trade. The map on the next page illustrates the importance of intermodal shipments relative to total shipments in each state. A high proportion of freight originating in New York and Florida, for example, is intermodal. In comparison, a small proportion of freight shipped from Wyoming is intermodal because it is dominated by coal that moves primarily by rail.

Although intermodal shipments account for a relatively small proportion of freight tonnage and ton-miles, they play a key role in business logistics and in international trade. The rapid growth in this type of shipment presents capacity and congestion challenges to the freight community and increases the need to improve the efficiency of intermodal connections at marine and air cargo facilities, land border crossings, intermodal rail terminals, and domestic access infrastructure. The growth of containerization has made intermodal shipments—both domestic and international—more timely, cost-effective, and reliable.

Source

1. U.S. Department of Transportation, Bureau of Transportation Statistics and U.S. Department of Commerce, U.S. Census Bureau, *1997 Economic Census: Transportation, 1997 Commodity Flow Survey* (Washington, DC: 1999), table 7.

---

[1] Intermodal freight as defined in the Commodity Flow Survey includes all shipments using two or more modes: air transportation (including truck and air); truck and rail; truck and water; rail and water; parcel, postal, and courier services; and other intermodal combinations.

[2] The Commodity Flow Survey underestimates truck and rail intermodal movement because imports are not included. Railroads handle millions of containers that arrive by ship and are trucked to nearby railyards for delivery by rail.

Intermodal Shipments as a Percentage of Total Shipments by State: 1997
(Commodity Flow Survey data only)

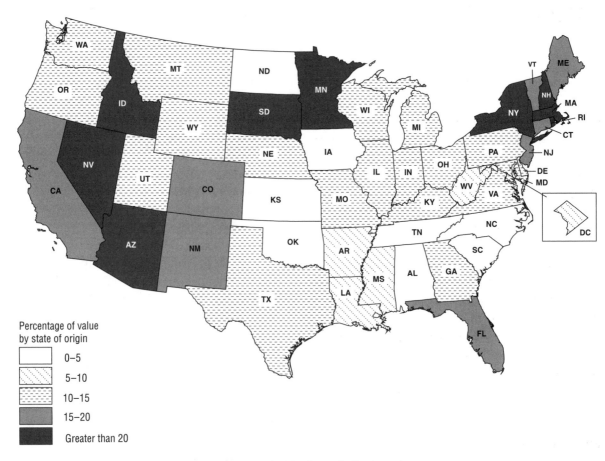

Percentage of value
by state of origin

- 0–5
- 5–10
- 10–15
- 15–20
- Greater than 20

SOURCE: U.S. Department of Transportation, Bureau of Transportation Statistics, Commodity Flow Survey data.

Major Commodity Shipments by the Trucking Industry

Trucking (for-hire and private) moved more freight in the United States in 1997 than any other mode, when measured by the value and tonnage of commodities. It was the dominant mode not only for commercial freight shipments as a whole, but also for the major commodity groups (table 1). For single mode shipments, Commodity Flow Survey (CFS) data show that trucking accounted for 71.7 percent of the value in 1997, down slightly from 75.3 percent in 1993. By tonnage, truck shipments accounted for 69.4 percent in 1997, up from 65.9 percent in 1993. However, when measured in ton-miles, trucking only accounted for 38.5 percent of the CFS shipments in 1997, a slight increase from 35.9 percent in 1993, reflecting the heavy use of this mode for local shipping.

Among the top 10 commodities by value, trucking's market share ranged from 56 percent to 92 percent. Electronic, electrical equipment, and office equipment was the largest commodity group in 1997 and trucking accounted for 56 percent of these shipments. Trucking also moved a large percentage of shipments for the majority of the next largest commodity groups: motorized and other vehicles (64 percent) and miscellaneous manufactured products (64 percent). Two in the top 10 commodity group—electronic, electrical equipment, and office equipment and

miscellaneous manufactured products—have the fastest growing freight markets. Between 1993 and 1997, the value of electronic, electrical equipment, and office equipment shipments rose by 56 percent, from $558 billion to $870 billion (1997 dollars). Miscellaneous manufactured products shipped in the United States increased from $252 billion to $420 billion, a 67 percent rise.

On average, each ton of electronic, electrical equipment, and office equipment shipped by truck in 1997 was carried an average of 650 miles and was valued at about $15,000 per ton. In contrast, a ton of miscellaneous manufactured products traveled about 300 miles and was valued at $2,600.

When measured by weight, trucks dominate shipments of 8 of the top 10 commodity groupings, with rail moving about 57 percent of coal and competing for 29 percent of cereal grains. In ton-miles, however, trucks moved only about 2 percent of coal (rail, 81 percent) and 9 percent of cereal grain (rail, 58 percent).

Source

1. U.S. Department of Transportation, Bureau of Transportation Statistics and U.S. Department of Commerce, U.S. Census Bureau, *1997 Economic Census: Transportation, 1997 Commodity Flow Survey* (Washington, DC: 1999), table 7.

Table 1

Trucking and Railroad Share of the Major Commodity Shipments in the United States: 1997

(Commodity Flow Survey Data Only)

SCTG code	Top 10 commodity groupings	All modes	Trucking	Rail	Trucking share (%)	Rail share (%)
	By value ($billions)					
	All commodities	*6,944*	*4,982*	*320*	*71.7*	*4.6*
35	Electronic, electrical equipment, and office equipment	870	484	3	55.7	0.3
36	Motorized and other vehicles (including parts)	571	367	77	64.2	13.5
40	Miscellaneous manufactured products	421	268	3	63.7	0.6
34	Machinery	417	320	6	76.7	1.5
30	Textiles, leather, and articles of textiles or leather	379	293	0.47	77.4	0.1
7	Other prepared foodstuffs and fats and oils	346	319	13	92.2	3.8
32	Base metal in primary or semifinished forms	286	242	26	84.7	9.1
24	Plastics and rubber	279	219	21	78.5	7.6
29	Printed products	260	178	0.27	68.4	0.1
41	Mixed freight	230	219	–	95.0	–
	By tonnage (millions)					
	All commodities	*11,090*	*7,701*	*1,550*	*69.4*	*14.0*
12	Gravel and crushed stone	1,815	1,672	51	92.1	2.8
15	Coal	1,217	217	687	17.8	56.5
17	Gasoline and aviation turbine fuel	963	518	5	53.8	0.6
31	Nonmetallic mineral products	910	860	23	94.5	2.5
2	Cereal grains	490	189	142	38.5	29.1
18	Fuel oils	482	244	7	50.7	1.4
19	Coal and petroleum products, n.e.c.	475	281	62	59.2	13.0
11	Natural sands	443	413	11	93.4	2.5
7	Other prepared foodstuffs and fats and oils	397	348	32	87.6	8.1
25	Logs and other wood in the rough	371	349	7	94.0	2.0
	By ton-miles (billions)					
	All commodities	*2,661*	*1,024*	*1,023*	*38.5*	*38.4*
15	Coal	542	9	439	1.7	81.0
2	Cereal grains	201	18	116	9.1	58.0
20	Basic chemicals	137	34	69	24.7	50.8
17	Gasoline and aviation turbine fuel	137	29	3	21.5	2.1
7	Other prepared foodstuffs and fats and oils	124	79	34	63.5	27.0
32	Base metal in primary or semifinished forms	117	68	36	57.5	30.9
26	Wood products	97	52	36	53.9	36.7
12	Gravel and crushed stone	93	58	11	62.8	11.8
31	Nonmetallic mineral products	91	64	14	69.7	15.4
27	Pulp, newsprint, paper, and paperboard	84	44	35	52.3	42.3

NOTE: – = data do not meet publication standards because of sampling variability or other reasons; n.e.c. = not elsewhere classified; SCTG = Standard Classification of Transported Goods.

SOURCE: U.S. Department of Transportation, Bureau of Transportation Statistics and U.S. Department of Commerce, U.S. Census Bureau, *1997 Commodity Flow Survey, United States,* EC97TCF-US (Washington, DC: 1999).

Chapter 5
Economic Growth

Introduction

Transportation is a vital component of the U.S. economy. As a sizable element of the country's Gross Domestic Product, transportation employs millions of people and consumes a large amount of the economy's goods and services. About one-fifth of household spending is on transportation. Transportation is also an important element of federal, state, and local government revenues and expenditures. For instance, the federal government's motor fuel tax collected about $18 billion from households in 1998, an average of $176 per household. In addition to discussing the size of transportation in the economy, transportation employment, fuel taxes, and transportation spending by households, this chapter presents data on labor productivity, gasoline prices, highway capital stocks, and international trade.

Demand for transportation-related goods and services represents about one-tenth of the U.S. economy and supports one in eight jobs. These goods and services encompass a whole range of activities from vehicle production and automobile insurance to road building and public transportation. The amount of goods and services produced by each worker, measured in dollars per hour of work (labor productivity), has increased markedly in most sectors of transportation over the past 45 years. In the rail industry, productivity gains have been particularly strong since deregulation in 1980. On average, a worker in the rail industry now produces more than three times as much as in 1980. This increased labor productivity has made transportation less expensive for consumers.

Transportation services are provided both by transportation companies, known collectively as the for-hire transportation sector, and by nontransportation companies. Transportation services provided by nontransportation companies for their own use are known as in-house transportation. A trucking fleet owned by a grocery chain is an example of in-house transportation. While data on the for-hire transportation sector have been readily available for many years, it has been impossible to estimate the value of in-house transportation until very recently. The Bureau of Transportation Statistics (BTS), in cooperation with the Bureau of Economic Analysis (BEA) in the U.S. Department of Commerce, has developed a method to measure the value added to the economy by these services. Using this method, BTS and BEA estimate that in 1996, in-house transportation contributed $142 billion to the economy compared with $236 billion by the for-hire sector.

Households spent on average $7,000 on transportation in 1999, nearly 20 percent of that year's average household income. This amount is second only to the amount they spent on housing. The vast majority of household spending on transportation goes for vehicle purchase, operation, and maintenance. While people are traveling a lot more now than they did in the mid-1980s, transportation expenditures have declined by 2 percent. Household spending on transportation, of course, varies according to a number of factors, including age and location. For example, people in the West spent more than those in any other region.

International trade is a growing part of the U.S. economy. The lowering of trade tariffs via the Free Trade Agreement of 1989 and the North American Free Trade Agreement (NAFTA) of 1993 have contributed to the increasing importance of North American trade. Canada has been and remains the top trading partner of the United States. In 1999, Mexico surpassed Japan to become America's second largest trading partner. Still, trade with other countries remains very important. About 66 percent of foreign trade in 1999 was with countries other than Canada and Mexico. The vast majority of these goods are transported by ship. International waterborne trade has, therefore, grown along with international trade, while domestic waterborne transportation over the past 15 years has stayed relatively constant.

Transportation Demand in GDP Growth

Purchases of transportation-related goods and services accounted for 10.6 percent of Gross Domestic Product (GDP) in 1999, or $990 billion (table 1) [1]. This broad measure, called transportation-related final demand, reflects all consumer and government purchases of goods and services and exports related to transportation. The list of purchases is diverse and extensive, including vehicles, parts, engines, fuel, maintenance, and auto insurance.

The share of transportation-related final demand in GDP has fluctuated slightly between 10.5 percent and 11.0 percent from 1975 through 1999. Only housing, health care, and food accounted for greater shares of GDP in 1999 (figure 1).

Source

1. U.S. Department of Transportation, Bureau of Transportation Statistics, 2000, based on data in U.S. Department of Commerce, Bureau of Economic Analysis, *Survey of Current Business* (Washington, DC: Various issues).

Table 1
Transportation-Related Components of U.S. GDP: 1975 and 1999
(Billions of current dollars)

	1975	1999
Personal consumption of transportation		
Motor vehicles and parts	54.8	320.7
Gasoline and oil	39.7	128.3
Transportation services	35.7	256.5
Total	*130.2*	*705.5*
Gross private domestic investment		
Transportation structures	1.4	6.4
Transportation equipment	1.9	193.5
Total	*3.3*	*199.9*
Exports (+)		
Civilian aircraft, engines, and parts	3.2	52.9
Automotive vehicles, engines, and parts	10.8	75.8
Passenger fares	1.0	19.8
Other transportation	5.8	27.0
Total	*20.8*	*175.5*
Imports (−)		
Civilian aircraft, engines, and parts	0.5	23.8
Automotive vehicles, engines, and parts	12.1	179.4
Passenger fares	2.3	21.4
Other transportation	5.7	34.1
Total	*20.6*	*258.7*
Net exports of transportation-related goods and services	*0.2*	*−83.2*
Government transportation-related purchases		
Federal	4.9	18.8
State and local	32.1	140.6
Defense-related	2.8	8.6
Total	*39.9*	*168.0*
Total transportation final demand[1]	173.6	990.2
Gross Domestic Product (GDP)	1,630.6	9,299.2
Total transportation in GDP (percent)	**10.6%**	**10.6%**

[1] Demand for goods and services produced in the United States, regardless of where they are consumed. The measure counts exported goods and services, but does not include imports.

SOURCE: U.S. Department of Transportation, Bureau of Transportation Statistics, calculated from data in U.S. Department of Commerce, Bureau of Economic Analysis, *Survey of Current Business* (Washington, DC: Various issues from 1975–December 2000.)

Figure 1
**U.S. Gross Domestic Product by Major
Societal Function: 1999**

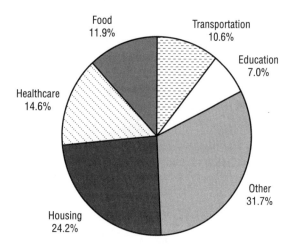

SOURCE: U.S. Department of Transportation, Bureau of Transportation
Statistics, calculated from data in U.S. Department of Commerce,
Bureau of Economic Analysis, *Survey of Current Business,* July 2000.

Transportation-Related Employment by Industry

Employment is an important indicator of economic growth and social well-being. In 2000, more than 10 million people were employed in for-hire transportation, vehicle manufacturing, and related industries, such as automobile sales and repair. These jobs accounted for about 7.5 percent of total civilian employment. The most recent data show that the automotive dealers and service station industry was the largest employer among transportation-related industries, followed by transportation equipment manufacturing, trucking and warehousing, air transportation, and auto repair and parking services (figure 1).

Transportation-related industry employment data, however, do not include transportation occupations in nontransportation industries, such as truck drivers working for wholesale and retail stores. Based on data from the U.S. Department of Labor's Bureau of Labor Statistics, the Bureau of Transportation Statistics estimated that employment in transportation occupations in nontransportation industries was about 5.5 million in 1998. When this component is included, total transportation employment would have accounted for about 12 percent, or 1 out of every 8 U.S. civilian jobs [1].

Source

1. U.S. Department of Transportation, Bureau of Transportation Statistics, *Transportation Indicators* (Washington, DC: September 2000).

Figure 1
Employment in Transportation-Related Industries: January 1980–January 2001
(Seasonally adjusted)

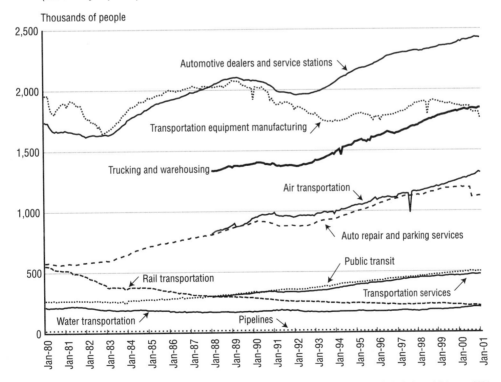

SOURCE: U.S. Department of Labor, Bureau of Labor Statistics, "Employees on Nonfarm Payrolls by Industry," February 2001.

For-Hire Transportation

The for-hire transportation industry contributed $303 billion to the U.S. economy in 1999 (table 1). Its share in Gross Domestic Product (GDP), however, has declined from 4.4 percent in 1960, to 3.6 percent in 1975, to 3.3 percent in 1999 (measured in current dollars) [1]. Many factors, including productivity improvements and the growth of in-house trucking services by companies that are not in the transportation business (e.g., grocery store chains), may explain this change.

Of all for-hire transportation industries, trucking and warehousing and air transportation contributed the largest share to U.S. GDP. In 1999, trucking and warehousing and air transportation contributed $116.6 billion and $95.0 billion,

respectively. Together, they accounted for more than two-thirds of transportation GDP. Not surprisingly, air transportation had the highest growth rate followed by transportation services over the 1960 to 1999 period (figure 1). Although the trucking and warehousing industry experienced considerable growth from 1975 to 1985, it has slowed down in recent years [1].

Source

1. U.S. Department of Commerce, Bureau of Economic Analysis, "Gross Domestic Product by Industry and the Components of Gross Domestic Income," available at http://www.bea.doc.gov/bea/dn2.htm, as of May 2001.

Table 1
U.S. Gross Domestic Product Attributed to For-Hire Transportation Industries
Millions of current dollars

Industry	1960	1965	1970	1975	1980	1985	1990	1995	1999
Gross Domestic Product	527,380	720,108	1,039,674	1,635,165	2,795,561	4,213,016	5,803,246	7,400,534	9,299,158
Transportation	**23,138**	**29,533**	**39,881**	**59,248**	**102,948**	**140,431**	**177,404**	**233,379**	**303,418**
Railroad transportation	8,400	9,069	10,049	12,555	20,752	22,002	19,819	23,594	23,431
Local and interurban passenger transit	1,906	2,176	2,880	3,488	5,271	7,731	9,077	12,439	17,117
Trucking and warehousing	7,518	10,653	15,029	24,154	40,094	56,326	69,428	89,036	116,627
Water transportation	1,818	2,190	2,855	3,987	7,180	8,317	10,044	11,627	14,395
Transportation by air	1,959	3,422	6,360	10,179	18,188	27,063	45,341	67,667	94,996
Pipelines, except natural gas	595	719	1,102	1,812	5,233	7,306	5,543	5,484	6,618
Transportation services	942	1,304	1,606	3,074	6,230	11,687	18,151	23,532	30,235

SOURCE: U.S. Department of Commerce, Bureau of Economic Analysis, "Gross Domestic Product by Industry and the Components of Gross Domestic Income," available at http://www.bea.doc.gov/bea/dn2.htm, as of May 2001.

Figure 1
For-Hire Transportation Shares in Gross Domestic Product: 1960 and 1999

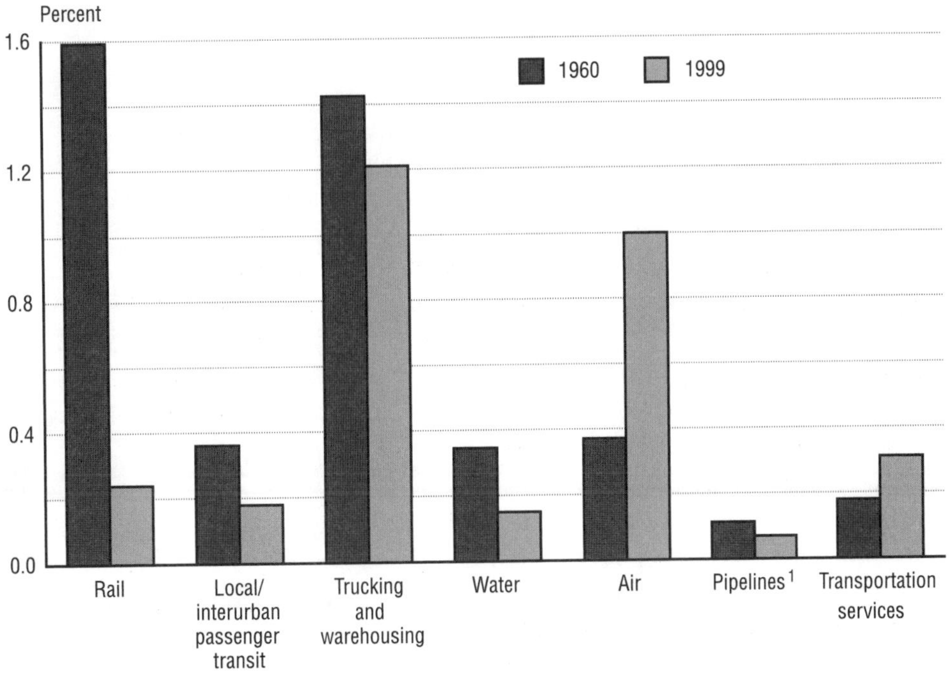

[1] Does not include natural gas.

SOURCE: U.S. Department of Commerce, Bureau of Economic Analysis, "Gross Domestic Product by Industry and the Components of Gross Domestic Income," available at http://www.bea.doc.gov/bea/dn2.htm, as of May 2001.

In-House Transportation

Companies that are not in the transportation business often have their own internal transportation operations (primarily trucking). For example, many grocery chains use their own trucks and employees to transport goods from warehouses to retail stores. Until recently, the value-added to the economy by in-house transportation was not known. Through joint research, the Bureau of Transportation Statistics and the Bureau of Economic Analysis in the U.S. Commerce Department have developed a method to

Figure 1
Gross Domestic Product by Selected Industries: 1996

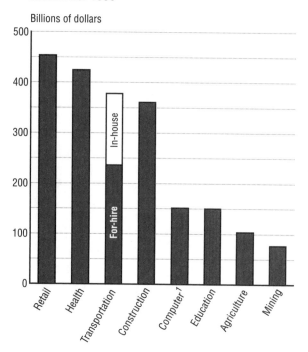

¹ Consists of computer and office equipment manufacturing and computer and data processing services.

SOURCE: U.S. Department of Transportation, Bureau of Transportation Statistics, special tabulation, September 2000.

Figure 2
Transportation GDP by Mode

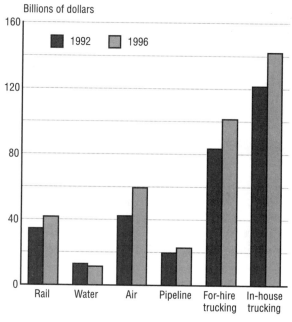

SOURCE: U.S. Department of Transportation, Bureau of Transportation Statistics, special tabulation, September 2000.

measure the value-added to the economy by these services. In 1996, the latest year for which data are available, in-house transportation contributed $142 billion to the economy. Together, in-house transportation and for-hire transportation services contributed about $378 billion or 4.8 percent of the U.S. Gross Domestic Product (GDP) [1, 2] (figure 1).

Trucking maintained a two-thirds share of transportation GDP, with in-house trucking contributing a larger share than for-hire trucking (figure 2). In 1996, in-house trucking accounted for 58 percent of trucking GDP and 38 percent of total transportation GDP. Air transportation, the fastest growing mode, was the next largest contributor to transportation GDP, followed by rail [1, 2].

Figure 3 shows that many industries rely more heavily on in-house transportation than for-hire transportation services to support their production. The agriculture, forestry, and fisheries industry sector is the most transportation-intensive. However, the second most transportation-intensive industry—construction—spends more on in-house transportation to produce a dollar of construction output.

Sources

1. U.S. Department of Transportation, Bureau of Transportation Statistics, *Transportation Satellite Accounts: A New Way of Measuring Transportation Services in America,* BTS99-R-01 (Washington, DC: 1999).

2. ____. *U.S. Transportation Satellite Accounts for 1996*, data, available at http://www.bea.doc.gov/bea/dn2.htm, as of May 2001.

Figure 3
Transportation Costs per Dollar of Output, by Major Industry: 1996

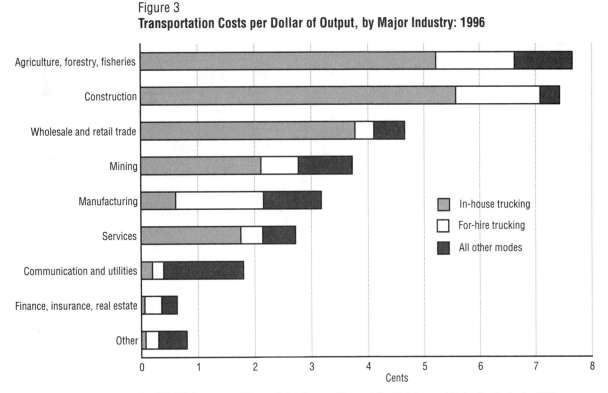

SOURCE: U.S. Department of Transportation, Bureau of Transportation Statistics, special tabulation, September 2000.

Transportation Labor Productivity

For the past four decades, transportation has been one of the leaders in U.S. productivity growth. As shown in figure 1, U.S. business sector productivity, measured in real output per employee, grew 122 percent between 1955 and 1998. In contrast, several transportation modes had much higher growth rates over this period. For example, between 1955 and 1997, railroad labor productivity grew 752 percent; pipeline grew 577 percent; air transportation grew 500 percent; and for-hire trucking grew 202 percent. In recent years, however, labor productivity growth in the trucking industry flattened out and air transportation fluctuated. When compared with the economy as a whole, labor productivity in the railroad and pipeline industries continues to increase at a faster rate, while the bus mode shows no growth [1]. Data for water transportation are not available.

Deregulation, technological change, and labor force reductions have all contributed to higher labor productivity in transportation. Specifically, air transportation labor productivity increased because of the introduction of larger and faster aircraft, computerized passenger reservation systems, the hub-and-spoke flight network, and changes in requirements for flight personnel. In the railroad industry, consolidation of companies, more efficient use of equipment and lines, increased ton-miles, and labor force reductions have played a role.

Source

1. U.S. Department of Labor, Bureau of Labor Statistics, Office of Productivity and Technology, "Historical Indexes of Output per Employee, All Published Industries, Productivity Trends for Transportation Industries," available at ftp://ftp.bls.gov/pub/special.requests/opt/dipts/oaehaiin.txt, as of September 2000.

Figure 1
Labor Productivity Trends by Mode
Index: 1955 = 100

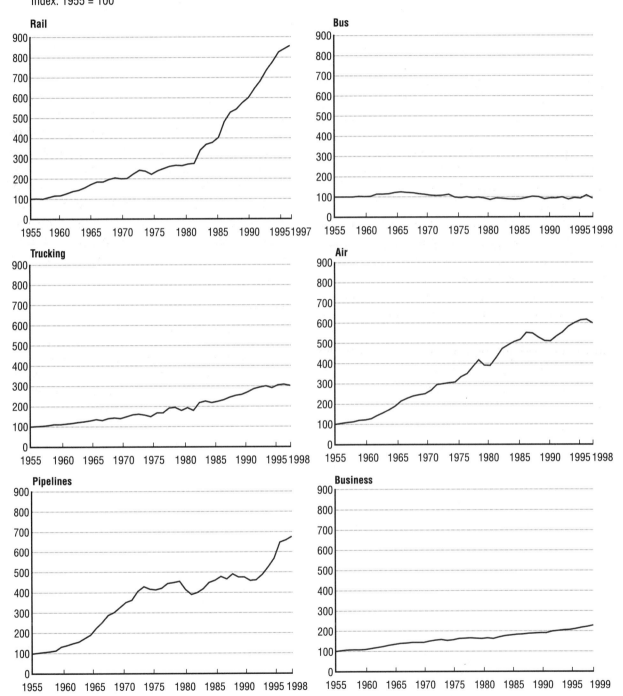

NOTES: Output is measured by quality-adjusted ton- and passenger-miles for railroad and air transportation, quality-adjusted ton-miles for trucking and pipelines, and passenger-miles for buses. *Quality-adjusted* refers to differences in services and handling, e.g., the difference between flying first class and coach or differences in the handling requirements and revenue generation of high- and low-value commodities. No data are available for water transportation. Most recent data available are provided.

SOURCE: U.S. Department of Labor, Bureau of Labor Statistics, Office of Productivity and Technology, available at http://www.bls.gov/iprdata1.htm, as of May 2001.

Consumer Prices for Transportation

Improvements in transportation labor productivity have made transportation less expensive for consumers. Since 1978, transportation prices increased less than those for other major consumer expenditure categories. For example, the price for the same amount of goods or services increased 172 percent for housing and 322 percent for health care between 1978 and 2000 (figure 1). By comparison, the overall price of transportation increased 148 percent. In more recent years, from 1994 to 2000, price inflation

for transportation was the lowest among the four major consumer expenditure categories.

Within transportation, the price for consumer-operated transportation (e.g., private passenger car transportation) increased more slowly than for purchased transportation services. Between 1978 and 2000, the price of consumer-operated transportation increased 139 percent, while the price of purchased transportation services increased 307 percent (figure 2).

Figure 1
Consumer Price Indexes for Selected Items: 1978–2000

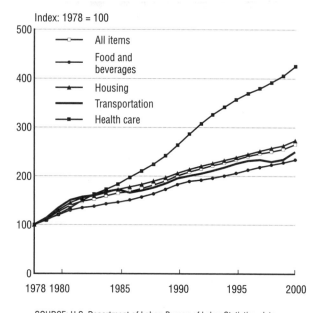

SOURCE: U.S. Department of Labor, Bureau of Labor Statistics, data available at http://www.bls.gov/cpihome.htm, as of May 2001.

Figure 2
Consumer Price Indexes for Purchased and Private Transportation Services: 1978–2000

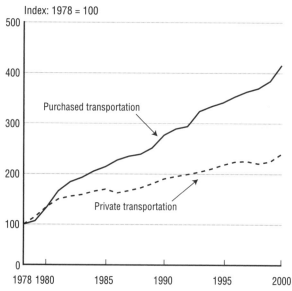

SOURCE: U.S. Department of Labor, Bureau of Labor Statistics, data available at http://www.bls.gov/cpihome.htm, as of May 2001.

Gasoline Prices

The average price of motor gasoline fuel in the United States increased from $1.03 per gallon in January 1999 to $1.64 per gallon in July 2000, a 59 percent increase within 18 months (figure 1). By the end of the year, however, the price had declined to $1.53. Although these fuel prices were far below record highs in real terms, the rapid rise attracted consumer attention and affected the profitability of transportation industries, whose profit margins, on average, have been less than 7 percent in the past few years [1]. Figure 1 shows that the consumption of motor fuels in the United States has not been very sensitive to changes in fuel prices in recent years. For the transportation sector, the price of fuel would have to increase 14 percent for a 1 percent reduction in fuel consumption to occur. Conversely, a small change in supply would cause a large change in price.

The impact of increases in fuel prices can also be measured by the added cost that industry incurs to produce $1 of net output, which is also known as industry Gross Domestic Product. Measured in this way, the impact of higher motor fuel prices would be the most severe on the railroad, transit, air, and trucking modes. According to a Bureau of Transportation Statistics (BTS) analysis, higher gasoline prices in 2000 would have cost transit an additional 9 cents to produce $1 of net output. The additional costs for air transportation and railroad were estimated to be 8 cents. For trucking, the estimate was 6 cents (figure 2). The impact of higher fuel prices on water transportation and pipelines would be less severe because they are less energy intensive than other modes. The additional fuel cost to produce $1 of net output was expected to be 2.8 cents for water transportation and 0.4 cents for pipelines [2, 3, 4].

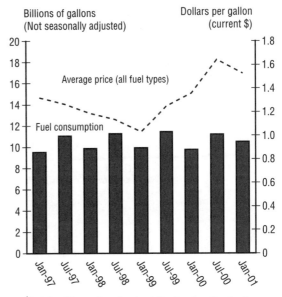

Figure 1

Price of Motor Gasoline[1] vs. Consumption: January 1997–January 2001

Billions of gallons (Not seasonally adjusted)

Dollars per gallon (current $)

[1]Includes all types of gasoline, in addition to automotive diesel.

NOTE: Monthly motor fuel consumption data are estimated based on a total of finished motor gasoline produced and imported, subtracted from the change in stocks and exports.

SOURCES: Fuel price data—U.S. Department of Labor, Bureau of Labor Statistics, Average Price Data, U.S. City Average, Gasoline (all types), monthly.
Fuel consumption data—U.S. Department of Energy, Energy Information Administration, *Petroleum Supply Monthly* (Washington, DC: various issues).

According to the recently published 1996 U.S. Transportation Satellite Accounts, developed jointly by BTS and the Bureau of Economic Analysis (U.S. Department of Commerce), fuel accounts for about 7 percent of the total operating costs of the for-hire trucking industry, 7 percent for the railroad industry, 9.2 percent for in-house trucking operations, 11 percent for the airline industry, and 8 percent for mass transit and local passenger transportation services [4].

Figure 2
Fuel Cost per Dollar of Net Output of For-Hire Transportation Industries

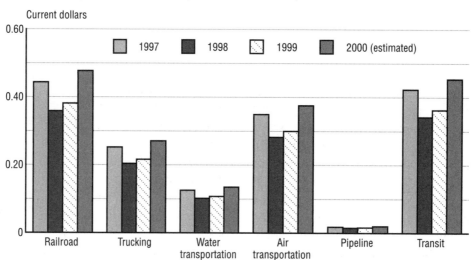

SOURCES: U.S. Department of Transportation, Bureau of Transportation Statistics, based on U.S. Department of Energy, Energy Information Administration, "Energy Consumption by Transportation Sector," monthly; and U.S. Department of Commerce, Bureau of Economic Analysis, "Gross Domestic Product by Industry and the Components of Gross Domestic Income," available at http://www.bea.doc.gov/bea/dn2.htm, as of May 2001.

Sources

1. U.S. Department of Commerce, Bureau of Economic Analysis, *Survey of Current Business,* various issues.

2. ___. "Gross Domestic Product by Industry," October 2000.

3. U.S. Department of Transportation, Bureau of Transportation Statistics, estimates based on U.S. Department of Energy, Energy Information Administration, "Energy Consumption by Transportation Sector," monthly reports.

4. ___. *U.S. Transportation Satellite Accounts for 1996,* data, available at http://www.bea.doc.gov/bea/dn2.htm, as of May 2001.

Household Spending on Transportation

Households spend more money, on average, on transportation than any other expenditure category except housing. In 1999, households on average spent about $7,000 on transportation, or 18.9 percent of their total spending (table 1). This share was slightly lower than that in 1984 (the first year for which data are available). Roughly 94 percent of household transportation expenditures went to purchase, maintain, and operate cars and other private vehicles. Purchased transportation services, including airline, intercity train and bus, and mass transit, accounted for less than 6 percent of household transportation expenditures in 1999 (table 2).

Measured in constant 1982 dollars, household transportation expenditures have decreased 2 percent between 1984 and 1998 (figure 1). During the same period, vehicle-miles traveled per household increased about 27 percent, indicating that transportation has become cheaper to consumers.

Household transportation expenditures vary by region (table 3). In 1999, on average, households in the West spent more on transportation than those in other regions. However, households in the Midwest and South spent a higher percentage of their income on transportation. Since 1994, however, regional differences in spending have decreased as automobiles have become relatively less expensive and more American households can afford multiple vehicles. Household transportation expenditures in the Northeast, which used to be the lowest among regions for both the amount and share in household spending, increased faster in terms of amount than that for other regions. However, the Northeast is the only region that showed an increase in the proportion of expenditures on transportation.

Spending on transportation differs among rural and urban households as well. During

Table 1
Consumer Expenditure Trends

	1984	1990	1999
Average annual household expenditures (current $)	$21,975	$28,381	$37,027
Category	**Percentage of total expenditures**		
Housing	30.4	30.7	32.6
Transportation	19.6	18.0	18.9
Food	15.0	15.1	13.6
Personal insurance and pensions	8.6	9.1	9.3
Apparel and services	6.0	5.7	4.7
Health care	4.8	5.2	5.3
Education	2.0	2.0	1.7
Other	13.7	14.1	13.9

SOURCES: U.S. Department of Labor, Bureau of Labor Statistics, "Consumer Expenditure Survey," 1984–1999, available at http://www.bls.gov, as of May 2001.

Table 2
Household Transportation Expenditures: 1999

Type of expenditure

Average annual household transportation expenditures (current $)	$7,011
Components and their shares	**Percent**
Vehicle purchases	**47.1**
Cars and trucks, used	23.4
Cars and trucks, new	23.2
Other vehicles	0.5
Gasoline and motor oil	**15.0**
Other vehicle expenses	**32.1**
Vehicle insurance	10.8
Maintenance and repairs	9.5
Vehicle rental, lease, license, and other charges	7.3
Vehicle finance charges	4.6
Purchased transportation services	**5.7**

SOURCE: U.S. Department of Labor, Bureau of Labor Statistics, "Consumer Expenditure Survey," 1999, available at http://www.bls.gov, as of May 2001.

Figure 1

Average Household Transportation Expenditures and Vehicle-Miles Traveled: 1984–1998

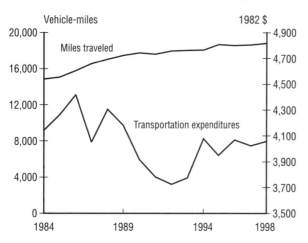

SOURCES: U.S. Department of Transportation, Bureau of Transportation Statistics:
Estimates of vehicle-miles traveled calculated from data in U.S. Department of Transportation, Federal Highway Administration, *Highway Statistics* (Washington, DC: 1984–1998). Estimates of transportation expenditures calculated from data in U.S. Department of Labor, Bureau of Labor Statistics, "Consumer Expenditure Survey," 1984–1998, available at http://www.bls.gov, as of May 2001.

Table 3

Annual Household Transportation Expenditures by Region: 1994 and 1999

	Northeast	Midwest	South	West
Transportation expenditures (in current dollars)				
1994	$5,111	$6,201	$6,141	$6,592
1999	$6,466	$6,939	$6,863	$7,802
Share of household total expenditures				
1994	15.7%	20.4%	20.4%	18.6%
1999	16.8%	19.1%	20.6%	18.4%

SOURCE: U.S. Department of Labor, Bureau of Labor Statistics, "Consumer Expenditure Survey," 1994 and 1998, available at http://www.bls.gov, as of May 2001.

percent for households in the 75 years and over age bracket.

Half of the transportation expenditures in young households were to purchase vehicles, compared with 37 percent for households in the oldest age group (figure 2). Moreover, younger households spent a smaller share of transportation expenditures on purchased transportation services, such as air travel, mass transit, and taxi fares [1].

Source

1. U.S. Department of Labor, Bureau of Labor Statistics, "Consumer Expenditure Survey," 1999, available at http://www.bls.gov, as of May 2001.

much of the 1990s, rural households, on average, spent more on transportation than urban households. In 1999, for instance, average urban household transportation expenditures were $6,975, while those of rural households were $7,276 [1].

Not surprisingly, the age of the head of the household also has an impact on transportation spending. Household transportation expenditures rise as the age of the head of the household increases, peaking between 45 and 54 years of age and then decreasing. In 1999, for example, households in which the head of the household was between 45 and 54 years of age spent, on average, $9,028 on transportation, while households in the under 25 years of age bracket spent a little more than half of that amount. Spending on transportation was lowest in households headed by people 75 years of age or older. However, transportation as a share of total household expenditures was highest in young households, averaging 23.2 percent. The percentage decreased gradually as age increased, reaching its lowest point at 14

Figure 2

Components of Household Transportation Expenditures by Age Group: 1999

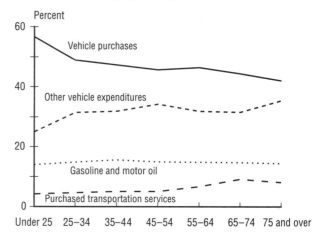

SOURCE: U.S. Department of Labor, Bureau of Labor Statistics, "Consumer Expenditure Survey," 1999, available at http://www.bls.gov, as of May 2001.

Fuel Tax Revenue

The Highway Trust Fund (HTF), which provides funding for surface transportation, has received its major source of revenue from federal motor fuel taxes paid by households (figure 1 and box). In 1970, for example, households paid $8.5 billion (chained 1998 dollars) in federal motor fuel taxes, accounting for about 50 percent of HTF revenue. By 1998, the share of federal motor fuel taxes paid by households increased to 69 percent of the HTF, or $18.3 billion.

Households paid an average of $176 each in 1998 in federal fuel taxes, five times the amount they did in 1966, when measured in current dollars (figure 2a). However, when the effect of inflation is removed, federal motor fuel taxes paid by

> **Where the Fuel Tax Revenues are Kept**
>
> States have collected taxes on gasoline since 1919, and in 1932 the U.S. Congress enacted the first federal tax on gasoline. These taxes were deposited in the General Fund. Beginning in 1956, federal motor fuel taxes were earmarked for the federal Highway Trust Fund. Since then, motor fuel taxes have increased several times (e.g., 9 cents per gallon in 1983, 14.1 cents per gallon in 1990, and 4.3 cents per gallon in 1993). Between December 1990 and October 1997, a percentage of the increase in federal motor fuel taxes was deposited in the General Fund for deficit reduction.

the average American household increased by only 27 percent between 1966 and 1998 (figure 2b), while household real disposable income rose by 60 percent. Hence, the share of federal motor fuel tax in household disposable income decreased from 0.37 percent in 1966 to 0.29 percent in 1998 (figure 3).

Improvements in automobile fuel economy were largely responsible for the slower growth of household motor fuel consumption and hence household expenditures on the motor fuel tax relative to the growth of household income and travel demand. Between 1966 and 1998, vehicle-miles traveled per household increased 68 percent, while motor fuel consumption per household increased only 15 percent.

Figure 1
Highway Trust Fund Revenue Sources: 1970–1998

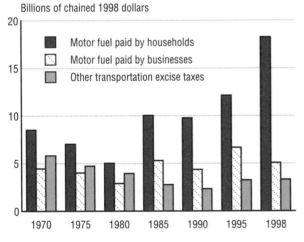

SOURCES:
U.S. Department of Transportation, Bureau of Transportation Statistics, "Federal Gas Tax: Household Expenditures from 1965 to 1995," *TranStat*, August 1997.
1998 data—U.S. Department of Transportation, Bureau of Transportation Statistics estimates based on U.S. Department of Commerce, Bureau of Economic Analysis, *Survey of Current Business*, various issues; U.S. Department of Labor, Bureau of Labor Statistics, "Consumer Expenditure Survey," 1996, 1997, and 1998; and U.S. Department of Transportation, Federal Highway Administration, *Highway Statistics 1998* (Washington, DC: 1999).

Figure 2
Federal Motor Fuel Tax per Household: 1966–1998

(a) Current Dollars

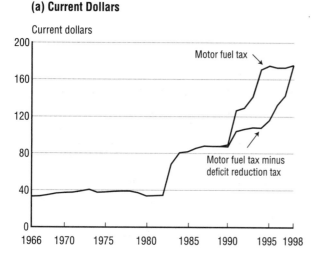

(b) Chained Dollars

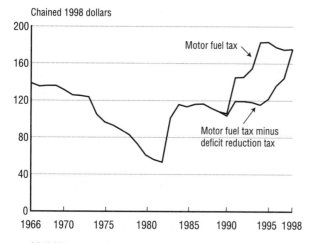

SOURCES:
U.S. Department of Transportation, Bureau of Transportation Statistics, "Federal Gas Tax: Household Expenditures from 1965 to 1995," *TranStat,* August 1997.
1998 data—U.S. Department of Transportation, Bureau of Transportation Statistics estimates based on U.S. Department of Commerce, Bureau of Economic Analysis, *Survey of Current Business,* various issues; U.S. Department of Labor, Bureau of Labor Statistics, "Consumer Expenditure Survey," 1996, 1997, and 1998; and U.S. Department of Transportation, Federal Highway Administration, *Highway Statistics 1998* (Washington, DC: 1999).

Figure 3
Share of Federal Motor Fuel Tax in Household Disposable Income: 1966–1998

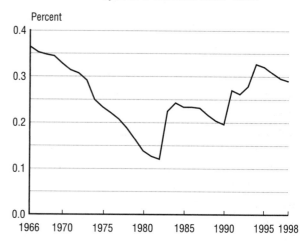

SOURCES:
U.S. Department of Transportation, Bureau of Transportation Statistics, "Federal Gas Tax: Household Expenditures from 1965 to 1995," *TranStat,* August 1997.
1998 data—U.S. Department of Transportation, Bureau of Transportation Statistics estimates based on U.S. Department of Commerce, Bureau of Economic Analysis, *Survey of Current Business,* various issues; U.S. Department of Labor, Bureau of Labor Statistics, "Consumer Expenditure Survey," 1996, 1997, and 1998; and U.S. Department of Transportation, Federal Highway Administration, *Highway Statistics 1998* (Washington, DC: 1999).

Highway Capital Stocks

Through decades of government investment, the United States has developed a large and extensive transportation system that is an important component of our national wealth and a contributor to productive capacity. Currently, however, adequate economic data on transportation infrastructure and vehicle capital stocks are only available for highways, although an effort is underway to expand knowledge in this area (see box).

In 1999, the accumulated public capital stock in highways and streets was valued at $1.3 trillion (current dollars). From 1988 to 1999, the value (in chain-type 1996 dollars) of highway capital stock increased by 22.5 percent. More dramatic increases in the value of highway capital stock occurred between 1953 and 1971 when the Interstate system was under development. Figure 1 shows the growth pattern in public capital in highways and streets between 1925 and 1999. Since the early 1970s, highway vehicle stocks have grown much faster than highway capital stocks, indicating that highways support much more rolling stock today than they did 20 years ago.

Transportation Infrastructure Capital Stock Account

All levels of government, along with the private sector, invest in transportation infrastructure. The resulting infrastructure assets play a key role in U.S. productive capacity, and also contribute to income and wealth generation. At the same time, infrastructure must be maintained to ensure adequate service. Despite its obvious importance, economic data on transportation infrastructure are inadequate.

The Bureau of Transportation Statistics of the U.S. Department of Transportation is developing a Transportation Infrastructure Capital Stock Account (TICSA) to overcome some of these data limitations. TICSA will provide comprehensive information on infrastructure investment, capital stock value, service value, asset retirement, and asset depreciation.

TICSA will include capital assets for highways and streets, airports and airways, ports and waterways, transit facilities, railroads, and pipelines. With such broad coverage, TICSA data will allow analysts to address such questions as:

1. What is the monetary value of transportation infrastructure used to support transportation operations in the U.S. economy?

2. What proportion of national income is invested in transportation infrastructure?

3. How much would need to be spent to maintain the current capacity of the transportation network or to increase its capacity to a certain level?

4. What is the rate of return of public investment in transportation infrastructure?

5. What is the relationship between transportation infrastructure investment and the growth in productivity in transportation industries?

6. How are transportation costs affected by the level of investment in transportation infrastructure, and how does this vary by mode?

Figure 1

Real Growth in Highway Capital Stocks Compared with Vehicle Stocks: 1925–1999

Chain-type index: 1925 = 100

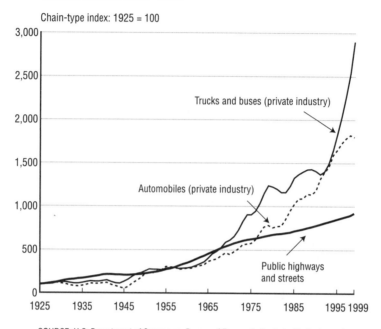

SOURCE: U.S. Department of Commerce, Bureau of Economic Analysis, "Industry and Wealth Data: Fixed Assets," available at http://www.bea.doc.gov/bea/dn2.htm, as of April 2001.

International Trade

Continuing growth of international trade is influencing the development of transportation systems and services within the United States. Increased international merchandise trade has spurred the development of marine and air cargo facilities, land border crossings, and domestic access infrastructure to connect international gateways with domestic U.S. origins and destinations. New technologies, including intelligent transportation systems, facilitate lower transportation costs and higher levels of service and speed.

Between 1997 and 1999, U.S. international merchandise trade rose 10.3 percent to $1.7 trillion (current dollars). Canada continued as the number one overall trade partner of the United States in 1999, a position the country has held for decades. Meanwhile, Mexico surpassed Japan to move into the number two position. In 1999, 10 nations accounted for almost 70 percent of all U.S. merchandise trade, and 5 of these were Asian Pacific countries (figure 1). Despite the recession in East and Southeast Asia in 1997, the overall U.S. trade relationship with many countries in the Pacific region, expanded between 1998 and 1999.[1]

In 1999, higher value manufactured goods dominated U.S. trade, accounting for $1,497 billion or 87 percent of the value of all merchandise trade. Motor vehicles, electrical machinery and appliances, office machines (including computers and other automated data processing

Figure 1
Top 10 U.S. Trade Partners by All Modes: 1999

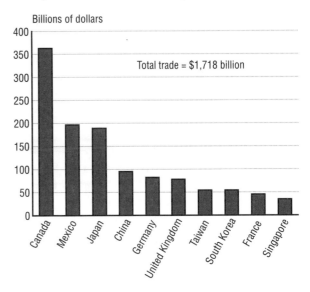

SOURCES: U.S. Department of Transporation, Bureau of Transportation Statistics, special tabulation, November 2000, based on U.S. Department of Commerce, U.S. Census Bureau, Foreign Trade Division, *U.S. Exports of Merchandise CD* and *U.S. Imports of Merchandise CD*, December 1999.

equipment) were among the top U.S. import and export commodities when measured by value. Transportation equipment was one of the leading U.S. manufactured exports, accounting for $53 billion in 1999. Agricultural goods accounted for approximately 5 percent of the share of U.S. international trade, and Japan was the top market for U.S. agricultural exports. Canada and Mexico were also leading purchasers and suppliers of U.S. agricultural commodities. Mineral fuels accounted for an approximate 5 percent share of U.S. international trade in 1999; the majority of this trade was U.S. imports of crude petroleum and related products. Venezuela was the leading supplier of

---

[1] U.S. overall merchandise trade with many Asian Pacific countries fell between 1997 and 1998 due to the region's recession. However, by 1999, trade with many of these same countries had risen to or exceeded the 1997 levels. Some of this trade growth was due to the expansion in imports from these countries, as these goods became relatively cheaper due to currency exchange rates.

petroleum products to the United States in 1999, followed by Canada and Saudi Arabia.

Between 1997 and 1999, the relative roles of the transportation modes in carrying U.S. international trade were in flux due to the continuing growth in trade within North America and internationally. During this period, U.S. international trade carried by truck increased 19 percent to $385 billion, air freight expanded 15 percent to $496 billion, while waterborne trade grew by less than 1 percent. Despite the small increase in waterborne trade during this time, over $631 billion of U.S. exports and imports moved by this mode in 1999, accounting for about 37 percent of the value of all U.S. international trade (table 1).

By value, Japan is the leading U.S. maritime trade partner, representing almost one-fifth of all U.S. waterborne trade. The ports of Long Beach and Los Angeles account for the majority of West Coast trade and also represented in 1999 over one-quarter of the value of overall waterborne trade for the United States (table 2).

Waterborne trade accounts for a much higher percentage of U.S. international trade tonnage compared with other modes. By weight, the top U.S. waterborne trade partner was Mexico, followed by many other U.S. trade partners for crude petroleum and petroleum products (table 3). Houston and other Gulf Coast ports accounted for the majority of U.S. international waterborne tonnage, a large component of which is the trade of bulk commodities and crude petroleum.

Growth in air cargo, especially of high-value, time-sensitive commodities, continued into 1999. Lower shipping costs and more frequent service have made air cargo a major factor in the way global business is conducted. Air cargo is carried both by all-passenger carriers as well as air freight carriers, including integrated express carriers, such as Federal Express, United Parcel Service (UPS), DHL, Airborne Express, CF/Emery, Burlington and

---

International Trade Data

Overall and modal trade totals cited here are based on annual data reported by the Foreign Trade Division of the U.S. Census Bureau in the *FT920 U.S. Merchandise Trade: Selected Highlights*, (December 1999) report, *U.S. Exports of Merchandise CD* (December 1999), and *U.S. Imports of Merchandise CD* (December 1999). Following the release of these products, the Census Bureau also makes available (on an annual basis) revised overall and country totals. These revised figures are used by Census and other federal agencies.

Due to the way U.S. international trade data has historically been collected and processed, accurately calculating the modal share of that trade for all modes of transportation (including disaggregated land modes) was not possible until 1997. Because of this difficulty, the mode of transportation data are not corrected in the revised figures provided by the Census Bureau. Therefore, this section relies on both the overall and mode of transportation data in the originally documented merchandise trade figures as cited in the report and CDs mentioned above.

Thus, this section on U.S. international trade analyzes changes between 1997 and 1999. At the same time, longer term trends are also noted and different reference years shown where necessary. Unless otherwise noted, the value of U.S. merchandise imports is based on U.S. general imports, customs value basis. Export value is f.a.s. (free alongside ship) and represents domestic and foreign exports valued at the port of exit (including the transaction price, inland freight, insurance, and other charges).

---

others. Air freight accounted for approximately 29 percent (by value) of U.S. international trade in 1999. Japan was the leading trade partner for U.S. air freight, followed by the United Kingdom and Germany (figure 2). New York's John F. Kennedy (JFK) International Airport was the leading gateway for international air shipments, accounting for $105 billion in 1999. Following JFK were San Francisco, Los Angeles International Airport, and Chicago.[2]

---

[2] San Francisco includes the San Francisco International Airport and other smaller regional airports. Chicago includes O'Hare, Midway, and other smaller regional airports.

Table 1
Value of U.S. International Merchandise Trade by Mode of Transportation: 1999

	Imports		Exports			
Mode	Current U.S. ($ millions)	Percent	Current U.S. ($ millions)	Percent	Total trade	Percentage of total
Total, all modes	**1,024,766**	**100.0**	**692,821**	**100.0**	**1,717,587**	**100.0**
Water	449,344	43.8	182,211	26.3	631,555	36.8
Air	258,883	25.3	236,649	34.2	495,533	28.9
Truck	195,349	19.1	190,064	27.4	385,413	22.4
Rail	60,948	5.9	17,466	2.5	78,414	4.6
Pipeline	12,058	1.2	258	0.04	12,316	0.7
Other and unknown	48,184	4.7	66,173	9.6	114,356	6.7

NOTES:
Water: Excludes in-transit data (merchandise shipped from one foreign country to another via a U.S. water port).
Imports: Excludes imports valued at less than $1,250. Import value is based on U.S. general imports, customs value basis.
Exports: Excludes exports valued at less than $2,500. Export value is f.a.s. (free alongside ship) and represents the value of exports at the port of export, including the transaction price and inland freight, insurance, and other charges.

SOURCES: Compiled by U.S. Department of Transportation, Bureau of Transportation Statistics, November 2000.
Total, water, and air data: U.S. Department of Commerce, U.S. Census Bureau, Foreign Trade Division, *U.S. Exports of Merchandise CD* and *U.S. Imports of Merchandise CD*, December 1999.
Truck, rail, pipeline, and other and unknown data: U.S. Department of Transportation, Bureau of Transportation Statistics, *Transborder Surface Freight Data*, 1999, and special tabulations.

Table 2
Top 10 U.S. Maritime Ports for International Trade by Value and Weight: 1999

Ranked by value	Port	Value ($ billions)	Percent	Ranked by weight	Port	Millions of metric tons	Percent
1	Long Beach, CA	89.0	14.1	1	Houston, TX	95.1	8.7
2	Los Angeles, CA	83.1	13.1	2	South Louisiana, LA	70.9	6.5
3	New York, NY	71.7	11.3	3	New Orleans, LA	69.8	6.4
4	Houston, TX	34.1	5.4	4	New York, NY	57.6	5.3
5	Seattle, WA	32.2	5.1	5	Corpus Christie, TX	56.9	5.2
6	Charleston, SC	29.1	4.6	6	Beaumont, TX	48.1	4.4
7	Oakland, CA	25.8	4.1	7	Morgan City, LA	42.8	3.9
8	Norfolk, VA	24.8	3.9	8	Long Beach, CA	35.7	3.3
9	Baltimore, MD	19.3	3.1	9	Los Angeles, CA	32.8	3.0
10	Tacoma, WA	17.0	2.7	10	Lake Charles, LA	28.7	2.6
	Top 10 total		**67.4**		**Top 10 total**		**49.1**

SOURCE: U.S. Department of Transportation, Maritime Administration, Office of Statistical and Economic Analysis, Annual Waterborne databanks, 1999.

(continued on the next page)

Table 3
Top 10 U.S. Maritime Trade Partners by Value and Weight: 1999

Ranked by value	Value Country	($ billions)	Percent	Ranked by weight	Country	Million short tons	Percent
	All countries	**$632**	**100.0**		**All countries**	**1,204**	**100.0**
1	Japan	116	18.4	1	Mexico	110	9.2
2	China	76	12.1	2	Venezuela	110	9.1
3	Germany	37	5.9	3	Canada	92	7.6
4	Taiwan	26	4.1	4	Japan	81	6.8
5	South Korea	26	4.1	5	Saudi Arabia	80	6.7
6	United Kingdom	24	3.7	6	Colombia	40	3.3
7	Mexico	16	2.6	7	Nigeria	40	3.3
8	Venezuela	15	2.4	8	Iraq	39	3.2
9	Brazil	14	2.2	9	China	36	3.0
10	Italy	14	2.2	10	South Korea	36	3.0
	Top 10 total	**364**	**57.7**		**Top 10 total**	**665**	**55.2**

NOTE: Excludes cargo in transit through the United States.

SOURCES: U.S. Department of Transportation, Bureau of Transportation Statistics, special tabulation, November 2000, based on U.S. Department of Commerce, U.S. Census Bureau, Foreign Trade Division, *U.S. Exports of Merchandise CD* and *U.S. Imports of Merchandise CD,* December 1999.

Figure 2
Top 10 U.S. Trade Partners by Air: 1999

Billions of dollars

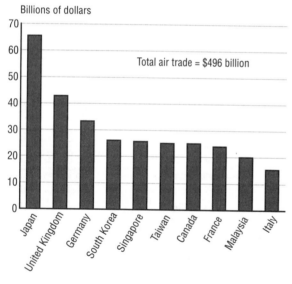

Total air trade = $496 billion

SOURCES: U.S. Department of Transportation, Bureau of Transportation Statistics, special tabulation, November 2000, based on U.S. Department of Commerce, U.S. Census Bureau, Foreign Trade Division, *U.S. Exports of Merchandise CD* and *U.S. Imports of Merchandise CD,* December 1999.

U.S. Waterborne Trade

U.S. domestic waterborne trade was fairly stable from the mid-1980s until the 1990s, when U.S. coastal trade (i.e., domestic traffic over the ocean or the Gulf of Mexico) declined due to a decrease in Alaskan crude oil shipments. Internal U.S. trade, which occurs on U.S. rivers and waterways, has remained fairly constant in recent years (figure 1). In 1999 when measured by tonnage, petroleum and petroleum product shipments were down 5.5 percent and food and farm products were up 9.3 percent over 1998 levels. Coal shipments were down 4.6 percent over this period [1].

Since the early 1990s, U.S. international water trade has paralleled world trade growth. At the end of 1999, the United States accounted for 15.3 percent of the value of world maritime trade (table 1). The U.S.-flag share of U.S. foreign waterborne trade increased slightly from 2.7 percent in 1998 to 3.1 percent in 1999 [2]. The highest value cargo in U.S. foreign trade is liner service, which consists primarily of container vessels (figure 2).

Because of low freight rates and profits in recent years, shipping companies have attempted to improve usage of their vessels and other assets through consolidation, partnerships, and vessel-sharing agreements. These arrangements as well as the growth in e-commerce have had an impact on the makeup of the industry, the provision of transportation services, and the geographic flow of goods internally and into and out of the United States.

Table 1
Selected Major Trading Nations in the World Maritime Arena: 1999

Country/territory	Share of world trade generated
United States	15.3
Germany	8.8
Japan	6.4
United Kingdom	5.1
France	5.1
Canada	4.0
Italy	3.9
Netherlands	3.4
Hong Kong, China	3.1
Belgium-Luxembourg	3.1
China	3.1

SOURCE: United Nations Conference on Trade and Development (UNCTAD), *Review of Maritime Transport*, Report of the UNCTAD Secretariat (New York, NY: 2000).

Figure 1
U.S. Domestic Waterborne Trade: 1985–1999

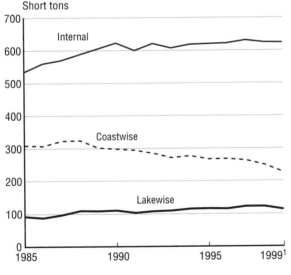

Short tons

[1] Estimate.

SOURCE: U.S. Army Corps of Engineers, Water Resources Support Center, *Waterborne Commerce of the United States, Calender Year 1998; Part 5: National Summaries*, available at http://www.wrsc.usace.army.mil/ndc/wcsc.htm, as of Oct. 18, 2000.

Figure 2
U.S. Foreign Waterborne Trade by Value: 1988–1999

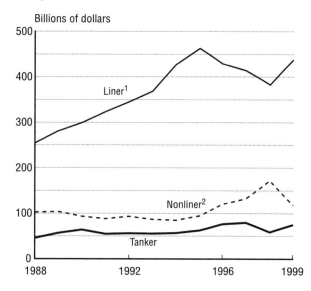

Billions of dollars

[1] Primarily container vessels.
[2] "Tramp" or nonscheduled service.

SOURCES: U.S. Department of Transportation, Maritime Administration, Office of Statistical and Economic Analysis, "U.S. Imports and Exports by Customs District Ports, U.S. Foreign Waterborne Transportation Statistics," available at http://www.marad.dot.gov/statistics/usfwts/index.html, and "U.S. Foreign Waterborne Commerce," adapted from U.S. Department of Commerce, U.S. Census Bureau, U.S. foreign waterborne commerce data, various years.

Sources

1. U.S. Army Corps of Engineers, Water Resources Support Center, *Waterborne Commerce of the United States, Calendar Year 1999; Part 5: National Summaries,* available at http://www.wrsc.usace.army.mil/ndc/wcsc.htm, as of Dec. 31, 2000.

2. U.S. Department of Transportation, Maritime Administration, "U.S. Waterborne Commerce," 1999, adapted from U.S. Department of Commerce, U.S. Census Bureau, U.S. waterborne commerce data, various years.

NAFTA Trade

The United States, Mexico, and Canada have signed two free trade agreements: the North American Free Trade Agreement (NAFTA) in 1993 and the Free Trade Agreement in 1989. Both agreements have led to the gradual reduction of tariffs on goods. These agreements have brought the share of U.S. merchandise trade with Canada and Mexico, now our two largest trading partners, to about 34 percent—Canada accounts for 22 percent and Mexico, 12 percent—in 1999.

Since NAFTA went into effect, the value of U.S. trade with Canada and Mexico has risen 63 percent in current dollars, from $343 billion to $559 billion (figure 1). In addition to the trade agreements, several other factors contributed to this increase, including the sustained economic expansion in the United States, U.S./Canada and U.S./Mexico exchange rates, and changes in industry manufacturing and distribution patterns.

Motor vehicles, parts, and accessories dominate NAFTA trade by value, as North American automobile manufacturing is increasingly integrated across the three countries. Other leading commodities traded among NAFTA partners are consumer electronics, telecommunications equipment, petroleum and petroleum products, and aircraft equipment and parts [1, 2].

In 1999, trucks transported about 69 percent of the value of NAFTA merchandise trade, a share that has remained constant since 1997. Rail accounted for about 14 percent of the share, and air and water modes accounted for approximately 4 to 6 percent. In recent years, trade by air has grown more rapidly than the other modes [3].

Six ports account for 65 percent of all North American trade by land, with Detroit, Michigan, and Laredo, Texas, handling the majority of trade on each U.S. border (figure 2). Trucks carry most of the trade at each of these ports, and the num-

Figure 1
U.S. Merchandise Trade with NAFTA Partners: 1994–1999

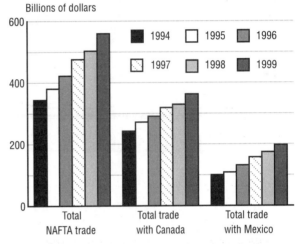

SOURCE: U.S. Department of Transportation, Bureau of Transportation Statistics, special tabulation, August 2000, based on data from U.S. Department of Commerce, Census Bureau, Foreign Trade Division.

ber of trucks entering at these border gateways has increased, in some cases, substantially (table 1). The origins and destinations of the trucks crossing at a particular port are often outside of the port state. For example, over 70 percent of the shipments that cross through the ports of Laredo and Buffalo have their respective origins or destinations outside of Texas or New York.

The maps on pages 163 and 164 show the top trade flows by truck between the United States and Canada and the United States and Mexico. Many of these flows represent relatively shorter hauls while others involved longer distance North American trade. These flows are increasingly characterized as trade and transportation corridors. The Transportation Equity Act for the 21st Century contained specific provisions for funding of trade corridor planning and border infrastructure enhancement to facilitate increases in North American trade.

Ten U.S. states accounted for about two-thirds of the value of North American land trade in 1999. They are Michigan, Texas, California, New York, Ohio, Illinois, Indiana, Pennsylvania, North Carolina, and Washington (table 2).[1]

Sources

1. U.S. Department of Commerce, U.S. Census Bureau, Foreign Trade Division, *FT920 U.S. Merchandise Trade: Selected Highlights, December 1994* (Washington, DC: 1994).

2. ____. *FT920 U.S. Merchandise Trade: Selected Highlights, December 1999* (Washington, DC: 1999).

3. U.S. Department of Transportation (USDOT), Bureau of Transportation Statistics (BTS), special tabulation, August 2000, based on the following: USDOT, BTS, Transborder Surface Freight Data; and Source 2 above.

[1] State origins and destinations are based on official U.S. international trade statistics. Because of the way these data are collected, some border state activity may be overrepresented.

Figure 2
Port Share of U.S. Land Trade with NAFTA Partners, by Value: 1999

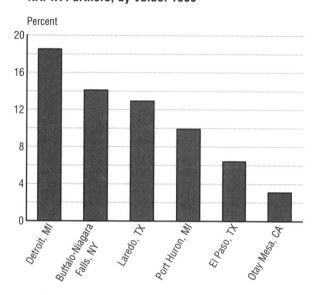

SOURCE: U.S. Department of Transportation (USDOT), Bureau of Transportation Statistics (BTS), special tabulation, August 2000, based on USDOT, BTS, Transborder Surface Freight data, December 2000.

Table 1
Major NAFTA Border Crossings: 1996 and 1999
(Trucks crossing into the United States)

Port name	1996 (thousands)	1999 (thousands)	Percentage change (1996–1999)	Average number of trucks per day (1999)
Detroit, MI	1,332	1,759	32.1	4,819
Laredo, TX	1,016	1,487	46.4	4,074
Buffalo-Niagara Falls, NY	996	1,188	19.3	3,255
Port Huron, MI	636	791	24.4	2,167
El Paso, TX	556	673	21.0	1,844
Otay Mesa, CA	531	546	2.8	1,496
Blaine, WA	402	492	22.4	1,348
Champlain-Rouses Pt., NY	279	399	43.0	1,093
Nogales, AZ	229	256	11.8	701
Brownsville, TX	226	304	34.5	833

SOURCE: U.S. Department of Transportation, Bureau of Transportation Statistics, special tabulation, August 2000, based on data from U.S. Department of the Treasury, U.S. Customs Service, Operations Management Warehouse database, August 2000.

U.S-Canada Top 20 State and Provincial Flows for Merchandise Trade by Truck: 1999

(a) U.S. exports to Canada by truck

Export/import value (current U.S. $)
$20 billion $10 billion $5 billion

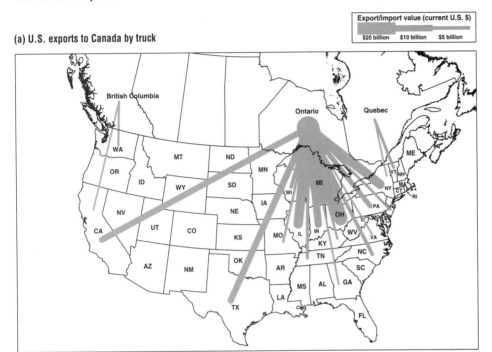

(b) Imports from Canada to the United States by truck

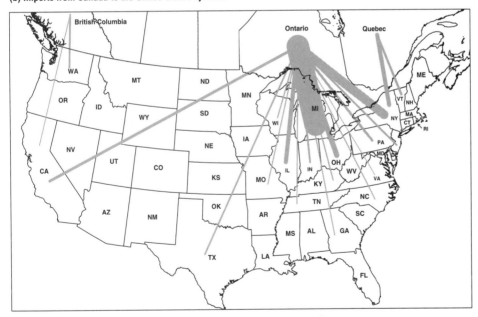

U.S. state: For U.S. exports to Canada, the U.S. state is based on the state of origin as reported on official U.S. trade documents, which typically refer to the state of origin where the goods were grown, manufactured, or otherwise produced. For U.S. imports from Canada, the U.S. state of destination reflects the state of the importer of record. This state may not always represent the ultimate physical destination of shipments.

Canadian Province: For U.S. exports to Canada, the Canadian province of clearance is the province in which Canadian Customs cleared the shipment, and may not always be the province of final destination. For U.S. imports from Canada, the Canadian province of origin typically refers to the province of origin where the goods were grown, manufactured or otherwise produced.

SOURCE: U.S. Department of Transportation, Bureau of Transportation Statistics, Transborder Surface Freight data, special tabulation, December 2000.

U.S-Mexico Top State Flows for Merchandise Trade by Truck: 1999

(a) U.S. exports to Mexico by truck

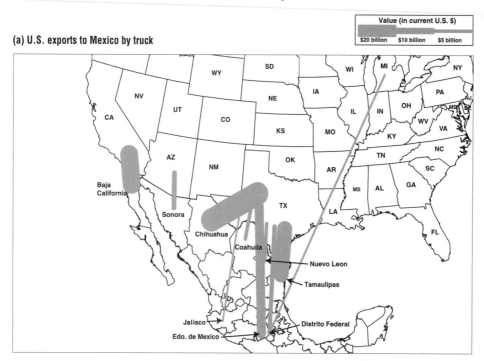

(b) Imports from Mexico to the United States by truck

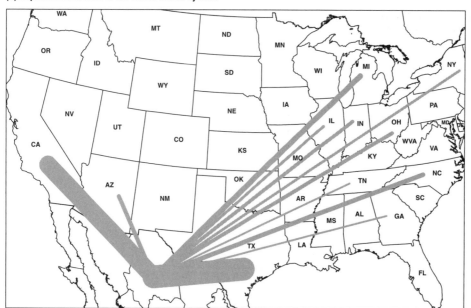

U.S. state: For U.S. exports to Mexico, the U.S. state is based on the state of origin as reported on official U.S. trade documents, which typically refer to the state of origin where the goods were grown, manufactured, or otherwise produced. For U.S. imports from Mexico, the U.S. state of destination reflects the state of the importer of record. This state may not always represent the ultimate physical destination of shipments.

Mexican state: For U.S. exports to Mexico, the Mexican state of destination is the state where the ultimate consignee is located, and may not always be the state of final destination. For U.S. imports from Mexico, it is not possible to obtain the Mexican state of origin due to the existing filing requirements of trade documentation.

SOURCE: U.S. Department of Transportation, Bureau of Transportation Statistics, Transborder Surface Freight data, special tabulation, December 2000.

Table 2
**Top 10 U.S. Origins/Destinations for
North American Merchandise Trade: 1999**
(All surface modes)

State	Value (billions of current U.S. dollars)
Michigan	80.3
Texas	71.1
California	46.0
New York	35.7
Ohio	26.1
Illinois	24.9
Indiana	14.0
Pennsylvania	14.0
North Carolina	11.6
Washington	10.3
Total top 10 states	**334.1**
Percentage of total NAFTA trade	**66.7**
All U.S. states	**501.2**

NOTE: Totals may not add due to rounding.
Total for all U.S. states includes data for shipments where the U.S. state of origin or destination was unknown.

SOURCE: U.S. Department of Transportation, Bureau of Transportation Statistics, Transborder Surface Freight data, special tabulation, September 2000.

Chapter 6

Energy and the Environment

Introduction

The U.S. Department of Transportation, under its human and natural environment strategic goal, is committed to protecting and enhancing communities and the natural environment affected by transportation. The economic and societal benefits provided by transportation also generate environmental impacts, and the sector's dependence on fossil fuels is at the root of many of these environmental problems. Construction of transportation infrastructure and facilities, and vehicle manufacturing, maintenance, use, and disposal affect the environment as well.

Transportation energy use has grown at 1.5 percent per year for the past two decades. Still, this growth rate is slower than that of the Gross Domestic Product and passenger-miles of travel, reflecting in part a general decline in the energy intensity of almost all modes. Today, however, the transportation sector consumes a greater share of petroleum (66 percent) than it did in 1973 (50 percent). The use of alternative and replacement fuels to reduce foreign oil dependence and environmental impacts has grown, but, despite incentives in place to promote these fuels, they still accounted for only a small faction of total motor vehicle fuel use in 1999.

Growth in energy consumption is causing a corresponding increase in greenhouse gas (GHG) emissions. The transportation sector emitted 1,819 million metric tons of carbon dioxide in 1999, an increase of 14.9 percent since 1990. Three-quarters of GHG emissions come from the use of highway vehicles. In addition to GHG emissions, transportation remains a primary source of emissions of three of the six air pollutants regulated under the Clean Air Act: carbon monoxide, nitrogen oxides, and volatile organic compounds. However, with the exception of nitrogen oxides, these emissions have been declining since 1990.

Using transportation vehicles generates noise and can result in hazardous materials and oil spills. New estimates suggest that, since 1992 when U.S. requirements for quieter aircraft went into effect, the percentage of the population exposed to airport noise has been cut in half. Another area of concern is oil spills—an average of 1.8 million gallons of oil is spilled into U.S. waters each year. In 1998, 51 percent of this oil was cargo carried by marine vessels, pipelines, railcars, and tank trucks.

Transportation infrastructure and its maintenance can also be sources of environmental damage. Each year the U.S. Army Corps of Engineers dredges an average of 271 million cubic yards of sediments from navigation channels. Contaminated sediments are confined in various ways, while the balance may be used beneficially to nourish beaches and wetlands. Sediments become contaminated from pollutants released into the nation's waters. Similarly, petroleum stored in underground tanks has a history of leaking into soils and ultimately into surface and underground waters. By 2000, after a decade of focused effort by the U.S. Environmental Protection Agency (EPA), there were almost 163,000 known petroleum tank releases around the country waiting to be cleaned up. The leaking of methyl-tertiary-butyl-ether (MTBE), largely from underground storage tanks, was recognized in 2000 as an issue serious enough for EPA to ask the U.S. Congress to ban or reduce its use as an additive in gasoline.

Rubber tires and lead-acid batteries are two of several transportation wastes quantified on an annual basis. States and local governments often promote the establishment of systems to recycle these wastes at the end of their lifetime. However, while over 93 percent of the lead content of batteries was reused in 1998, only 24 percent of the 4.5 million tons of scrap tires generated were recycled. This left almost 3.5 million tons of car, truck, and motorcycle tires to be disposed of in landfills or incinerated.

Preservation of wetlands, urban sprawl, invasive species, and environmental justice are areas of concern that have emerged fairly recently. The United States has an estimated 105 million acres of wetlands. An equal amount may have been lost since the 1600s, drained to develop rural and urban areas. Transportation impacts wetlands when roads and railroads are built and people and cargo are moved through them and when airports and other facilities are placed in them.

How land is used for transportation is also a part of urban sprawl. Here, transportation enables and follows the radial development of commercial, industrial, and residential communities out from urban areas. Transportation also enables the legal, illegal, and unintended importation of non-native species of plants and animals. Once established, many of these species cause environmental and economic damage; in some cases, killing off native species. Disproportionately using land in minority and low-income communities for transportation and other infrastructure has given rise to the environmental justice movement. Today, environmental justice has become part of U.S. Department of Transportation operations. The central aim is to redress lack of meaningful participation by these communities in transportation decisionmaking.

Energy Use

As the economy has grown, so too has transportation energy use. From 1980 to 1999, transportation energy use grew from 19.7 quadrillion (quads) British thermal units (Btu) to 26.0 quads, an annual growth rate of 1.5 percent [1]. The overall growth rate is lower than that of the economy (as measured by Gross Domestic Product (GDP)) and the growth rate in passenger-miles, but not population (figure 1). It is influenced by a combination of factors, including changes in transportation intensity of U.S. GDP, vehicle fuel efficiency, and personal travel propensity.

For decades, the transportation sector has accounted for between 25 percent and 27 percent of total U.S. energy consumption (table 1). In 1998, highway vehicles accounted for about 80 percent of transportation energy use. Passenger cars use about 42 percent of the sector's total, followed by light trucks with 20 percent, and heavier trucks with 17 percent. Among the nonhighway

Figure 1

Transportation Energy Use and Other Trends: 1980–1999

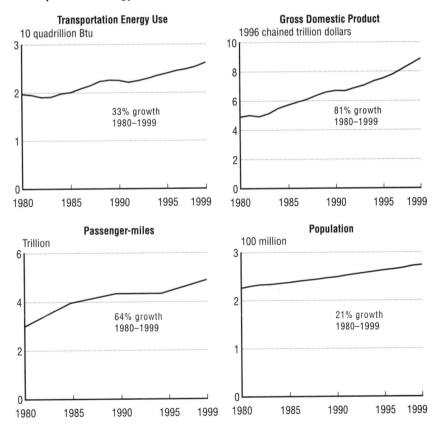

SOURCES: U.S. Department of Transportation, Bureau of Transportation Statistics, *National Transportation Statistics 2000* (Washington, DC: 2001); U.S. Department of Commerce, Bureau of Economic Analysis, *Survey of Current Business*, various issues.

Table 1

Energy Consumption by End-Use Sector

(Quadrillion BTU)

Year	Residential/ commercial	Industrial	Transportation
1980	26.551	32.189	19.696
1985	27.645	29.067	20.071
1990	29.973	31.687	22.541
1995	32.897	34.052	23.975
1999	35.015	35.882	26.193

SOURCE: U.S. Department of Energy, Energy Information Administration, *Monthly Energy Review* (Washington, DC: Various issues).

modes, air transportation is the biggest and fastest growing energy user. The pipeline mode, which accounted for about 3 percent of total transportation energy use, is the only mode that does not depend directly on petroleum. Typically, pipelines use natural gas and/or electric pumps to move products (figure 2).

Source

1. U.S. Department of Energy, Energy Information Administration, *Monthly Energy Review, May 2000,* DOE/EIA-0035(2000/05) (Washington, DC: 2000).

Figure 2

Transportation Energy Use by Mode: 1998

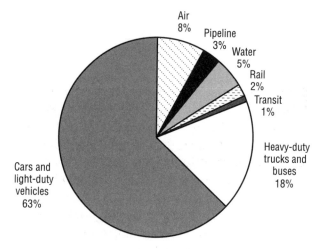

SOURCE: Compiled from various sources, as cited in U.S. Department of Transportation, Bureau of Transportation Statistics, *National Transportation Statistics 2000* (Washington, DC: 2001).

Petroleum Consumption

In the United States, petroleum consumption has risen faster in the transportation sector than in any other since 1973, before the first oil embargo. Continued growth in transportation activities has contributed, in large part, to the increase in oil consumption. While the oil price shocks of 1973–74 and 1979–80 depressed demand for a while, they did little to shake transportation's dependence on oil. Only a small fraction of transportation's energy needs are met by nonpetroleum sources, such as natural gas, methanol, and ethanol. Nonpetroleum sources are used primarily as gasoline blending agents to meet requirements of the Clean Air Act Amendments of 1990.

From 1973 to 1999, the residential and commercial buildings sector cut petroleum use in half, and the utilities sector reduced oil use by more than 60 percent. Over the same period, industrial sector oil use hovered between 4 million barrels per day (mmbd) and 5 mmbd, primarily because petroleum is an important feedstock for the petrochemicals industry. In contrast, oil use in the transportation sector rose from 9.05 mmbd in 1973 to 12.75 mmbd in 1999, an increase of about 41 percent. Due to these changes in consumption patterns among sectors, transportation today accounts for two-thirds of total U.S. petroleum demand compared with about 50 percent before 1973 [1] (figure 1).

The U.S. Department of Energy expects the heavy concentration of oil demand in the transportation sector to continue. Between 1998 and 2020, overall U.S. petroleum consumption is pro-

Figure 1
Transportation's Share of U.S. Petroleum Use: 1973–1999

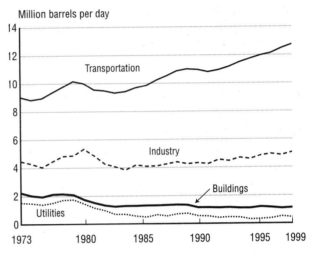

Million barrels per day

SOURCE: U.S. Department of Energy, Energy Information Administration, *Annual Energy Review 1999* (Washington, DC: July 2000), table, 5.12.

jected to increase by 6.2 mmbd. Transportation demand, particularly for "light products,"[1] accounts for much of this projected rise in consumption [2].

Sources

1. U.S. Department of Energy, Energy Information Administration, *Annual Energy Outlook 2000*, DOE/EIA-0383(2000) (Washington, DC: December 1999).

2. _____. *Annual Energy Review 1999*, available at www.eia.doe.gov/emeu/aer/petro.html as of June 23, 2000.

---

[1] Light products include gasoline, diesel, heating oil, jet fuel, and liquefied petroleum gases. They are more difficult and costly to produce than heavy products, such as residual fuel oil.

Alternative and Replacement Fuels

Spurred by energy and environmental legislation, the use of alternative and replacement fuels in motor vehicles is growing, but not enough to indicate a trend away from the use of petroleum in the transportation sector. Between 1992 and 1999, estimated alternative fuel use grew by 5.8 percent annually (table 1). Nevertheless, alternative fuels comprise a tiny fraction of total motor vehicle fuel use—0.17 percent in 1992 and 0.21 percent in 1999. This growth is in proportion to the rise in the number of alternative fuel vehicles (table 2) [2].

Replacement fuels—alcohols and ethers (oxygenates)—are blended with gasoline to meet the requirements of the Clean Air Act Amendments of 1990. They comprise a larger proportion of the motor fuel market than alternative fuels, as shown in figure 1. Unlike petroleum, which is composed entirely of hydrogen and carbon atoms, alcohols and ethers contain oxygen and are derived from energy sources other than petroleum.

In areas where carbon monoxide emissions are a problem, fuel providers have been required since 1992 to add oxygenates to gasoline to promote more complete combustion. Gasoline that contains oxygenates is referred to as reformulated gasoline (RFG). Beginning in 1994, areas failing to attain air quality standards for ozone were required to use RFG, which must contain 2 percent oxygen by weight. In 1999, oxygenates made up 3.2 percent of the gasoline pool [2].

The most popular oxygenate is methyl-tertiary-butyl-ether (MTBE), a combination of methanol and isobutylene. Natural gas is used to make MTBE. The discovery of MTBE in drinking water supplies has raised concerns about its use as a gasoline additive, however. At this time, MTBE is not classified as a carcinogen, but studies have

shown that it can cause cancer in animals. Moreover, trace amounts of MTBE in water supplies produces an unpleasant odor and taste [1]. Many issues remain regarding the use of MTBE as a replacement fuel. These are just a few that decisionmakers must face when considering the use of alternative and replacement fuels.

Table 1

Fuel Consumption in the United States: 1992 and 1999
(Thousand gasoline-equivalent gallons)

Type of fuel	1992	1999
Alternative fuels		
Liquefied petroleum gas	208,142	242,141
Compressed natural gas	16,823	86,286
Liquefied natural gas	585	5,828
Methanol (85%)[1]	1,069	1,073
Methanol, neat (100%)	2,547	447
Ethanol (85%)[1]	21	2,075
Ethanol (95%)[1]	85	59
Electricity	359	1,431
Subtotal	**229,631**	**339,340**
Replacement fuels/oxygenates		
MTBE[2]	1,175,000	3,331,000
Ethanol in gasohol	701,000	956,900
Traditional fuels		
Gasoline[3]	110,135,000	125,111,000
Diesel	23,866,000	35,796,800
Total fuel consumption	**134,230,631**	**161,247,140**

[1] The remaining portion of 85% methanol and both ethanol fuels is a gasoline. Data include gasoline portion of the fuel.
[2] Methyl-tertiary-butyl-ether (MTBE) includes a small amount of other ethers, primarily tertiary-amyl-methyl-ether and ethyl-tertiary-butyl-ether.
[3] Includes ethanol in gasohol and MTBE.

SOURCE: U.S. Department of Energy, Energy Information Administration, *Alternatives to Traditional Transportation Fuels 1998* (Washington, DC: 2000), available at http://www.eia.doe.gov/cneaf/solar.renewables/alt_trans_fuel98/atf_99.html, as of May 2001.

Table 2
Estimated Number of Alternative Fueled Vehicles in the United States, by Fuel: 1992 and 2000

Type of fuel	1992	2000 (preliminary data)
Liquefied petroleum gas[1]	221,000	268,000
Compressed natural gas	23,191	100,530
Liquefied natural gas	90	1,900
Methanol, 85%[2]	4,850	18,365
Methanol, neat	404	195
Ethanol, 85%[2]	172	34,680
Ethanol, 95%[2]	38	13
Electricity	1,607	8,661
Total	**251,352**	**432,344**

[1] Numbers rounded to nearest thousand. These estimates are not equal to the sum of federal fleet data (for which exact counts are available) and nonfederal fleet estimates.
[2] The remaining portion of 85% methanol and both ethanol fuels is gasoline.

SOURCE: U.S. Department of Energy, Energy Information Administration, *Alternatives to Traditional Transportation Fuels 1999*, available at http://www.eia.doe.gov, as of October 2000.

(MTBE is discussed in more detail in the environment section.)

Sources

1. U.S. Department of Energy (USDOE), Energy Information Administration (EIA), *Annual Energy Outlook 2000*, DOE/EIA-0383(2000) (Washington, DC: December 1999).

2. ____. *Alternatives to Traditional Transportation Fuels 1998*, available at www.eia.doe.gov/cneaf/solar.renewables/alt_trans_fuel98/table10.html, as of May 31, 2000.

Figure 1
Transportation Fuel Consumption in the United States: 1999

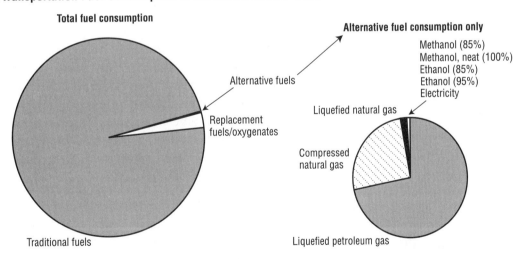

NOTES: The remaining portion of 85% methanol and ethanol fuels is gasoline. Figure is not proportional.

SOURCE: U.S. Department of Energy, Energy Information Administration, *Alternatives to Traditional Transportation Fuels 1999* (Washington, DC: 2000).

World Crude Oil Prices

World oil prices tripled between January 1999 and July 2000 as a result of oil production cutbacks by the Organization of Petroleum Exporting Countries (OPEC), with the cooperation of Mexico, Norway, and Russia (figure 1). This oil price hike prompted concern that oil dependence may once again become a serious concern for the transportation sector and the economy as a whole.

The economic costs of previous oil price shocks are estimated to be in the trillions of dollars. Of course, the size of economic losses depends on the importance of oil in the economy and the ability to substitute other energy sources for oil. The transportation sector, with its inelastic demand, has shown little movement toward replacing oil with other energy sources.

A Bureau of Transportation Statistics (BTS) analysis of the economic impact of the 1999–2000 increase in fuel prices concluded that, to drive the same distance and produce the same Gross Domestic Product as in 1999, U.S. households and businesses would spend an additional $67 billion (28 percent more) on transportation fuel in 2000. Households would absorb more than half of the additional cost and for-hire transportation firms about one-third. The rest of the cost would be absorbed by nontransportation firms. On a per household basis, U.S. households would have to spend $344 more in 2000 on motor fuel to travel the same distance as in 1999 [1]. In fact, households spent, on average, $1,550 on motor fuel, or $312 more than the average in 1999 (figure 2). The difference between

Figure 1
World Crude Oil Prices
(Weekly data, not seasonally adjusted)

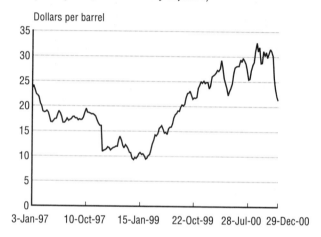

SOURCE: U.S. Department of Energy, Energy Information Administration, *Crude Oil Watch*, available at http://www.eia.doe.gov/oil_gas/petroleum/data_publications/crude_watch/crude.html, as of May 2001.

what BTS estimated households would spend and what they actually spent may have been caused by reduced household travel in response to higher gasoline prices, the use of more efficient vehicles, or switching to other modes of transportation. However, data are not available at this time to substantiate these or other possible explanations.

Source

1. U.S. Department of Transportation, Bureau of Transportation Statistics, "The Economic Impact of the Recent Increase in Oil Prices," *Transportation Indicators: A Prototype*, May 2000.

Figure 2
Average Motor Fuel Expenditures
per Household: 1997–2000

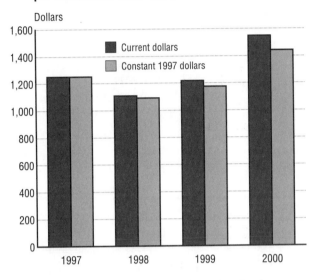

SOURCES: Bureau of Transportation Statistics estimates based on energy consumption and expenditure data from U.S. Department of Energy, Energy Information Administration.
Household data from U.S. Department of Commerce, Census Bureau.

Energy Intensity of Passenger Travel and Freight Transportation

The amount of energy required to carry passengers and freight has declined. Between 1980 and 1998, automobile energy use per passenger-mile of travel (pmt) by car fell by 12 percent (figure 1). This has occurred even though the average fuel economy of new car and light truck fleets leveled off in the 1990s [1].

Commercial air carriers reduced energy use per passenger-mile by more than 30 percent over the 1980 to 1998 period, due largely to higher occupancy [1]. Flying a full plane requires considerably less than twice the amount of fuel of a half-full one but yields twice the passenger-miles. Airlines have been increasingly successful in filling their planes; in some cases, reconfiguring seating to fit more passengers. Moreover, although newer airplanes are more efficient, this probably has less effect on energy intensity than the greater number of passengers.

The energy intensity of Amtrak intercity rail and intercity bus declined as well (−22 percent and −33 percent, respectively). At 713 British thermal unit (Btu) per pmt in 1998, intercity buses are considered the most energy-efficient mode of transportation. Energy use per pmt on transit buses, however, increased 51 percent over this period to 4,238 Btu per pmt [1].

Because of data limitations and availability, less is known overall about the energy intensity of freight transportation, particularly the water-borne and heavy truck modes. Some data are available, however. Energy use per vehicle-mile has decreased, albeit slowly. The decrease in energy use per vehicle-mile combined with a general increase in truck size and weight limits suggest that truck energy use per ton-mile has

---

It is important to note that intermodal comparisons should be considered approximations. Modal data are collected in different ways and based on different assumptions. Passenger-mile data are more relevant for passenger vehicles, while vehicle-mile or ton-mile data are more relevant for freight vehicles. Modes also perform different functions and serve different travel markets.

---

also decreased [2]. For rail freight, energy intensity declined about 38 percent between 1980 and 1997 [3].

Sources

1. Davis, Stacy C., *Transportation Energy Data Book, Edition 19* (Oak Ridge, TN: Oak Ridge National Laboratory, 1999), table 2.12.

2. U.S. Department of Transportation, *The Changing Face of Transportation* (Washington, DC: 2000).

3. U.S. Department of Transportation, Bureau of Transportation Statistics, *National Transportation Statistics 1999* (Washington, DC: 1999).

Figure 1
Energy Intensities of Passenger Modes: 1980–1998

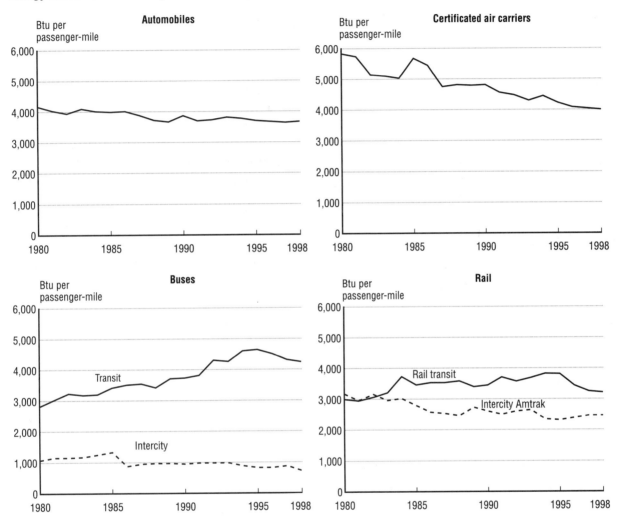

KEY: Btu = British thermal units.

SOURCE: Stacy C. Davis, *Transportation Energy Data Book, Edition 20* (Oak Ridge, TN: Oak Ridge National Laboratory, 2000), table 2.12.

Car and Light Truck Fuel Efficiency

Passenger cars and light trucks are more fuel-efficient today than they were in 1978, when fuel economy standards were first implemented. Technologies like fuel injection engines, lockup torque in transmissions, and improved rolling resistance of tires have played a major role in this change. Between 1978 and 1988, new passenger car average fuel economy shot up from 19.9 miles per gallon (mpg) to 28.8 mpg, while light trucks improved somewhat from 18.2 mpg (1979) to 21.3 mpg. Since then, new car fuel economy has remained flat (figure 1).

The Corporate Average Fuel Economy (CAFE) standard for new cars has held constant at 27.5 mpg since 1990 (table 1). On average, new foreign and domestic cars and light trucks meet the CAFE standard, but several high-end imports were below it in 1999 [3].

In recent years, efficiency gains have been offset by increases in vehicle weight and power and by consumer shifts to less efficient vehicles, such as light trucks, especially sport utility vehicles, minivans, and pickup trucks. For example, the average weight of new cars (foreign and domestic) rose from a low of 2,805 pounds in 1987 to 3,116 pounds in 1999. The average weight of new cars today is still lower than the 3,349-pound weight of new cars in 1978. Furthermore, in response to consumer demand for new high performance cars, the ratio of horsepower to 100 pounds of weight increased from 3.98 in 1987 to 5.21 in 1999. For the domestic car fleet, the average is even higher—5.30 horsepower per 100 pounds [3].

The popularity of light trucks continues to grow. Twice as many cars as light trucks were sold in the United States in 1990. By 2000, however, almost an equal number of cars (8.8 million) and light trucks (8.5 million) were sold [2]. Clearly, many consumers are finding what they want in

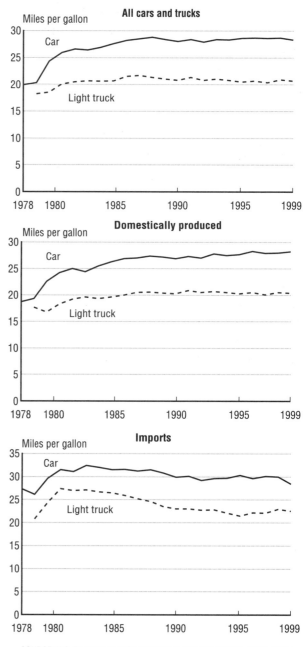

Figure 1

New Passenger Car and Light Truck Fuel Economy Averages: Model Years 1978–1999

SOURCE: U.S. Department of Transportation, National Highway Traffic Safety Administration, Automotive Fuel Economy Program, *Twenty-Fourth Annual Report to Congress, Calendar Year 1999* (Washington, DC: June 2000).

Table 1
Changes in Fuel Economy Standards

New cars		New light trucks	
Model year	mpg	Model year	mpg
1978	18.0	1982	17.5
1979	19.0	1983	19.0
1980	20.0	1984	20.0
1981	22.0	1985	19.5
1982	24.0	1986	20.0
1983	26.0	1987–1989	20.5
1984	27.0	1990	20.0
1985	27.5	1991–1992	20.2
1986–1988	26.0	1993	20.4
1989	26.5	1994	20.5
1990–1999	27.5	1995	20.6
		1996–1999	20.7

SOURCE: U.S. Department of Transportation, National Highway Traffic Safety Administration, Automotive Fuel Economy Program, *Twenty-Fourth Annual Report to Congress, Calendar Year 1999* (Washington, DC: June 2000).

light trucks rather than cars: roominess, more carrying capacity, greater visibility, and a perception of safety (at least for themselves). However, this trend has implications for energy consumption and for emissions, because light trucks, on average, are less fuel-efficient than cars.

A variety of technologies can increase motor vehicle fuel efficiency. In the near term, improving vehicle aerodynamics to reduce drag and lowering the rolling resistance of tires can make a difference. In the longer term, improved electronic transmission controls that allow optimum gear selection for peak efficiency and continuously variable transmissions can provide additional efficiency gains. Several automobile manufacturers are marketing hybrid engines, cars that run alternatively on gasoline and electric-powered engines. These cars are rated at 48 to 64 mpg (combined highway and city) for the 2001 model year. More advanced technologies, such as the diesel hybrid engine, are expected to obtain even higher efficiencies [1].

Sources

1. U.S. Department of Energy and U.S. Environmental Protection Agency, *Energy Technology and Fuel Economy,* available at http://www.fueleconomy.gov, as of February 2001.

2. Compiled from data provided by Ward's AutoInfo-Bank as cited in U.S. Department of Transportation, Bureau of Transportation Statistics, "Transportation Indicators," February 2001.

3. U.S. Department of Transportation, National Highway Traffic Safety Administration, Automotive Fuel Economy Program, *Twenty-Fourth Annual Report to Congress, Calendar Year 1999* (Washington, DC: June 2000).

Transportation Environmental Indicators

Indicators are quantitative data that can be used to assess the magnitude of problems, help set priorities, develop performance measures and track progress toward goals, or educate stakeholders. To assess problems and measure progress, trend data are needed. The full range of environmental impacts of the transportation system is extensive but few good indicators are available.

Figure 1 is a conceptual diagram of the environmental impacts of transportation from a life cycle perspective. Phases (or stages) of transportation include fuel production, vehicle manufacturing, fixed infrastructure development, travel (or vehicle use), maintenance, and disposal. Activities occurring during the phases result in environmental outcomes (e.g., pollution releases and changes in wetlands acreage). Outcomes can, in turn, affect the environment and human health, creating impacts that are usually negative (e.g., cancers, birth defects, asthma, stunted tree growth, and fish kills). Impacts, which can be chronic or acute, are highly dependent on two variables: concentration and exposure.

Activity, outcome, or impact data can be the source for indicators. However, outcome indicators are most commonly used for transportation. Activities are only indirectly related to environmental consequences. Increases in passenger car vehicle-miles traveled may or may not result in increased pollutant releases. Similarly, the volume of oil transported by marine vessels is not indicative of harm caused by oil spills at sea. Most available impact data do not directly identify sources, such as transportation. For instance, the U.S. Environmental Protection Agency (EPA) reports annually on changes in the nation's air quality (described elsewhere in this chapter). These data come from monitoring stations that measure concentrations of pollutants in the atmosphere. The sources of the pollutants may be factories, powerplants, dry cleaning facilities, printing shops, storage tanks, and so on, as well as vehicles.

Readily available data for outcome indicators are not comprehensive, especially for all modes and life cycle phases. National trend data for outcomes are estimated, modeled, or collected only for some pollutants.

The most often used transportation environmental indicator comprises six criteria air pollutants regulated under the Clean Air Act (described elsewhere in this chapter). The data are estimated annually by EPA and show the relative outcome contribution of these pollutants by mode (except pipelines) during the travel phase. With the emergence of the global climate change issue, an additional indicator is available. EPA and the Energy Information Administration now annually estimate the amount of six greenhouse gases emitted by the transportation sector.

Figure 1
Impacts of Transportation on the Environment

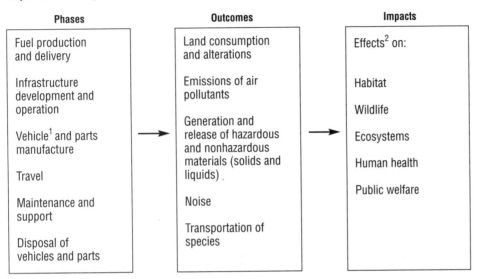

Phases	Outcomes	Impacts
Fuel production and delivery	Land consumption and alterations	Effects[2] on:
Infrastructure development and operation	Emissions of air pollutants	Habitat
Vehicle[1] and parts manufacture	Generation and release of hazardous and nonhazardous materials (solids and liquids)	Wildlife
Travel		Ecosystems
Maintenance and support	Noise	Human health
Disposal of vehicles and parts	Transportation of species	Public welfare

[1] Vehicle here includes highway vehicles, airplanes, marine vessels, railroad cars and locomotives, and transit equipment.
[2] Dependent on ambient levels or concentrations of pollutants and exposure to those outputs.

SOURCE: U.S. Department of Transportation, Bureau of Transportation Statistics, based on U.S. Environmental Protection Agency, *Indicators of the Environmental Impacts of Transportation* (Washington, DC: October 1999), figure 1-1.

Transportation Sector Carbon Emissions

Most scientists believe that rising concentrations of greenhouse gases in the Earth's atmosphere could cause global climate change. Greenhouse gases, such as carbon dioxide, methane, and nitrous oxide, can occur naturally or can be produced by human activities. Carbon dioxide is the predominant greenhouse gas produced by human activity, accounting for 83 percent of all U.S. greenhouse gas emissions in 1999. Nearly all carbon dioxide emissions are produced by the combustion of fossil fuels. Thus, there is a high correlation between energy use and carbon emissions [1].

Today, almost all of transportation's energy needs are supplied by oil. The combustion of petroleum in the transportation sector alone is responsible for about 27 percent of all greenhouse gases emitted in the United States. Figure 1 shows carbon emissions from energy consumption in transportation and other sectors. From 1990 to 1999, transportation-related carbon dioxide emissions grew 14.9 percent. This is less than the commercial sector growth, about the same as the residential sector, but more than that recorded in the industrial sector. In absolute numbers, however, transportation sector carbon emissions grew the most—about 64.3 million metric tons of carbon (mmtc) during this period. Table 1 breaks down transportation sector emissions by fuel type.

According to the U.S. Department of Energy, carbon emissions from energy consumption could rise from 1,485 mmtc in 1998 to 1,979 mmtc by 2020 under a "business as usual" scenario. The transportation sector could contribute about 710 mmtc, or 36 percent of the total. The transportation emissions growth rate is higher than that of other end-use sectors due

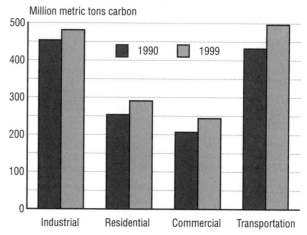

Figure 1
U.S. Carbon Dioxide Emissions from Energy Use by Sector: 1990 and 1999

NOTES: Electric utility emissions are distributed across end-use sectors. Numbers may not add to totals due to rounding. Tons of carbon can be converted to tons of carbon dioxide gas by multiplying by 3.667. One ton of carbon equals 3.667 tons of carbon dioxide gas.

1999 data are preliminary.

SOURCE: U.S. Department of Energy, Energy Information Administration, *Emissions of Greenhouse Gases in the United States 1999*, DOE/EIA-0573(99) (Washington, DC: October 2000).

to several factors, including expected increases in travel and a leveling off of light-duty vehicle fuel efficiency [2].

Because of growing concerns about the potentially adverse impacts of global climate change (e.g., loss of coastal land to rising oceans and greater frequency of violent weather), several international meetings have addressed global climate change. In 1997, parties to the United Nation's Framework Convention on Climate Change met in Kyoto, Japan, and agreed to the Kyoto Protocol setting emissions targets for individual industrialized countries. Since then, the Convention parties have met in Buenos Aires, Bonn, and the Hague to discuss unresolved issues,

Table 1
U.S. Carbon Dioxide Emissions from Transportation: 1990 and 1999
(Million metric tons of carbon)

Fuel	1990	1999	Growth rate 1990–99
Motor gasoline	260.6	299.1	14.8%
Liquefied petroleum gas	0.4	0.3	−25.0%
Jet fuel	60.1	66.3	10.3%
Distillate fuel	75.7	100.1	32.2%
Residual fuel	21.9	17.5	−20.1%
Lubricants	1.8	1.8	0.0%
Aviation gasoline	0.8	0.7	−12.5%
Total petroleum	*421.1*	*485.8*	*15.3%*
Natural gas	*9.8*	*9.5*	*−3.1%*
Electricity	*0.7*	*0.8*	*14.3%*
Transportation total	**431.8**	**496.1**	**14.9%**
Total CO₂ emissions (energy use-related)	**1,345.2**	**1,495.0**	**11.1%**
Total CO₂ emissions	**1,347.0**	**1,526.7**	**13.3%**

NOTES: Electric utility emissions are distributed across end-use sectors. Numbers may not add to totals due to rounding. Tons of carbon can be converted to tons of carbon dioxide gas by multiplying by 3.667. One ton of carbon equals 3.667 tons of carbon dioxide gas.

1999 data are preliminary.

SOURCE: U.S. Department of Energy, Energy Information Administration, *Emissions of Greenhouse Gases in the United States 1999*, DOE/EIA-0573(99) (Washington, DC: October 2000).

EPA and EIA Data Differ

Both the Energy Information Administration (EIA) and the U.S. Environmental Protection Agency (EPA) estimate annual U.S. greenhouse gas (GHG) emissions. EPA's data are the official inventory for the United States for reporting required under the United Nations Framework Convention on Climate Change (UNFCCC). Although EPA uses EIA fuel consumption data as a basis for some of its estimates, there are differences in the two agencies' methodologies that result in different datasets. For instance, EPA estimated total 1998 U.S. transportation sector carbon dioxide emissions at 450.3 million metric tons of carbon (mmtc), while EIA reported 482 mmtc.

The Intergovernmental Panel on Climate Change (IPCC) was set up as the scientific body under UNFCCC, and EPA largely adheres to IPCC methodology guidelines designed to assure data harmonization among all reporting countries. EIA has more discretion in deciding which IPCC guidelines to follow. For instance, EIA's data cover 50 states and the District of Columbia, while EPA must include all U.S. territories, as well. Some numbers EPA gets from EIA are revised. EIA fuel consumption data are gathered in physical units and EPA converts them to energy equivalents. In some cases, EPA emission estimates (e.g., for industrial coal) are lower than EIA's to avoid double counting problems.

EIA releases its data five to six months before EPA does and its data could be considered preliminary estimates. EPA data undergo external, as well as internal, review before they are released in time to meet a United Nations deadline of April each year. While EPA data are not as timely as are EIA data, EPA provides more detail of interest to transportation. For instance, EPA breaks down GHG data by modes and by various GHGs, such as carbon dioxide, nitrous oxide, and methane.

---

such as international emissions trading, rules for joint implementation projects and the clean development mechanism, and compliance and data development issues.

The United States signed the Kyoto Protocol, but it has not been submitted to the U.S. Senate for advice and consent. Many members of Congress have expressed opposition to the Protocol for several reasons. Some say redirecting our resources to meeting this goal could reduce economic growth and hurt U.S. competitiveness relative to countries that have not made binding commitments to reducing emissions (i.e., developing countries). Proponents of control argue that steps need to be taken now to reduce future impacts of climate change and that emissions reductions could create opportunities for businesses selling energy-efficient technologies.

Ultimately, strategies to reduce greenhouse gas emissions will affect all energy-using sectors of the economy, including transportation. In 1999, the U.S. Department of Transportation established a Center for Climate Change and Environmental Forecasting to identify and evaluate options to reduce emissions from and impacts on transportation.

Sources

1. U.S. Department of Energy, Energy Information Administration, *Annual Energy Outlook 2000*, DOE/EIA-0383(2000) (Washington, DC: December 1999).

2. ____. *Emissions of Greenhouse Gases in the United States 1999*, DOE/EIA-0573(99) (Washington, DC: October 2000).

Key Air Pollutants

Despite significant increases in the U.S. population, gross domestic product, and vehicle-miles traveled since 1980, carbon monoxide (CO), volatile organic compounds (VOC), particulates, and lead emissions have declined, leading to improved air quality. These decreases are due primarily to vehicle tailpipe and evaporative emissions standards established by the U.S. Environmental Protection Agency (EPA), improvements in vehicle fuel efficiency, and the ban on leaded fuel for motor vehicles. Only nitrogen oxide (NO_X) emissions, which contribute to the formation of ground-level ozone, remain above their 1990 level (figure 1). In September 1998, EPA issued a rule to reduce NO_X emissions in 22 eastern states, but implementation was held up by a court case.

Although progress has been made in reducing transportation-related pollutants, mobile sources still account for a sizable percentage of several key pollutants. In 1998, for example, transportation contributed about 61 percent of all CO emissions, 41 percent of NO_X, 36 percent of VOC, and 13 percent of lead [2]. With the exception of lead, highway vehicles were the primary transportation source of these pollutants. The use of lead in aircraft fuel is responsible for nearly all transportation-related lead emissions. The Federal Aviation Administration, EPA, and the aviation industry are examining ways to reduce lead emissions. Figure 2 (page 188) shows 1998 emissions by mode.

In 1997, EPA added ammonia to its National Emission Trends database, which covers both mobile and stationary sources of pollution. Gaseous ammonia reacts in the air with sulfur dioxide and NO_X to form ammonium sulfate and nitrate particles that are found in particulate matter of 2.5 microns in diameter or smaller. In 1998, mobile sources, primarily onroad gasoline-powered vehicles, accounted for about 8 percent of total ammonia emissions.

The decline in emissions of some pollutants from transportation vehicles directly impacts the nation's air quality, which is a measure of the concentration of pollutants in the atmosphere. Since 1980, air quality trends show continuous improvement nationwide. The maps (page 189) compare nonattainment areas[1] in September 1996 and 1999. Over this period, the number of nonattainment areas for one or more pollutants declined from 174 to 119. The number of people living in nonattainment areas and, therefore, exposed to poor air quality declined from 127 million to just under 103 million [1, 3].

Sources

1. U.S. Environmental Protection Agency, Office of Air Quality Planning and Standards, *National Air Quality and Emissions Trends Report, 1995* (Research Triangle Park, NC: 1997).

2. ____. *National Air Pollutant Emission Trends: 1900–1998*, EPA 454/R-00-002 (Research Triangle Park, NC: March 2000), also available at http://www.epa.gov/ttn/chief/trends/, as of May 18, 2001.

3. ____. *National Air Quality and Emissions Trends Report, 1998*, 454/R-00-003 (Research Triangle Park, NC: March 2000), also available at http://www.epa.gov/oar/aqtrnd98/, as of May 18, 2001.

---

[1] Areas where air pollution levels persistently exceed national air quality standards.

Figure 1
National Transportation Emissions Trends Index: 1970–1998
1970 = 1.0; 1990 = 1.0 for PM-2.5 and ammonia

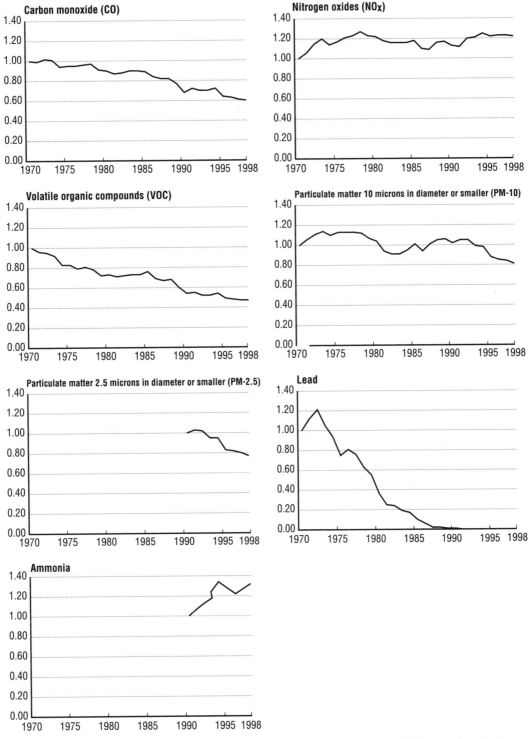

SOURCE: U.S. Environmental Protection Agency, Office of Air Quality Planning and Standards, *National Air Pollutant Emission Trends: 1900–1998,* EPA 454/R-00-002 (Research Triangle Park, NC: March 2000), also available at http://www.epa.gov/ttn/chief/trends/, as of May 18, 2001.

Figure 2
Modal Share of Key Transportation-Related Air Pollutants: 1998

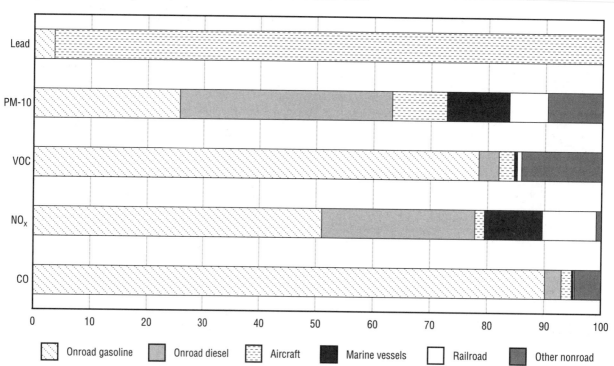

KEY: CO = carbon monoxide; NO$_x$ = nitrogen oxides; VOC = volatile organic compounds; PM-10 = particulate matter 10 microns in diameter or smaller.

NOTE: Other nonroad includes gasoline and diesel recreational vehicles, recreational marine vessels, airport service vehicles, and railroad maintenance equipment. Does not include farm, construction, industrial, logging, light commercial, and lawn and garden equipment.

SOURCE: U.S. Environmental Protection Agency, Office of Air Quality Planning and Standards, *National Air Pollutant Emission Trends: 1900–1998*, EPA 454/R-00-002 (Research Triangle Park, NC: March 2000), also available at http://www.epa.gov/ttn/chief/trends/, as of May 18, 2001.

Location of Nonattainment Areas for Criteria Pollutants

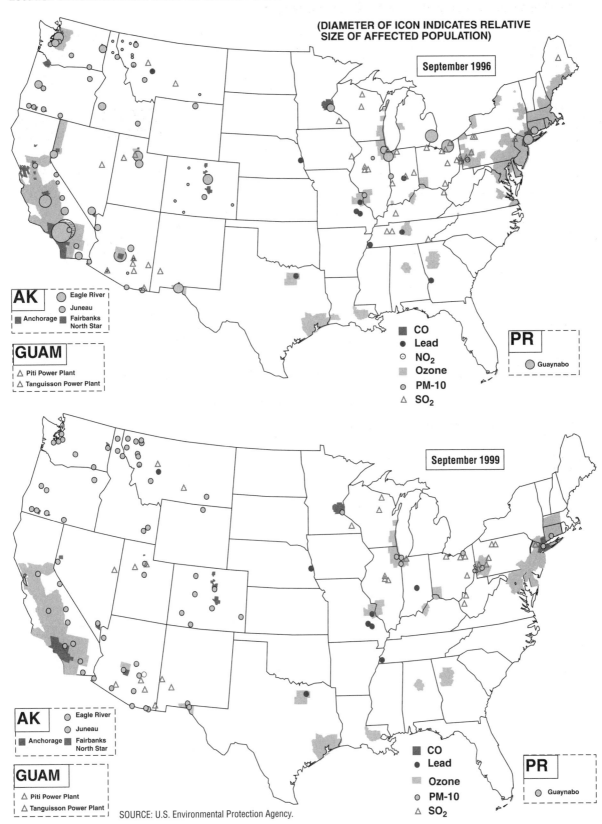

(DIAMETER OF ICON INDICATES RELATIVE SIZE OF AFFECTED POPULATION)

September 1996

September 1999

AK
Eagle River
Anchorage   Juneau
Fairbanks North Star

GUAM
Piti Power Plant
Tanguisson Power Plant

CO
Lead
NO₂
Ozone
PM-10
SO₂

PR
Guaynabo

SOURCE: U.S. Environmental Protection Agency.

Mobile Source Toxic Air Pollution Emissions

Transportation vehicles emit hazardous air pollutants (HAPs). These chemicals have the potential to cause serious health effects in humans, such as cancer, reproductive disorders, and developmental and neurological problems, and cause damage to the ecosystem. The U.S. Environmental Protection Agency (EPA) estimated that 4.3 million tons of 188 HAPs (as specified in the Clean Air Act Amendments of 1990) were released nationwide in 1996. Half of the total came from mobile sources; the balance, from stationary sources, such as factories, powerplants, and shops.

Mobile source air toxics are constituents of or impurities in petroleum feedstock, are formed during the fuel combustion process or afterward in the atmosphere, or result from engine wear. Benzene, toluene, and xylene, for instance, are volatile organic compounds (VOC) that occur naturally in petroleum. They are concentrated during the gasoline refining process and then released during vehicle fueling and in vehicle exhaust.

The air concentration of 13 mobile source air toxics (MSATs) has been monitored at some sites, nationwide.[1] The annual average concentration of benzene declined 37 percent in metropolitan areas between 1993 and 1996 (figure 1), while toluene decreased by 44 percent. EPA attributes these decreases to the use of reformulated fuel in many parts of the country [2]. The nationwide trends for other MSATs, such as 1,3-butadiene and styrene, do not show appreciable air quality improvements or are relatively flat.

EPA issued a ruling in December 2000 designating 21 HAPs as MSATs [1] (table 1). Among this set of HAPs, transportation is the source of 86 percent of the nation's air emissions of methyl-tertiary-butyl-ether (MTBE), 84 percent of ethylbenzene, 79 percent of xylene, 76 percent of benzene, 74 percent of toluene, 70 percent of acetaldehyde, and 60 percent of 1,3-butadiene. EPA is relying on vehicle-based programs already in place or proposed (e.g., reformulated gasoline and sulfur control requirements) to significantly reduce onroad MSAT emissions. In addition, EPA set new gasoline toxic emissions performance standards to reduce emissions such as benzene. For nonroad emissions, EPA plans to conduct research to improve emissions inventory data before proposing any control programs.

Sources

1. U.S. Environmental Protection Agency (EPA), National Vehicle and Fuels Emission Laboratory, "Control of Emissions of Hazardous Air Pollutants from Mobile Sources," 65 *Federal Register* 48058, 2001

2. _____. Office of Air Quality Planning and Standards, *National Air Quality and Emissions Trends Report, 1998*, EPA 454/R-00-003 (Research Triangle Park, NC: 2000).

---

[1] The total number of monitoring sites varies by pollutant. There are 84 sites measuring benzene and 78 measuring toluene in metropolitan areas. Thirty of the nation's air toxic monitoring locations are in California.

Figure 1
National Trend in Annual Average Benzene Concentrations in Metropolitan Areas: 1993–1998

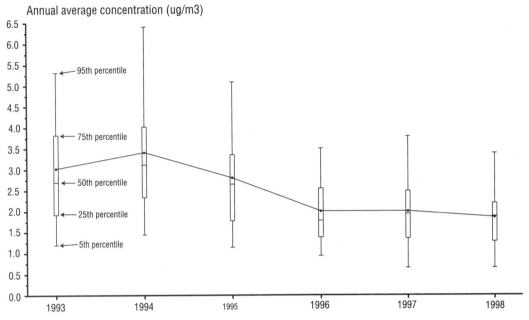

Annual average concentration (ug/m3)

Sites included in national trend
● Sufficient trend data (84)
● Insufficient trend data (595)

SOURCE: U.S. Environmental Protection Agency, Office of Air Quality Planning and Standards, *National Air Quality and Emissions Trends Report, 1998*, available at http://www.epa.gov/oar/aqtrnd98/, as of April 21, 2001.

Table 1
Mobile Source Air Toxics (MSATs): 1996

MSAT	Highway motor vehicles		Nonroad vehicles and engines		Total mobile sources	
	Short tons	National total (percent)	Short tons	National total (percent)	Short tons	National total (percent)
Acetaldehyde	28,700	29.0	40,800	41.0	69,500	70.0
Acrolein	5,000	16.0	7,400	23.0	12,400	39.0
Arsenic compounds	0.25	0.06	2.01	0.51	2.26	0.57
Benzene	168,200	48.0	98,700	28.0	266,900	76.0
1,3-butadiene	23,500	42.0	9,900	18.0	33,400	60.0
Chromium compounds	14	1.2	35	3.0	49	4.2
Dioxin/furans	0.0001	0.2	NA		0.0001	0.2
Diesel exhaust (PM)	data not yet available					
Ethylbenzene	80,800	47.0	62,200	37.0	143,000	84.0
Formaldehyde	83,000	24.0	864,000	25.0	169,400	49.0
Lead compounds	19	0.8	546	21.8	565	22.6
Manganese compounds	5.80	0.2	35.50	1.3	41.30	1.5
Mercury compounds	0.20	0.1	6.60	4.1	6.80	4.2
MTBE	65,100	47.0	53,900	39.0	119,000	86.0
n-Hexane	63,300	26.0	43,600	18.0	106,600	44.0
Naphthalene	data not yet available					
Nickel compounds	10.70	0.9	92.80	7.6	103.50	8.5
POM (sum of 7 PAHs)	42	4.0	19.30	2.0	61.30	6.0
Styrene	16,300	33.0	3,500	7.0	19,800	40.0
Toluene	549,900	51.0	252,200	23.0	802,100	74.0
Xylene	311,000	43.0	258,400	36.0	569,400	79.0
Totals	**1,394,892**		**1,695,337**		**2,312,329**	

KEY: MTBE = methy-tertiary-butyl-ether; NA = not applicable; PAHs = polycyclic aromatic hydrocarbons; PM = particulate matter; POM = polycyclic organic matter.

NOTE: EPA estimates these data based on engine type. Thus, highway motor vehicles includes both gasoline- and diesel-powered vehicles such as light duty vehicles and trucks, heavy duty vehicles, and motorcycles. The nonroad vehicles and engines category data are estimated based on engine types normally used by aircraft, marine vessels, and locomotives. However, this category can also include engines for lawn, construction, and other equipment that the Bureau of Transportation Statistics does not consider to be transportation-related sources of nonroad emissions. Currently, it is not possible to subtract these data from the totals, as is done for criteria pollutants.

SOURCE: U.S. Environmental Protection Agency, National Vehicle and Fuels Emission Laboratory, "Control of Emissions of Hazardous Air Pollutants from Mobile Sources," 65 *Federal Register* 48058, 2001.

Aircraft Noise

A series of U.S. laws passed between 1968 and 1990 established aircraft noise as an environmental pollutant. The entire fleet of large civil subsonic turbojet airplanes operating at airports in the contiguous United States were converted to the quieter Stage 3 status by the end of 1999 (see box). Individually, all operators had met or exceeded the interim compliance requirement of the Airport Noise and Capacity Act of 1990. As shown in figure 1, throughout the transition period (1992 to 1999), operators made steady progress toward the final goal [1].

National data and modeling of airport noise indicate there has been a decline in the numbers and percentage of the population exposed to noise levels of 65 dB of day-night noise levels and above since 1975 (figure 2). During this same period, annual aircraft departures rose from 4.5 million to over 8 million [2]. Four different methodologies (for 1995, 1980 to 1985, 1990, and 1990 to 1998) were used to estimate the exposure data. Actual data do not exist for many of the nation's airports, such as New York City's John F. Kennedy International Airport. Airport authorities are not required to produce noise exposure maps and reports except when applying for federal funds to participate in the voluntary Noise Compatibility Program. Accordingly, the current Nationwide Airport Noise Impact Model, which is used to esti-

> **Measuring Aircraft Noise**
>
> Sound is measured on a logarithmic (nonlinear) scale in decibel (dB) units. There are different dB scales. Transportation noise is usually measured in dBAs, the so-called A-weighted scale that emphasizes sound frequencies that people hear best. On this scale, a 10 dBA increase in sound level is generally perceived by humans as a doubling of sound.
>
> For airport noise exposure, the U.S. Department of Transportation, Federal Aviation Administration, has adopted a dB measurement called day-night noise level (DNL) established by a federal interagency group. The DNL is a yearly day-night average sound level, a measure of exposure to cumulative events over time. Aircraft engine noise standards, on the other hand, have been set based on a measurement of effective perceived noise level, or EPNdB, which accounts for the presence of different tones in sound.
>
> Contour sound maps of airports are constructed from sound levels measured on the ground. People living or working within DNL 65 dB or higher contours are considered to be subject to significant sound. In general, sound levels are highest in the immediate area of flight pathways and increase in proximity to the airport. Sound levels also differ between takeoffs and landings and type and size of aircraft.
>
> Stage 3 aircraft standards differ based on aircraft size and operations and range from 89 to 106 EPNdB. For landings, aircraft must meet the appropriate standard measured over a reference point 2,000 meters from the runway threshold. For takeoffs, the reference point is 6,500 meters from the start of an aircraft's takeoff roll.

Figure 1

Stage 3 Airplanes as a Percentage of Fleets: 1992–1999

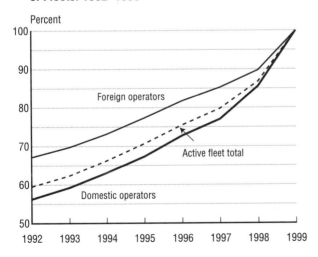

SOURCE: U.S. Department of Transportation, Federal Aviation Administration, *Report to Congress: Progress Report on the Transition to Quieter Airplanes* (Washington, DC: Annual editions).

Figure 2
People Living in High Noise Areas Around U.S. Airports

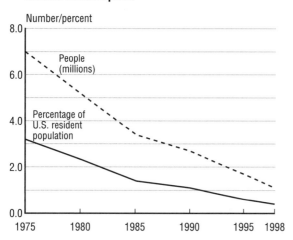

NOTE: The *DOT Performance Plan (FY 2001) and Report (FY 1999)* lists a preliminary estimate of 680,000 people exposed in 1999.

SOURCES: Exposure: U.S. Department of Transportation, Federal Aviation Administration, Office of Environment and Energy, personal communications.
Population: U.S. Department of Commerce, Census Bureau, *Statistical Abstract of the United States 1999* (Washington, DC: 2000), table 2.

mate 1995 data and beyond, contains approximations of noise contours for many commercial airports, including 14 of the nation's 50 busiest. These 14 airports accounted for about one-quarter of all air carrier operations in 1998 [3].

Despite declines in exposure and aircraft noise, 58 percent of the airport operators surveyed in 2000 cited noise as their most serious environmental challenge [3]. Aircraft operators have two ways to meet Stage 3 standards: put new aircraft built to the standards in service and retrofit existing aircraft engines with hushkits to muffle noise. Among those surveyed, most airport operators claimed that the continuing noise problem is caused by the retrofitted aircraft because they are still noisier than aircraft built to meet Stage 3 standards [3]. Federal Aviation Administration data on Stage 3 aircraft do not differentiate between these two types of aircraft.

Sources

1. U.S. Department of Transportation, Federal Aviation Administration, *Report to Congress: 1998 Progress Report on the Transition to Quieter Airplanes* (Washington DC: August 1999).

2. U.S. Department of Transportation, Office of the Secretary, *The Changing Face of Transportation*, draft for public comment, September 2000, fig. 5-31.

3. U.S. General Accounting Office, *Aviation and the Environment: Airport Operations and Future Growth Present Environmental Challenges*, GAO/RCED-00-153 (Washington, DC: August 2000), also available at http://www.gao.gov/reports.htm, as of May 2001.

Oil Spills

Failures in transportation systems (vessels, pipelines, highway vehicles, and railroad equipment) or errors made by operators can result in spills of oil and hazardous materials. Better information is available about the extent of spill incidents than about the overall consequences of these spills on the environment and human health. The impact of each spill, for instance, will depend on the concentration and nature of the pollution, the location and volume of the spill, weather conditions, and the environmental resources affected.

When an oil spill occurs in U.S. waters, the responsible party is required to report the spill to the U.S. Coast Guard. The Coast Guard collects data on the number, location, and source of spills, volume and type of oil spilled, and the type of operation that caused spills. Between 1994 and 1999, an annual average of 2.1 million gallons of various types of oil were spilled by all sources (figure 1). While it varies from year to year, not all the oil spilled is cargo. In 1998, for instance, 51 percent of the volume of oil spilled was cargo being moved by transportation equipment such as tankers, barges, pipelines, railroads, and tank trucks [1].

Data for 1989 to 1998 show that marine vessel and pipeline spills varied considerably each year, from a low of 40 percent of the total volume spilled in 1991 to a high of 90 percent in 1989 [2] (table 1). A major incident in any one year can cause major fluctuations in data from year to year. For instance, the 10 million gallon Exxon Valdez spill represented 91 percent of the crude oil spilled in 1989. In 1996, a pipeline

Figure 1
Reported Oil Spills by Type: 1994–1999
Annual average

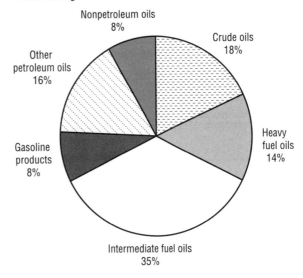

SOURCE: U.S. Department of Transportation, U.S. Coast Guard, *Volume of Spills by Source*, Oil Spill Compendium Data Tables, July 1999, available at http://www.uscg.mil, as of June 8, 2000.

ruptured, spilling about 958,000 gallons of intermediate fuel oil into the Reedy River in South Carolina. This one incident represented 98 percent of the total volume of oils spilled into U.S. waters by pipelines that year.

Sources

1. American Petroleum Institute, *Oil Spills in U.S. Navigable Waters: 1989–1998* (Washington, DC: Feb. 22, 2000).

2. U.S. Department of Transportation, U.S. Coast Guard, *Polluting Incident Compendium*, 2000, available at http://www.uscg.mil, as of June 7, 2000.

(continued on next page)

Table 1
Reported Oil Spills in U.S. Waterways: 1989–1999
Thousands of gallons

	1989	1990	1991	1992	1993	1994	1995	1996	1997	1998	1999
Marine vessels	12,694	6,387	696	665	1,177	1,334	1,624	1,681	381	621	576
Pipelines	215	317	49	200	362	62	12	978	224	48	36
Facilities	449	1,059	446	505	350	677	869	406	205	16	368
Other[1]	33	32	10	236	146	349	77	24	72	33	148
Unknown	88	119	674	269	32	78	56	29	60	17	45
Total	**13,479**	**7,915**	**1,876**	**1,876**	**2,067**	**2,499**	**2,638**	**3,118**	**943**	**885**	**1,173**

[1] Depending on the year, this category may include other transportation sources such as aircraft and railroad equipment.

NOTE: Numbers may not add to totals due to rounding.

SOURCE: U.S.Coast Guard, "Oil Spill Compendium Data Tables," Volume of Spills by Source, updated July 1999, available at http://www.uscg.mil, as of June 8, 2000.

Dredged Material

The nation's ports and navigation channels must be regularly dredged to maintain proper depths to accommodate shipping. In conducting this work between 1990 and 1999, the U.S. Army Corps of Engineers produced an average of 271 million cubic yards of dredged materials per year at an annual average cost of $572 million [1]. U.S. port authorities spend an additional $100 million per year on average to dredge their berths and connecting channels [2], but data on the total amount of material dredged are only occasionally available.

In 1998, the U.S. Environmental Protection Agency (EPA) estimated that about 10 percent (about 1.2 billion cubic yards) of the sediment underlying the nation's surface water was "sufficiently contaminated with toxic pollutants to pose potential risks to fish and to humans and wildlife who eat fish" [3]. Further, EPA noted that about 3 million to 12 million cubic yards of material dredged each year are "sufficiently con-

taminated to require special handling and disposal." National Army Corps of Engineers data, which are aggregated on an annual basis from individual dredging contracts, do not identify how much material is contaminated, although the data show how dredged material is managed (figure 1). Several of the reporting categories (especially confined, open water/upland, and mixed) may include contaminated sediments.

Sources

1. U.S. Army Corps of Engineers, Water Resources Support Center, Navigation Data Center, *Dredging Information System*, 2000, available at http://www.wrsc.usace.army.mil/ndc, as of February 2001.

2. U.S. Department of Transportation, Maritime Administration, Office of Ports and Domestic Shipping, *United States Port Development Expenditure Report* (Washington, DC: November 1999).

3. U.S. Environmental Protection Agency, Office of Water, *EPA's Contaminated Sediment Management Strategy*, EPA-823-R-98-001 (Washington, DC: April 1998).

(continued on next page)

Figure 1

Disposal/Use of Material Dredged by the U.S. Army Corps of Engineers

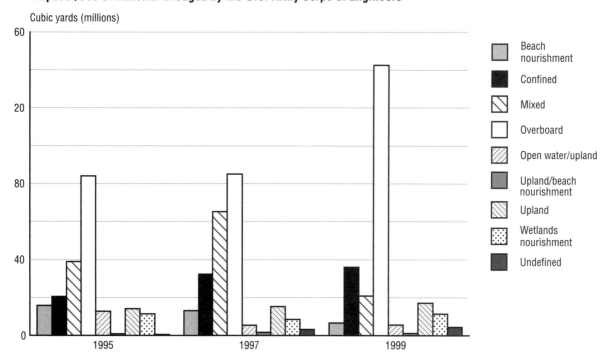

Key to terms used:

Beach nourishment—beach restoration in which hydraulically pumped dredge material is directly placed onto an eroded beach.

Confined—placement of dredged material within diked nearshore or upland confined placement facilities that enclose and isolate the dredged material from adjacent waters.

Mixed—dredging operation that uses more than one dredged material placement alternative.

Overboard—placement of dredged material in rivers, lakes, estuaries, or oceans via pipeline or surface release from hopper dredges.

Open water/upland—combination of open water and upland placement of dredged material.

Upland/beach nourishment—combination of upland placement and beach nourishment using dredged material.

Upland—placement of dredge material on land above adjacent water surface elevation.

Wetlands nourishment—wetland restoration in which hydraulically pumped dredge material is directly placed in a wetland area.

Undefined—undefined or unknown at the time of data entry.

SOURCE: U.S. Army Corps of Engineers National Data Center, available at http://www.wrsc.usace.army.mil/ndc, as of May 17, 2001.

Leaking Underground Storage Tanks

Underground tanks for storing petroleum products, such as fuels for transportation, have a history of leaking petroleum into the nation's underground water. The U.S. Environmental Protection Agency (EPA) started collecting annual data on the problem and its resolution in fiscal year (FY) 1990 under the Underground Storage Tank Program. By the end of FY 2000, EPA regions reported that there were 713,666 active underground tanks in the nation and that almost 1.5 million tanks had been closed [3].

Between 1990 and 2000, the numbers of confirmed releases of petroleum from underground storage tanks (USTs) climbed at an annual rate of 17 percent (table 1). By the end of FY 2000, cleanups had been initiated at 89 percent of the confirmed release sites, and 61 percent of those cleanups had been completed. Almost 163,000 known releases still need to be cleaned up.

As with oil spills in U.S. waters, these data do not reveal the overall environmental impact of releasing petroleum products into underground and surface waters. Furthermore, the data gathered show the number of incidents rather than volume; thus, even the full extent of the problem is not clear. For example, the amount of water contaminated by releases from underground tanks is not known.

In 2000, concern arose about the leaking of methyl-tertiary-butyl-ether (MTBE) from storage tanks and other sources. MTBE is a constituent of reformulated gasoline, which is used in nonattainment areas of the country to lower ozone levels. Once released, MTBE moves rapidly through underground water. This substance has been detected in drinking water, with the highest levels in areas of the country using reformulated gasoline. The major source of groundwater contamination from MTBE appears to be from leaking USTs [1]. Other sources include aboveground tanks, pipelines, and recreational boats. An expert panel convened by EPA to review the MTBE issue reported that, while 80 percent of USTs have been upgraded, there continue to be reports of releases from some of them due to "inadequate design, installation, maintenance, and/or operation." EPA has proposed regulations that would ban or limit the use of MTBE as a gasoline additive [2].

Sources

1. U.S. Environmental Protection Agency, *Achieving Clean Air and Clean Water: The Report of the Blue Ribbon Panel on Oxygenates in Gasoline*, Executive Summary and Recommendations (Washington, DC: July 27, 1999).

2. ____. "EPA Administrator Carol M. Browner Remarks as Prepared for Delivery," press release, Mar. 20, 2000.

3. U.S. Environmental Protection Agency, Office of Underground Storage Tanks, *Corrective Action Measures Archive*, Jan. 13, 2000, available at http://www.epa.gov/swerust1/cat/camarchv.htm, as of May 2001.

(continued on next page)

Table 1
Leaking Underground Storage Tank Releases and Cleanups

	FY 1990	FY 1992	FY 1994	FY 1996	FY 1998	FY 2000
Total confirmed releases	87,528	184,457	270,567	317,488	371,387	412,392
Cleanups initiated	51,770	129,074	209,797	252,615	314,965	367,603
Percentage of total	59%	70%	78%	80%	85%	89%
Cleanups completed	16,905	55,444	107,448	152,683	203,247	249,759
Percentage of total	19%	30%	40%	48%	55%	61%

NOTE: Data are cumulative.

SOURCE: U.S. Environmental Protection Agency, Office of Underground Storage Tanks, *Corrective Action Measures Archive*, available at http://www.epa.gov/, as of December 2000.

Transportation Wastes

As highway vehicles, aircraft, marine vessels, and railroad locomotives and cars and their various parts are maintained over their lifetime, numerous wastes are generated. At the end of their useful life, transportation equipment is generally dismantled with some portions recycled and the rest discarded. The U.S. Environmental Protection Agency (EPA) makes estimates, based on a material flows model, on the amounts of municipal solid waste (MSW) generated each year. In 1998, the United States generated 220 million tons of MSW [3]. Some transportation wastes (e.g., tires and batteries) are included in these data, but others, such as transportation equipment, discards from automobile dismantling operations, and motor oils, are not included.

Most trend data available on transportation wastes pertain to highway vehicles. For instance, EPA makes annual estimates on the disposal of lead-acid batteries and rubber tires from passenger cars, trucks, and motorcycles (figures 1 and 2). Recovered batteries and tires are reused in some form and therefore do not end up in municipal waste landfills and incinerators. Batteries are dismantled, and, in 1997, over 93 percent of the lead content and a significant portion of the polypropylene casings were recycled [3].

The transportation sector consumed an estimated 1,176 million gallons of lubricants in 1997 [1]; these motor oils become wastes throughout a vehicle's life cycle. Means of disposal include burning as fuel, dumping illegally, landfilling, rerefining, and incinerating. Trend data on disposal are not collected and the most recent data were estimated for 1991.

The used motor oils that are burned as fuel or incinerated contribute to the transportation sector's carbon dioxide emissions. EPA estimates that 50 percent of the carbon value in lubricants used by the transportation sector is ultimately released. The balance is sequestered in the products [2].

Sources

1. U.S. Department of Energy, Energy Information Administration, *State Energy Data Report 1997,* 1997, available at http://www.eia.doe.gov/pub/state.data/pdf/SEDR97.pdf, table 15.

2. U.S. Environmental Protection Agency, Office of Policy, Planning and Evaluation, *Inventory of U.S. Greenhouse Gas Emissions and Sinks: 1990-1997,* EPA 236-R-99-003 (Washington, DC: 1999), table A-10.

3. U.S. Environmental Protection Agency, Office of Solid Waste, *Characterization of Municipal Solid Waste in the United States: 1998 Update* (Washington, DC: July 1999).

(continued on next page)

Figure 1
Disposition of Used Lead-Acid Batteries
Passenger cars, trucks, and motorcycles

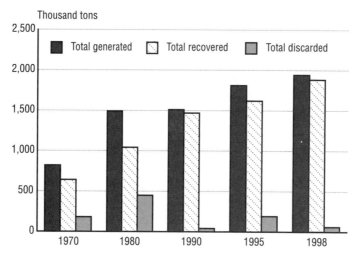

SOURCE: U.S. Environmental Protection Agency, Office of Solid Waste, *Characterization of Municipal Solid Waste in the United States* (Washington, DC: Various years).

Figure 2
Disposition of Used Rubber Tires
Passenger cars, trucks, and motorcycles

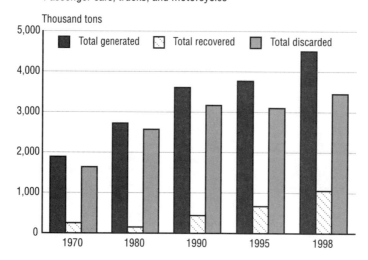

SOURCE: U.S. Environmental Protection Agency, Office of Solid Waste, *Characterization of Municipal Solid Waste in the United States* (Washington, DC: Various years).

Wetlands

It is only during the last few decades that the United States has considered wetlands a natural resource worth enhancing and preserving. This change in thinking occurred after the loss by draining of an estimated half of the wetlands acreage believed to exist in the 1600s [5]. In 1993, the Administration issued a "no net loss of wetlands" policy statement, and four years later called for a national goal of an annual net gain of 100,000 acres of wetlands by 2003.

There were an estimated 105.5 million acres of wetlands in 1997, according to a study done by the U.S. Fish and Wildlife Service of the U.S. Department of the Interior (DOI), in cooperation with other agencies [3]. The study responded to problems the General Accounting Office found in previous estimates done separately by DOI and the Department of Agriculture [2]. In the new study, DOI estimated that a net loss of almost 650,000 acres of wetlands occurred between 1986 and 1997. Urban development, which includes transportation activities, accounted for an estimated 30 percent of all wetland losses.

Transportation infrastructure and use has contributed to the loss of wetlands. Today, developers of roads, airports, rail systems, and marine facilities must determine, as part of the National Environmental Policy Act process, whether their projects will impact wetlands. If so, they may need to obtain a Clean Water Act Section 404 permit from the U.S. Army Corps of Engineers.

The only time the Corps has collected nationwide data on permits was between May 1997 and September 1998 (table 1), when it was restructuring permits. According to these data, multiple residential projects received the most permits (20 percent) and impacted 26 percent of the wetlands acreage listed. Transportation ranked second in total number of requested and author-

Table 1
Wetland Acreage Impacted and Nationwide Permit (NWP) 26[1] Requests and Authorizations: May 1997–September 1998

Category	Wetlands acreage impacted	Number of NWPs requested	Number of NWPs authorized
Residential multiple	1,097.5	2,008	1,905
Transportation	**603.0**	**1,869**	**1,779**
Industrial	313.7	591	560
Retail multiple	311.5	466	436
Impoundment	222.6	553	515
Retail individual	213.0	401	390
Agricultural	197.8	709	689
Storm water	191.1	656	580
Institutional	157.4	333	315
Mining, other	94.7	178	168
Treatment facility	42.5	125	115
Mining aggregates	39.3	69	67
Silviculture	39.3	19	17
Other	705.5	2,179	2,047
Total	**4,198.0**	**10,156**	**9,583**

[1] An NWP 26 is a type of permit

SOURCE: David Olson, U.S. Army Corps of Engineers, Regulatory Program Office, personal communication, June 2000.

ized permits (18 and 19 percent, respectively) and in total wetlands acreage impacted. While these data provide some insight into transportation infrastructure's relative impact on wetlands, there are no data on impacts from runoffs of salt, oils, and rubber from highways and other facilities, and air pollutants emitted by vehicles, locomotives, airplanes, and vessels as they move along or through wetland areas. Furthermore, data showing total numbers of acres provide no information on the quality of the remaining wetlands as measured by their value to society [1].

The Corps does not break down wetlands permit data by mode. The Federal Highway Administration has collected data on wetlands acreage impacted by the Federal Aid Highways system since 1996 (table 2). However, Federal Aid Highways constitute only 4 percent of the total miles of public roads in the country [4]. Although the Federal Aviation Administration (FAA) does not collect data on wetlands impacted by airports, airport runway expansion often involves an evaluation of wetland impacts. As part of its dredging program, the Corps identifies the amount of material dredged from navigation channels used each year to nourish wetlands. From 1994 to 1999, an average of 30 million cubic yards per year (7 percent of all Corps-dredged material) was used for this purpose.

When it is determined that a transportation project will impact a wetland, federal policy requires compensatory mitigation to restore, create, or enhance wetlands. According to Federal Aid Highway Program data, 2.7 times as many acres of wetlands were created than lost between 1996 and 2000 during highway construction or maintenance. Corps data for May 1997 to September 1998 show that 995.8 acres of wetlands were mitigated under transportation projects, resulting in a ratio of 1.7:1. FAA evaluation of mitigation projects focuses on ensuring that habitats are not created that would attract wildlife known to affect aircraft operations.

Table 2
Wetlands Lost and Created Under the Federal Aid Highway Program: 1996–2000

Fiscal year	Acres impacted	Acres mitigated	Ratio of wetlands created to wetlands lost
1996	1,568	3,554	2.3:1
1997	1,699	4,484	2.6:1
1998	1,167	2,557	2.2:1
1999	2,354	5,409	2.3:1
2000	2,041	7,671	3.8:1
Total	**8,829**	**23,675**	**2.7:1**

SOURCE: U.S. Department of Transportation, Federal Highway Administration, *Wetlands Mitigation Data Report for the Federal-Aid Highway Program, Fiscal Year 2000* (Washington, DC: 2001).

Sources

1. U.S. Congress, Congressional Research Service, "Wetlands Issues," Mar. 15, 2000.

2. U.S. Congress, General Accounting Office, *Wetlands Overview: Problems with Acreage Data Persist,* GAO/RCED-98-150 (Washington, DC: July 1998).

3. U.S. Department of the Interior, Fish and Wildlife Service, *Status and Trends of Wetlands in the Conterminous United States: 1986 to 1997* (Washington, DC: December 2000).

4. U.S. Department of Transportation, Federal Highway Administration, *Highway Statistics 1998* (Washington, DC: 2000), table HM-14.

5. U.S. Environmental Protection Agency, Office of Water, "Status and Trends," available at http://www.epa.gov/owow/wetlands/vital/status.html, as of May 2001.

Urban Sprawl

There is no standard definition of "sprawl." However, the word generally applies to the expanding growth of suburbs and exurbs around a mature urban area. The characteristics of sprawl can include:

- dispersed commercial and industrial sites;
- low-density residential population;
- single-use zoning (i.e., separate residential areas; shopping centers; strip commercial, industrial, and office parks);
- noncontiguous or leapfrog development; and
- heavy reliance on highway vehicles for transportation.

Local and state governments directly impact local growth through activities such as transportation planning and land-use zoning. However, the federal government plays an indirect role in local growth decisions through spending programs, tax policies, regulatory activity, and administrative actions [4].

Over the past several decades, academics, planners, local government officials, environmentalists, and others have debated the positive and negative impacts of sprawl. However, wide disagreement still exists on many issues (table 1). In addition, a 1998 Transportation Research Board review of studies on sprawl found that various costs and benefits have been identified but are not fully quantified [2]. Data used to prove and disprove whether sprawl exists and is detrimental include: comparisons between population growth and growth of developed land, loss of farmland, changes in vehicle-miles traveled, construction of new homes, the percentage of Americans living in metropolitan areas, and housing costs.

Potential environmental impacts of sprawl are listed in table 2, but, again, are not quantified. While most experts agree that road congestion can be a symptom of sprawl, their environmental impact analyses can differ. Pollutant emissions rates vary with vehicle speed, and the optimal speed varies by pollutant. It is generally agreed that emissions rates are higher during stop-and-go, congested traffic conditions than during free flow conditions [3].

Despite the data gaps and uncertainties of sprawl, state and local governments began in the 1990s to consider and, in some cases, foster "smart growth" and "livable communities" ideas and principles. Both of these concepts apply to urban, as well as suburban and exurban, areas. Indeed, some analyses suggest that the late 20th century decline in urban areas is linked to suburban growth [1].

As a first step toward quantifying livability, the Bureau of Transportation Statistics is supporting a National Research Council study to develop a set of Livability Indicators.

Sources

1. National Governors' Association, *Growing Pains: Quality of Life in the New Economy,* 2000, available at http://www.nga.org, as of May 2001.

2. National Research Council, Transportation Research Board, *The Costs of Sprawl—Revisited* (Washington DC: National Academy Press, 1998).

3. U.S. Department of Transportation, Federal Highway Administration, *Transportation Air Quality: Selected Facts and Figures* (Washington DC: January 1999).

4. U.S. General Accounting Office, *Community Development: Local Growth Issues—Federal Opportunities and Challenges,* GAO-RCED-00-178, 2000, available at http://www.gao.gov, as of March 2001.

Table 1
Alleged Negative and Positive Impacts of Sprawl

Substantive concern	Alleged negative impacts	Alleged positive impacts
Public-private capital and operating costs	Higher infrastructure costs Higher public operating costs More expensive private residential and nonresidential development costs More adverse public fiscal impacts Higher aggregate land costs	Lowers public operating costs Lessens expensive private residential and nonresidential development costs Fosters efficient development of "leapfrogged" areas
Transportation and travel costs	More vehicle-miles traveled Longer travel times More automobile trips Higher household transportation spending Less cost-efficient and effective transit High social costs of travel	Shortens commuting times Lessens congestion Lowers governmental costs for transportation
Land/natural habitat preservation	Loss of agricultural land Reduced farmland productivity Reduced farmland viability (water constraints) Loss of fragile environmental lands Reduced regional open space	Enhances personal and public open space
Quality of life	Aesthetically displeasing Weakened sense of community Greater stress Higher energy consumption More air pollution Lessened historic preservation	Creates low-density living options Lowers crime rates Enhances value or reduced costs of public and private goods Fosters greater economic well-being
Social issues	Fosters suburban exclusion Fosters spatial mismatch Fosters residential segregation Worsens city fiscal stress Worsens inner-city deterioration	Fosters localized land-use decisions Enhances municipal diversity and choice

SOURCE: National Research Council, Transportation Research Board, *The Costs of Sprawl—Revisited* (Washington DC: National Academy Press, 1998), table 7, p. 42.

Table 2
Growth-Related Environmental Issues and Impacts

Growth issue	Environmental issue	Potential impacts
Haphazard expansion of suburban communities	Water runoff	Increased pollution of streams, rivers, and marine environments Increased flooding Loss of biodiversity in streams Soil erosion Decreased recharge of aquifers Lower drinking water quality
Poor land-use planning	Consumption of open spaces	Loss of contiguous green spaces Loss of natural habitats for native species Loss of wetlands Fragmentation and loss of forestland Increased flooding Increased mountain mudslides and slope collapses Increased prevalence of non-native, invasive species Health impacts from proximity to wild animals and confined-animal feeding operations Loss of green infrastructure for metropolitan areas Less access to recreation areas Higher temperatures or "heat islands" in metropolitan areas Reduced plant photosynthesis
Traffic congestion	Air pollution	Increased smog and other pollutants Increased health impacts, such as asthma Noncompliance with federal standards and limits on new road construction
	Public safety	Increased response times for fires and medical emergencies Road rage
	Energy use	Wasted petroleum
Urban depopulation and decay	Contaminated land and buildings	Increased human exposure to toxic substances
	Public infrastructure	Decreased maintenance and greater service interruptions for water, sewer, road repair, and waste disposal

SOURCE: Adapted from National Governors' Association, *Growing Pains: Quality of Life in the New Economy,* 2000, available at http://www.nga.org/Releases/
PR-05June2000Growth.asp, as of May 2001.

Transportation and Environmental Justice

The Environmental Justice (E J) movement began in the United States in 1982 during protests over the siting of a landfill in a predominately African-American and low-income county in North Carolina. The issue was and is unfair treatment of minority and low-income communities with respect to the development, implementation, and enforcement of environmental laws, regulations, and policies.

In 1994, the Clinton Administration issued Executive Order 12898 on Environmental Justice, requiring all federal agencies to make E J part of their missions. The U.S. Department of Transportation (DOT) subsequently issued a *DOT Order to Address Environmental Justice in Minority Populations and Low-Income Populations* in 1997. This order applies to all policies, programs, and activities undertaken, funded, or approved by DOT components. Although E J has generated controversy for federal agencies, the actual number of administrative complaints filed has been relatively low. At any given time, DOT usually has fewer than a dozen complaints pending, under investigation, or being processed through alternative dispute resolution.

Viewed narrowly, E J applied to transportation would be about avoiding, minimizing, and mitigating disproportionately high environmental and health impacts from transportation in disadvantaged neighborhoods where they exist. Transportation E J has, however, evolved to encompass a broader array of issues, some of which have environmental bases or outcomes. Among the issues are: meaningful participation in transportation planning; access to job-related transportation, especially transit services; the location of infrastructure, such as, highways and inter-

changes, bus barns, and waste transfer stations, that may adversely impact neighborhoods; the connection between vehicle air pollution and asthma; transportation noise; and the lack of complaint investigation and findings in favor of complainants.

Examples of transportation-related E J cases include:

- **Access to Appropriate Public Transportation.** A civil rights suit was brought against the Los Angeles Country Metropolitan Transportation Authority (MTA) by two groups, the NAACP Legal Defense and Education Fund and Environmental Defense, for spending a disproportionate amount of money on a rail system that served mainly white residential neighborhoods. In a 1996 consent decree, MTA agreed to invest over $1 billion in bus system improvements over 10 years [1].

- **Impact of Trucks on Residential Neighborhoods.** The Federal National Environmental Justice Advisory Council conducted fact-findings on the siting and operations of waste transfer stations (WTSs) in New York City and Washington, DC, in 1998 and 1999. WTSs tend to be in urban areas and clustered in low-income and minority communities. They are facilities where municipal waste is unloaded from collection vehicles and then stored temporarily before being reloaded onto long-distance transport vehicles for shipment to landfills or incinerators. WTSs increase noise, odor, litter, and traffic in a neighborhood and impact air quality because of idling diesel-fueled trucks and from particulate matter such as dust and glass [2].

- **Involvement in Transportation Planning.** In metropolitan Atlanta, E J groups raised concerns about disparate impacts related to job access, storm-water runoff cleanup, exposures to small particle air toxics and diesel exhaust, pedestrian safety, noise, and community destruction by highways. DOT now has an E J equity analysis underway of Atlanta's regional transportation planning process. The first phase began in late 1999 and is examining the public participation and data-collection aspects of Atlanta's process. The second phase will be a quantitative analysis of the distribution of transportation benefits and burdens to low-income and minority communities.

- **Location of Waste Dumps.** The presence of National Priorities List (NPL) toxic waste sites (more commonly called Superfund sites) in disadvantaged communities and the slow pace at which they are cleaned up has been a major issue for E J groups. There are over 1,000 Superfund sites, and many of them result from activities related to transportation. Among the sites are facilities that treated wood products with preservative, some of which became ties for railroad tracks; petroleum refineries; barge cleaning and maintenance operations; tire recycling facilities; and railroad yards. Five of the 12 sites added to the NPL in July 2000 are related to transportation: one preserved wood, two refined petroleum, and two maintained marine vessels [3].

Despite the fact that concerned communities, advocacy groups, and government agencies have used various data-collection and analysis methods to try to quantify (and prove or disprove) environmental *injustice*, these studies have usually produced contradictory and contentious findings. Problems with the studies have involved spatial scale issues (e.g., whether to use ZIPcode or census data to define concentrations of low-income and/or minority populations) and difficulties in modeling the complexities of the human impact of transportation. Another problem has been determining cause and effect, since demographics of neighborhoods change over time. In addition, a risk assessment may be needed to determine whether public health is being impacted from, for example, a landfill in the community and, if so, to what extent.

Sources

1. Environmental Defense, *Transportation Equity in Los Angeles: The MTA and Beyond,* 2000, available at http://www.environmentaldefense.org/programs/Transportation/Equity/b_justice.html, as of March 2001.

2. U.S. Environmental Protection Agency, National Environmental Justice Advisory Council, *A Regulatory Strategy for Siting and Operating Waste Transfer Stations,* EPA 500-R-00-002 (Washington, DC: March 2000).

3. U.S. Environmental Protection Agency, Office of Solid Waste and Emergency Response, *New Final NPL Sites,* 2000, available at http://www.epa.gov/superfund/sites/newfin.htm, as of March 2001.

Introduction of Harmful Species

Transportation and world trade enables the introduction of both desirable and harmful non-native animal and plant species and pathogens into the United States. Non-native species arrive via air or marine transportation from locations around the globe and via surface transportation from Canada and Mexico. They are imported legally or illegally or arrive as stowaways among cargo or shipping equipment.

Once inside the country, non-native species may become invasive and adversely affect native species. Not all such introductions have been problematic, however. Non-native corn, wheat, rice, other food crops, and livestock now generate more than 98 percent of the U.S. food system [2]. More than 205 known non-native species were introduced or first detected in the United States in the 1980s and early 1990s. Of these, 59 were expected to cause economic or environmental harm [4]. Estimated annual costs and damages total more than $100 billion dollars each year [3].

Methods to control the entry of non-native species include placing harmful species on "black lists" and regulating pathways. The United States tries to control entry primarily using the species-by-species approach. However, one pathway—ship ballast waters released into the Great Lakes—is regulated. Other pathways include ship dunnage; ship and air cargo containers (and the cargo itself), shipping crates, and packaging; personal baggage and clothing; and military equipment returning from overseas conflicts.

Transportation is not always the carrier of non-native species, and proving it is can be challenging. For instance, several theories surround the entry in 1999 of the West Nile Virus. One is that the virus was carried across the Atlantic Ocean from Europe by migratory birds. Because the virus was first reported in the United States in the Queens borough of New York City, another theory suggests that it arrived (via humans or animals) aboard aircraft landing at John F. Kennedy or LaGuardia Airports [1]. By the summer of 2000, the virus (with mosquitoes as its vector) had spread to 11 states (see map on page 212). A few examples of non-native species introductions for which transportation was apparently the enabler are the following:

- The **zebra mussel** entered the United States and was deposited in the Great Lakes in the 1980s when ship ballast water was discharged from European freighters. It has spread to 20 states, as far south as the mouth of the Mississippi River. While filter-feeding by this mussel has improved water quality in the Great Lakes, it has cost an estimated $3.1 billion over 10 years for control efforts and to fix damages to water intake pipes, filtration equipment, and electric generating plants.

- The **brown tree snake** is thought to have been introduced to Guam in military cargo shipments just after World War II. More recently, the snake has been found in the wheel wells of aircraft departing and arriving from Guam. The population of the snake has increased tremendously, causing the extinction of native Guam birds. In addition, it damages electrical and telephone grids, resulting in power outages that have cost Guam an estimated $1 million a year.

- The **Asian long-horned beetle** may have arrived in packing materials or pallet wood in shipments from China. In New York State and the Chicago area, the beetle is attacking a broad range of tree species, eventually killing them.

A number of aquarium fish and plants have been legally imported and then inadvertently or purposefully released. The aquatic plant, hydrilla, was imported for use in aquariums and discarded into the wild in Florida. It is now likely being spread across the United States by plant fragments attached to recreational boats.

The globalization of trade, increased volume of cargo shipments, and rising tourism increase the chances of more accidental introductions [2]. In addition, technological changes in transportation have altered the way non-native species are introduced. For instance, dry ship ballast was a significant pathway for insects and plants in the 1880s. Ships now use water as ballast and, while this pathway is still important today, port areas may no longer be the major point of entry for non-native species. Today, containerized cargo from both ships and aircraft are not always unpacked prior to arrival at an inland destina-

tion, creating the potential for release of stowaways in other locations in the United States.

Sources

1. *The Lancet,* "Genetic Analysis of West Nile New York 1999 Encephalitis Virus," vol. 354, Dec. 4, 1999.

2. Pimentel, D., L. Lach, R. Zuniga, and D. Morrison, "Environmental and Economic Costs Associated with Non-Indigenous Species in the United States," Cornell University, College of Agriculture and Life Sciences, Ithaca, NY, available at http://www.news.cornell.edu/releases/Jan99/species_costs.html, as of May 2001.

3. U.S. Congress, Congressional Research Service, *Harmful Non-Native Species: Issues for Congress,* RL30123 (Washington, DC: Sept. 15, 1999).

4. U.S. Congress, Office of Technology Assessment, *Harmful Non-Indigenous Species in the United States,* September 1993, available at http://www.ota.nap.edu, as of May 2001.

Distribution of the West Nile Virus: 2000

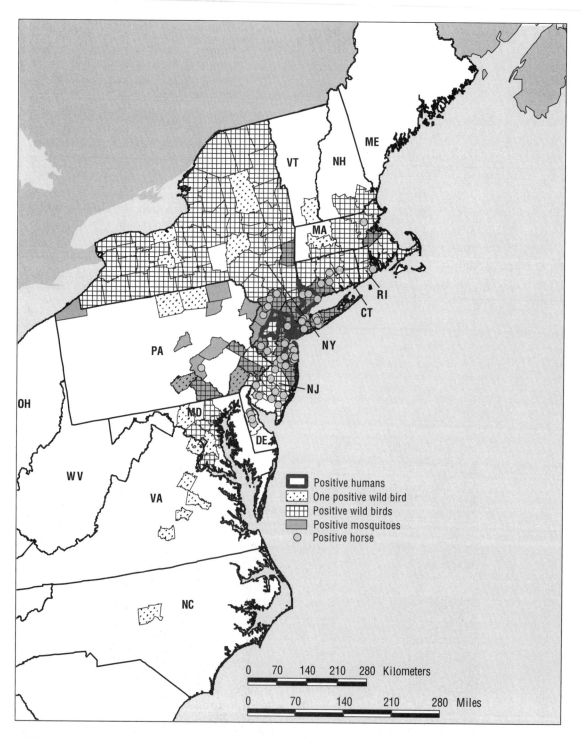

SOURCE: U.S. Department of Agriculture, Animal and Plant Health Inspection Service, available at http://www.aphis.usda.gov/oa/wnv/index.html, as of May 8, 2001.

Chapter 7
National Security

Introduction

One of the U.S. Department of Transportation's (DOT's) strategic goals is to ensure that the nation's transportation system is secure and available for defense mobilization and that our borders are safe from illegal intrusion. Our economic well-being and national security are dependent on a secure transportation system that can move people, goods, and military personnel and equipment without fear of intentional disruption or damage by terrorists or other criminal elements. Since the terrorist attack of September 11, 2001, these goals have become even more critical.

The ability to move military personnel and equipment within the United States and then "project" those forces overseas depends on three transportation components: ground transportation, sealift, and airlift. In each of these components, DOT plays a key role in mobilizing and coordinating the public and private transportation resources and systems necessary to deploy U.S. forces overseas.

As the events of September 11 showed, transportation systems, both overseas and in the United States, can be a target of terrorists and criminals, particularly because they are accessible, attract broad media coverage when attacked, and may be associated with national symbols, such as airlines. In 1998, there were 1,033 terrorist and criminal attacks aimed at transportation systems worldwide—a 20 percent increase over 1997 and a 107 percent increase over 1995. These attacks resulted in 1,700 deaths and 2,200 injured people. In the United States alone, 27 incidents were recorded in 1998, nearly double the total from the previous year.

Our national security is also dependent on key transportation-related sectors of the economy: the oil industry, shipbuilding, and aircraft manufacturing. Since 1997, the United States has imported more than half the oil that it consumes. The U.S. transportation system consumes much more oil today than it did 20 years ago, increasing U.S. vulnerability to oil disruptions, and making the availability of oil a national security concern. The United States' shipbuilding industry has experienced long-term decline. The United States today ranks just ahead of Romania, but behind countries such as Croatia and Finland in merchant shipbuilding. In contrast, while the United States produces fewer aircraft than it did 20 years ago, the U.S. aircraft manufacturing industry remains competitive internationally. Our Armed Forces' reliance on ships and aircraft make the maintenance of a strong manufacturing base in these industries a vital national security concern.

> This report was predominantly written prior to the September 11, 2001, terrorist attacks on the United States.

Finally, our national security depends on the ability of the United States to secure the nation's borders from the illegal intrusion of drugs, contraband, and aliens. The increasing flow of international trade and passenger travel means that more cars, trucks, and railcars are crossing U.S. borders, and more ships are arriving at U.S. ports. With increasing traffic and the flow of goods come more opportunities to smuggle illegal drugs, contraband, and aliens. The U.S. Coast Guard (USCG) is the lead federal agency for maritime drug and alien interdiction and shares the lead for air interdiction with the U.S. Customs Service. In fiscal year 1999, USCG seized a record 111,689 pounds of cocaine, with an estimated street value of $3.7 billion. In 2000, USCG interdicted 4,217 illegal aliens at sea and expects the number to rise in coming years. Securing the nation's borders, therefore, is yet another example of how transportation and national security are inextricably linked.

Movement of Military Forces and Materiel

Our nation's civilian transportation infrastructure provides vital strategic mobility for materiel and forces in times of national emergency. Since the end of the Cold War, U.S. Armed Forces have shifted from anticipating a possible global conflict with a dangerous and powerful adversary to being prepared for rapid deployment in localized incidents. At the same time, fewer U.S. troops are permanently stationed in foreign countries, increasing reliance on reserve forces. Therefore, the smaller, more mobile, U.S. military force structure places different demands on our transportation system [2].

One of the first military actions undertaken in a conflict is force deployment or "projection"— moving troops and equipment. During Operation Desert Shield/Desert Storm, the U.S. Department of Transportation mobilized and coordinated the public and private transportation resources and systems necessary to deploy U.S. forces to the Persian Gulf. Force projection relies on three transportation components: sealift, airlift, and ground transportation [2].

The ability of the United States to respond to military emergencies requires adequate U.S.-controlled maritime shipping capacity to move equipment, fuel, supplies, and ammunition [3]. The National Defense Reserve Fleet (NDRF) supports the Department of Defense (DOD) during national emergencies and consists of U.S. vessels strategically docked throughout the United States. The number of ships in the NDRF has declined since 1975 (figure 1) and today comprises 312 ships, 91 of which are Ready Reserve Force (RRF) ships. RRF ships can be tendered to the Navy's Military Sealift Command during armed conflicts and humanitarian emergencies in 4 to 30 days, depending on their location and readiness [4].

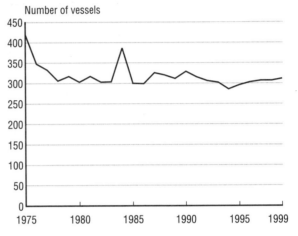

Figure 1
National Defense Reserve Fleet: 1975–1999

SOURCE: U.S. Department of Transportation, Maritime Administration, *Marad '99* (Washington, DC: May 2000).

In addition to the NDRF, which consists of government-owned vessels, DOD also relies on commercial transportation providers for 90 percent of its peacetime freight and personnel movements and an estimated 95 percent of its wartime movements. A major portion of this commercial transportation capacity includes the use of U.S.-flagged vessels and the U.S. merchant marine under the Maritime Administration's Maritime Security Program (MSP). The MSP was established to help ensure the existence of and access to as many as 47 modern and militarily useful U.S.-flagged oceangoing commercial vessels with U.S. crews for DOD sealift requirements [3].

The Civil Reserve Air Fleet (CRAF) is another key component of the nation's mobility resources. Selected aircraft from commercial U.S. airlines are contracted to CRAF to support DOD airlift requirements when military aircraft needs exceed capabilities. The CRAF program provides incentives for civil carriers to commit their air-

Table 1

Members of the Civil Reserve Air Fleet

Long-range international	Short-range international	Aeromedical evacuation
Air Transport International	Alaska Airlines	Delta Airlines
American Airlines	American Trans Air	Trans World Airlines
American Trans Air	Atlas Air	US Airways
Atlas Air	DHL Airways	
Continental Airlines	Evergreen International	**Domestic**
Delta Airlines	Gemini Air Cargo	America West Express
DHL Airways	Hawaiian Airlines	Midwest Express
Emery Worldwide	Lynden Air Cargo	Pan Am Airways
Evergreen International	Miami Air International	Southwest Airlines
Federal Express Corp	North American Airlines	Sun World International
Hawaiian Airlines	Spirit Airlines	
North American Airlines	US Airways Shuttle	**Alaskan**
Northwest Airlines		Northern Air Cargo
Omni Air Express		Lynden Air Cargo
Polar Air Cargo		
Tower Air		
Trans World Airlines		
United Airlines		
United Parcel Service		
World Airways		

SOURCE: U.S. Department of Transportation, Federal Aviation Administration, Office of Aviation Policy and Plans, personal communication, Apr. 18, 2001.

craft. As of December 2000, 31 carriers and 702 aircraft were enrolled in CRAF [1] (table 1).

Finally, the nation's rail and highway systems play critical roles in the movement of military equipment and personnel. When a contingency arises, vast amounts of military equipment and personnel are moved from continental U.S.-based military installations to various seaports and airports. Most of this equipment travels over U.S. highways [2].

The Strategic Highway Network (STRAHNET) system of public highways provides access, con-tinuity, and emergency transportation of personnel and equipment in times of peace and war. The 61,000-mile system, designated by the Federal Highway Administration in partnership with DOD, comprises about 45,400 miles of Interstate and defense highways and 15,600 miles of other public highways. STRAHNET is complemented by about 1,700 miles of connectors—additional highway routes linking more than 200 military installations and ports to the network [2] (see map).

Strategic Highway Network (STRAHNET)

——————	STRAHNET links and connectors
————	U.S. Interstate
●	Major military deployment sites

SOURCE: U.S. Department of Transportation, Federal Highway Administration, 1999.

Sources

1. U.S. Department of Transportation, Federal Aviation Administration, Office of Aviation Policy and Plans, personal communication, Apr. 18, 2001.

2. U.S. Department of Transportation, *The Changing Face of Transportation* (Washington, DC: 2000), pp. 7-1–7-6.

3. U.S. Department of Transportation, Maritime Administration, "Proceedings of the National Conference on the Marine Transportation System: Ports, Waterways, and Intermodal Connectors," November 1998.

4. U.S. Department of Transportation, Maritime Administration, Office of Ship Operations, *The National Defense Reserve Fleet*, available at http://www.marad.dot.gov/offices/press-gm.htm, as of June 28, 2000.

Terrorist Threats to Transportation

The terrorist attacks of September 11, 2001, have totally transformed the threat environment under which the United States operates. This chapter was predominantly written before September 11, and thus it does not reflect analysis of the terrorist threat that has been done since those attacks took place. It is based on publicly available data through 1999 and represents an analysis of those data only.

In 1999, the number of persons killed or wounded in international terrorist attacks fell sharply because of the absence of any single attack causing mass casualties. While the number of casualties dropped in 1999, the number of terrorist attacks rose 43 percent from the previous year (table 1). Moreover, terrorist threats through 1999 were increasingly aimed at U.S. interests. From 1994 to 1999, the proportion of attacks targeted at U.S. interests rose from 20 percent to 43 percent of the total number of international terrorist attacks (figure 1).

Transportation systems are an attractive target for both international and indigenous terrorist groups[1] (figure 2). In recent years, there have been violent attacks against transit passengers, vehicles, and systems worldwide, including Tokyo, where subway passengers were poisoned by a release of sarin nerve gas in 1998 [2]. In 1998, nearly 1,700 deaths and 2,200 injuries resulted from violent acts against transportation worldwide.[2] [3]

According to the Federal Bureau of Investigation, during the 1990s, domestic U.S. terrorist

---

[1] International terrorism is terrorism that involves citizens or the territory of more than one country. Domestic or indigenous terrorism involves groups or individuals whose activities are directed at their own government or population without foreign involvement.

[2] The U.S. Department of Transportation, Office of Intelligence and Security, is in the process of compiling 1999 data and plans on releasing its 1999 report in late-2001.

Table 1
International Terrorist Incidents and Casualties: 1994–1999

Year	1994	1995	1996	1997	1998	1999
Incidents	322	440	296	304	274	392
Casualties	988	6,454	3,225	914	6,693	939

SOURCE: U.S. Department of State, *Patterns of Global Terrorism: 1999* (Washington, DC: 2000).

Figure 1
International Terrorist Attacks Against U.S. Interests as a Proportion of Total Attacks: 1994–1999

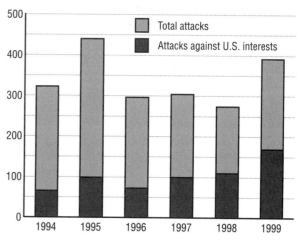

SOURCE: U.S. Department of State, *Patterns of Global Terrorism: 1999* (Washington, DC: 2000).

This report was predominantly written prior to the September 11, 2001, terrorist attacks on the United States.

Figure 2
Worldwide Violent Acts Against Transportation: 1995–1998

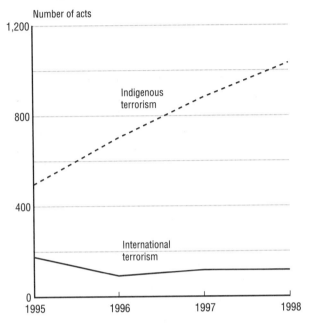

Number of acts

SOURCE: U.S. Department of Transportation, Office of the Secretary of Transportation, Office of Intelligence and Security, *Worldwide Terrorist and Violent Criminal Attacks Against Transportation—1998* (Washington, DC: 1999).

incidents (actual, suspected, and prevented) ranged from a low of 1 in 1994 to a high of 25 in 1997. In the early 1990s, bombings and arson predominated. By the late 1990s, letter bombs and large-scale vehicle bombs became the major con-

cern, particularly following the bombing of the Federal Building in Oklahoma City in 1995. Antigovernment organizations and "hate" groups were increasingly linked to these incidents. A similar phenomenon has occurred in many countries overseas, where indigenous terrorists are motivated more by domestic grievances and ethnic conflict than by geopolitical causes [1]. Since September 11, obviously, aircraft used as bombs and suicide terrorist attacks have emerged as major threats.

Finally, increasing U.S. dependence on sophisticated electronic information and communications systems for commerce, energy, vital human services, and transportation systems is a cause for concern due to the threat from electronic or cyber terrorism. Such threats prompted the creation of the President's Commission on Critical Infrastructure Protection to review the physical and electronic vulnerabilities of the nation's key infrastructure sectors, including transportation.

Sources

1. Federal Bureau of Investigation, *Terrorism in the United States—1997* (Washington, DC: 2000).

2. U.S. Department of Transportation, *The Changing Face of Transportation* (Washington, DC: 2000).

3. U.S. Department of Transportation, Office of the Secretary of Transportation, Office of Intelligence and Security, *Worldwide Terrorist and Violent Criminal Attacks Against Transportation—1998* (Washington, DC: 1999).

Vulnerability of Transportation Infrastructure to Terrorism

Transportation infrastructure, both overseas and in the United States, is increasingly a target for terrorists. In 1998, there were 1,033 terrorist and criminal attacks aimed at transportation systems—a 20 percent increase over 1997 and a 107 percent increase since 1995.[1] These attacks resulted in 1,700 deaths and 2,200 injured people. In the United States alone, 27 incidents were recorded in 1998, nearly double the total from the previous year [2].

Transportation infrastructure draws terrorists because it is accessible; attracts broad media cov-

---

[1] The U.S. Department of Transportation, Office of Intelligence and Security, is in the process of compiling 1999 data and plans on releasing its 1999 report in late 2001.

Table 1
Percentage of Worldwide Violent Attacks on Transportation, by Mode: 1998

Mode	Percent
Highways	24
Maritime/piracy	21
Bus	18
Pipelines	12
Rail	10
Aviation	7
Bridges	2
Other	2
Subway	1

NOTE: Maritime/piracy includes both attacks on maritime facilities, including ports, and piracy of vessels.

SOURCE: U.S. Department of Transportation, Office of the Secretary of Transportation, Office of Intelligence and Security, *Worldwide Terrorist and Violent Criminal Attacks Against Transportation—1998* (Washington, DC: 1999).

Table 2
Worldwide Casualties by Transportation Mode: 1998

Mode	Deaths	Injuries
Bus	647	1,029
Highways	579	336
Rail	161	607
Maritime/piracy	105	37
Aviation	77	13
Pipelines	74	154
Bridges	10	14
Subways	3	4

SOURCE: U.S. Department of Transportation, Office of the Secretary of Transportation, Office of Intelligence and Security, *Worldwide Terrorist and Violent Criminal Attacks Against Transportation—1998* (Washington, DC: 1999).

erage when attacked; may be associated with national symbols, such as national airlines; and large numbers of people can be affected by a single act. While all transportation modes have been targeted, attacks on highways and maritime accounted for almost half of all incidents in 1998 (table 1). Prior to the terrorist attacks of September 11, 2001, civil aviation accounted for a relatively small percentage of terrorist attacks on transportation, comprising only 7 percent of such attacks in 1998. Even before September 11, however, terrorism experts recognized that aviation was an attractive target for terrorists because it is the most visible national symbol of transportation. In 1998, attacks against buses accounted for the greatest number of deaths and injuries for a single mode (table 2).

An area of concern is the growing number of Americans traveling to foreign locations on

This report was predominantly written prior to the September 11, 2001, terrorist attacks on the United States.

Figure 1
Acts of Violence Against Transportation by Geographic Region: 1998

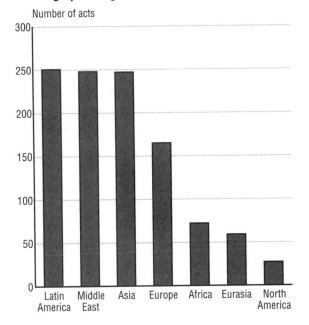

SOURCE: U.S. Department of Transportation, Office of the Secretary of Transportation, Office of Intelligence and Security, *Worldwide Terrorist and Violent Criminal Attacks Against Transportation* (Washington, DC: 1998).

cruises. In 1998, between 6 million and 8 million Americans took cruises to over 200 ports around the world. Moreover, Americans represent more than 80 percent of the passengers on all cruises worldwide, presenting terrorists with a large number of vulnerable targets [2].

Violent acts against domestic transportation doubled between 1997 and 1998 (none of these involved international terrorists). Of the 27 attacks in 1998 (figure 1), 11 were aimed at rail, including sabotage and derailment, attempted bombings, bomb threats, and one case of an incendiary device placed on railroad tracks. The remaining incidents included three bus hijackings; two planned or threatened attacks against bridges; three attacks against aviation; two pipeline bombings; and six maritime incidents that involved bombings, threats against cruise lines, and piracy [2].

Increasingly, sophisticated electronic information and communications systems are used in day-to-day transportation operations, causing concern about the possibility of electronic or "cyber-based" disruptions of key support services. During the late 1990s, the security of the nation's transportation system, potential countermeasures, and the need for improvements prompted the creation of the President's Commission on Critical Infrastructure Protection. The Commission identified three areas where transportation was potentially vulnerable to cyber-terrorists: the Global Positioning System for civil aviation navigation; air traffic control as part of the National Airspace System; and computer-based systems that control modern pipeline operations. Since release of the Commission's report, the government has taken steps to improve coordination of counter-terrorism efforts and has begun working with the transportation industry to identify new threats and vulnerabilities [1].

Sources

1. Executive Office of the President, "Presidential Decision Directive 62: Protecting American's Critical Infrastructure," Fact Sheet, May 1998.

2. U.S. Department of Transportation, Office of the Secretary of Transportation, Office of Intelligence and Security, *Worldwide Terrorist and Violent Criminal Attacks Against Transportation—1998* (Washington, DC: 1999).

International Terrorism and Civil Aviation

Prior to September 11, 2001, the number of terrorist attacks aimed at civil aviation had declined between 1995 and 1999. In fact, incidents of unlawful interference with civil aviation, primarily hijackings and sabotage, had been decreasing since the 1970s (figure 1), while the number of flights, enplanements, and passenger-miles flown by scheduled air carriers had increased dramatically. Nevertheless, because civil aviation is a highly visible national symbol of transportation, terrorism experts recognized that it would remain a tempting target for terrorists [2].

In 2000, attacks against civil aviation worldwide claimed only 2 lives and wounded 27 others. Although the number of fatalities in attacks

Table 1
Incidents Against Aviation by Category: 1996–2000

Category	Number of incidents
Hijackings	64
Airport attacks	30
Off-airport facility attacks	13
Attacks on general aviation	13
Commandeerings[1]	13
Shootings at aircraft	10
Bombings	3

[1] Unlike a hijacking, which occurs in flight, a commandeering occurs when the aircraft is on the ground.

SOURCE: U.S. Department of Transportation, Federal Aviation Administration, Associate Administrator for Civil Aviation Security, personal communication, Apr. 18, 2001.

Figure 1
Hijackings Worldwide: 1970–2000

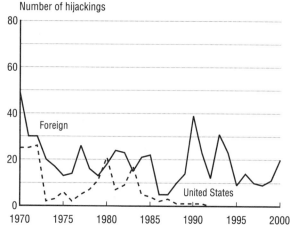

Number of hijackings

NOTE: There were no hijackings in the United States after 1991.

SOURCE: U.S. Department of Transportation, Federal Aviation Administration, Associate Administrator for Civil Aviation Security, personal communication, Apr. 18, 2001.

on aviation had been declining in recent years, aviation has historically been a high profile target for terrorists. Airlines are identified with a nation; therefore, terrorists can equate an attack against a U.S. flag airline with an attack on the United States [4]. Table 1 breaks out worldwide incidents by category.

The terrorist threat to aviation has been continually evolving. For example, after the Federal Aviation Administration (FAA) responded to a rash of hijackings in the 1970s by deploying metal detectors at domestic airports, terrorists began to board aircraft and leave explosive devices in the aircraft via carry-on baggage at various overseas locations. Similarly, after FAA began examining carry-on baggage, terrorists were successful in placing explosive devices on board aircraft via checked baggage without actually boarding the aircraft [5]. Now, terrorists have

This report was predominantly written prior to the September 11, 2001, terrorist attacks on the United States.

exploited a new area of vulnerability by adopting the tactic of suicide hijackings.

The bombing of Pan Am Flight 103 over Lockerbie, Scotland, in December 1988 had stimulated some of the most significant changes in aviation security prior to the September 11 terrorist attacks. Specifically, the Aviation Security Improvement Act of 1990 strengthened the role of the federal government in civil aviation security. Among other things, the Act instructed FAA to fund the development of Explosive Detection Systems (EDSs), establish EDS certification standards, and test and certify EDSs for eventual deployment [5].

Although air carriers have borne the primary responsibility for applying security measures, the White House Commission on Aviation Safety and Security, established after the loss of TWA Flight 800 in July 1996, further strengthened the federal role. Following Commission recommendations, FAA purchased and deployed advanced security technologies, including more than 100 EDS devices for checked baggage screening and more than 570 explosives trace detection devices for use at screening checkpoints at more than 90 U.S. airports. The major carriers assume operational costs for installed EDSs and other technologies [1].

Prior to the September 11 attacks, the most stringent security measures were on flights bound for or arriving from overseas destinations, because the vast majority of criminal and terrorist acts against civil aviation up until that time had taken place overseas. Now, new security measures are in place on domestic flights, and additional security measures are being considered. As we have seen, the decline in terrorist attacks on aviation during the 1990s did not mean that the threat had diminished.

Sources

1. Flynn, C., Associate Administrator for Civil Aviation Security, Federal Aviation Administration, U.S. Department of Transportation, "DOT Flagship Initiatives on National Security: Status Report on Implementation of the Recommendations of the White

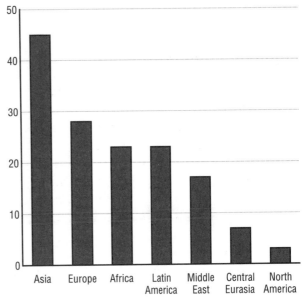

Figure 2

Incidents Against Aviation by Geographic Region: 1996–2000

Number of incidents

SOURCE: U.S. Department of Transportation, Federal Aviation Administration, Associate Administrator for Civil Aviation Security, personal communication, Apr. 18, 2001.

House Commission on Aviation Safety and Security," briefing paper, December 2000.

2. U.S. Department of Transportation, Federal Aviation Administration, Associate Administrator for Civil Aviation Security, personal communication, Apr. 18, 2001.

3. 14 CFR Part 129 (9 June 2000). U.S. Department of Transportation, Federal Aviation Administration. Operations: Foreign Air Carriers and Foreign Operators of U.S.-Registered Aircraft Engaged in Common Carriage. Information available at http://www.faa.gov/avr/avrhome.htm, as of Apr. 21, 2001.

4. U.S. Department of Transportation, Office of the Secretary of Transportation, Office of Intelligence and Security, *Worldwide Terrorist and Violent Criminal Attacks Against Transportation—1998* (Washington, DC: 1999).

5. U.S. General Accounting Office, Resources, Community, and Economic Development Division, *Aviation Security: Additional Actions Needed To Meet Domestic and International Challenges* (Washington, DC: January 1994).

World Petroleum Reserves

Because transportation depends on petroleum for about 95 percent of its energy needs, the long-term availability of petroleum supplies is a key concern. The U.S. Geological Survey (USGS) estimates that total world oil resources are about 2,311 billion barrels. This estimate includes expected but still undiscovered conventional petroleum, revisions made to known (discovered) oil reserves, and remaining reserves. Undiscovered conventional oil reserves are estimated to be 732 billion barrels worldwide (table 1). This estimate is 20 percent higher than earlier USGS assessments, reflecting the expectation that greater reserves than were previously thought to exist will be discovered in the Middle East, the northeast Greenland Shelf, the West Siberia and Caspian Sea areas of the former Soviet Union, and the Niger and Congo delta areas of Africa. USGS also notes for some areas, such as Canada, Mexico, and China, estimated undiscovered reserves are lower than previously reported [2].

The United States has 11 percent (83 billion barrels) of the estimated worldwide total of undiscovered oil, 76 billion barrels of reserve additions, and 32 billion barrels of remaining reserves [2]. Alaska, Texas, California, and offshore areas of the Gulf of Mexico account for the majority of proved oil reserves in the United States.

In the last 100 years, an estimated 710 billion barrels of oil have been produced worldwide. The United States has produced about 171 billion barrels or nearly 50 percent of its total oil endowment [2]. According to the Energy Information Administration, proved reserves have been declining an average of 2 percent per year [1]. Although worldwide resources are plentiful, the availability of these resources is affected by production costs, technologies, markets, and national policies. These uncertainties plus the fact that U.S. oil reserves are declining have implications for U.S. oil import vulnerability and transportation's overwhelming reliability on petroleum.

Table 1
World Petroleum Endowment
(Billion barrels)

	World (excluding U.S.)	United States
Undiscovered conventional	649	83
Reserve growth (conventional)	612	76
Remaining reserves	859	32
Total	**2,120**	**191**
Cumulative production	**539**	**171**
Total oil endowment	**2,659**	**362**

SOURCE: U.S. Department of the Interior, U.S. Geological Survey, *World Petroleum Assessment 2000, Executive Summary* (Reston, VA: April 2000).

Sources

1. U.S. Department of Energy, Energy Information Administration, *U.S. Crude Oil, Natural Gas, and Natural Gas Plant Liquids Reserves 1999* (Washington, DC: 2000).

2. U.S. Department of the Interior, *U.S. Geological Survey, U.S. Geological Survey World Petroleum Assessment 2000—Description and Results* (Washington, DC: June 2000), also available at http://energy.cr.usgs.gov/energy/WorldEnergy/DDS-601, as of Feb. 24, 2001.

Transportation's Dependence on Imported Oil

Transportation is the only sector of the economy that consumes much more oil today than it did 20 years ago, making it highly vulnerable to oil disruptions. Beginning in 1997, the United States imported more than half of the crude oil and petroleum products that it consumed (figure 1), with net imports reaching 9.9 million barrels a day (mmbd) in 1999. The transportation sector, alone, consumed nearly 13 mmbd, which is equivalent to all domestic production plus approximately 40 percent of imports [2].

Oil imports emerged as a national security issue in the 1970s when they grew to a significant fraction of total oil consumption. Today, Canada, Saudi Arabia, Venezuela, Mexico, and Iraq are the top five suppliers of U.S. oil [2] (table 1). Of these, Saudi Arabia, Venezuela, and Iraq are members of the Organization of Petroleum Exporting Countries (OPEC).[1] In 1999, OPEC supplied about 46 percent (4.9 mmbd) of net imports, or 25 percent of total U.S. oil consumption (figure 2).

The U.S. Department of Energy, Energy Information Administration (EIA), expects non-OPEC oil production to increase in the future. Much of this increase will come from the former Soviet Union. Other areas expected to increase production levels include the North Sea area, Canada, Mexico, Australia, Colombia, and Brazil [1].

Nevertheless, as U.S. consumption increases and domestic production decreases, dependence on foreign oil supplies is rising. Whether a high level of oil imports poses serious strategic and economic problems for the United States depends on several factors, such as oil prices,

[1] OPEC includes Algeria, Indonesia, Iran, Iraq, Kuwait, Libya, Qatar, Saudi Arabia, United Arab Emirates, and Venezuela.

Figure 1
U.S. Petroleum Production and Consumption: 1975–1999

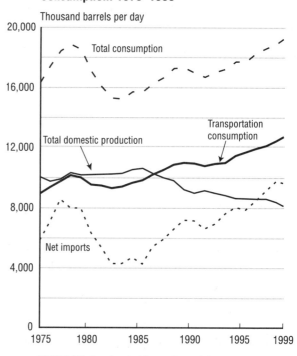

SOURCE: U.S. Department of Energy, Energy Information Administration, *Monthly Energy Review* (Washington, DC: April 2000), table 3.1a; and *Annual Energy Review 1998* (Washington, DC: 1999), table 5.12b.

ability of markets to respond to changes in supply and demand, OPEC's market share, and the importance of oil to the economy.

Sources

1. U.S. Department of Energy, Energy Information Administration, *Annual Energy Outlook 2000,* DOE/EIA-0383 (2000) (Washington, DC: December 1999).

2. ____. *Monthly Energy Review* (Washington, DC: April 2000), tables 1.3, 1.5, 3.1a, and 3.1b.

Table 1
Major Suppliers of U.S. Crude Oil and Petroleum Products
(Thousand barrels per day)

Year	Canada	Saudi Arabia	Venezuela	Mexico	Iraq	Nigeria	Colombia	United Kingdom	Angola	Norway	Virgin Islands	Algeria	Kuwait
1975	846	715	702	71	2	762	9	14	75	17	407	282	16
1980	455	1,261	481	533	28	857	4	176	42	144	388	488	27
1985	770	168	605	816	46	293	23	310	110	32	247	187	21
1990	934	1,339	1,025	755	518	800	182	189	237	102	282	280	86
1995	1,332	1,344	1,480	1,068	0	627	219	383	367	273	278	234	218
1999	1,539	1,478	1,493	1,324	725	657	468	365	361	304	280	259	248

NOTE: The country of origin for petroleum products may not be the country of origin for the crude oil used to produce the products. Refined products imported from western European refining areas may have been produced from Middle Eastern crude oil.

SOURCE: U.S. Department of Energy, Energy Information Administration, *Monthly Energy Review* (Washington, DC: April 2000), tables 3.1b, 3.3a–3.3h.

Figure 2
U.S. Oil Imports

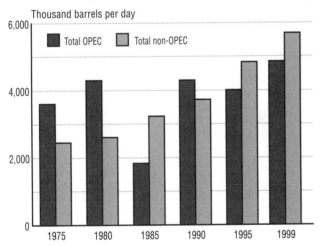

SOURCE: U.S. Department of Energy, Energy Information Administration, *Monthly Energy Review* (Washington, DC: April 2000), tables 3.1b, 3.3a–3.3h.

U.S. Merchant Shipbuilding and Repair

Because of the need to ship military forces and materiel around the globe, maintaining a strong manufacturing base capable of designing and building ships is a national security concern. Ships also provide much of the capacity needed to move international trade. Shipbuilding is, thus, a key industry in the United States and around the world.

In 1999, South Korea overtook Japan as the world leader in merchant shipbuilding in terms of gross tonnage. These two countries accounted for 69 percent of the gross tonnage of merchant ships on order as of July 2000. The United States ranked 11th, with about 1 percent of the world's gross tonnage on order [1] (table 1). Nevertheless, the U.S. shipbuilding industry has made some progress in its efforts to reemerge as an active participant in the commercial shipbuilding market (figure 1). The United States has 19 major private shipyards that can build vessels over 122 meters in length. More than 200 privately owned firms repair ships, but only 73 are classified as major repair yards with the capacity to handle vessels over 122 meters in length.

Over the last 10 years, the U.S. shipbuilding industry has invested more than $2.2 billion in capital improvement projects, the majority of which were targeted at increasing efficiency and competitiveness (figure 2). Investments were made in new shipyard layouts, and new cranes, transporters, automated equipment, and highly mechanized production systems were purchased [3]. Several government programs also have provided assistance in revitalization efforts. These include an expanded Ship Financing Program (Title XI) of the Merchant Marine Act of 1936, as

Table 1

World Orderbook as of July 2000

Self-propelled vessels of 100 gross tons and over

Rank	Country of build	Number of vessels	Total gross tons
1	Korea (South)	373	23,033,607
2	Japan	374	16,476,608
3	China, People's Republic of	191	4,215,232
4	Germany	71	1,966,963
5	Italy	53	1,875,957
6	China, Republic of (Taiwan)	37	1,663,082
7	Poland	80	1,611,161
8	Croatia	32	707,276
9	Finland	8	681,600
10	France	14	654,144
11	United States	20	579,081
12	Romania	80	578,297
13	Spain	29	529,153
14	Denmark	12	462,025
15	Netherlands	120	421,654
16	Ukraine	17	385,654
17	Russia	45	292,686
18	Philippines	9	233,176
19	Turkey	43	227,376
20	Bulgaria	15	160,822
	Total top 20	**1,623**	**56,755,554**
	Top 20% of total	90.0%	98.4%
	World total	1,793	57,655,516

SOURCE: Lloyds Maritime Information Service, World Orderbook data, as of March 2001.

Figure 1
**U.S. Commercial Shipbuilding Orderbook
History: As of December 31, 1999**
Ships of 1,000 gross tons and over

Number of ships

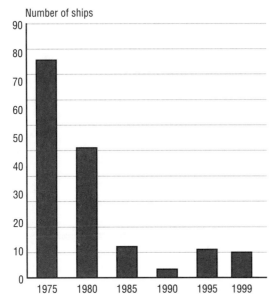

Figure 2
**Capital Investments in the U.S. Shipbuilding
and Repair Industry**

$ in millions

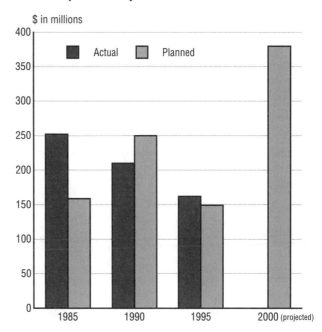

amended, and the National Shipbuilding and Conversion Act of 1993.

Revitalization efforts, however, have been complicated by an overall decline in world shipbuilding price levels. In 1998, world newbuilding price levels were less than most recorded world newbuilding prices in 1997. This decline continued into 1999, possibly due to a worldwide decrease in vessel orders and resulting competition [2].

Sources

1. Lloyds' Maritime Information Service, World Orderbook, datafile, July 2000.

2. United Nations Conference on Trade and Development, *Review of Maritime Transport 1999* (New York, NY: United Nations, 1999), p. 35.

3. U.S. Department of Transportation, Maritime Administration, *MARAD '99* (Washington, DC: May 2000), pp. 16–20.

U.S. Aircraft Manufacturing

Aircraft play a key role in the national security of the United States. Thus, maintaining a strong manufacturing base with a trained and skilled workforce capable of designing and building aircraft and aircraft components is an issue of national security. In 1999, the aerospace industry employed 846,000 workers, representing 4.6 percent of all manufacturing jobs in the United States. Although the number of U.S. aircraft produced has declined sharply since the late 1970s (figure 1), the U.S. aerospace industry as a whole—which includes the production of civil and military aircraft as well as space and missile systems—remains internationally competitive and has generated strong sales, profits, and net exports.

Commercial aircraft sales recovered from the recession that struck the industry in the late 1980s and early 1990s. The sales of general aviation aircraft rebounded from a low of 899 produced in 1992 to 2,496 in 1999—but this was nowhere near the record high of 17,817 aircraft produced in 1978 [1]. Much of the decline in general aviation aircraft production in the late 1970s and early 1980s coincided with increasing lawsuits against manufacturers. Liability costs rose and production and sales fell sharply. The decline in production and sales was reversed after enactment of the General Aviation Revitalization Act of 1994, which limited lawsuits against manufacturers [3].

Production of large transport-category aircraft over the last 20 years has experienced annual increases and decreases but no decline comparable to that of general aviation. In 1979, the United States produced 376 transport-category aircraft, compared with 620 in 1999. The United States' sole remaining manufacturer of such air-

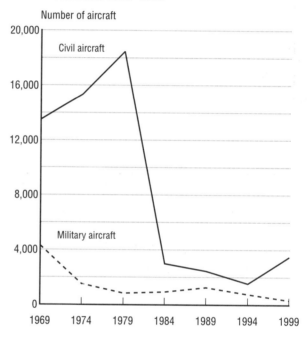

Figure 1
U.S. Civil and Military Aircraft Production: 1969–1999

Number of aircraft

SOURCE: Aerospace Industries Association, *Aerospace Facts and Figures, 2000/2001* (Washington, DC: 2000).

craft, the Boeing Company, retains a sizeable portion of the world market but faces growing competition from its chief European competitor, Airbus Industrie [2] (figure 2).

The U.S. aerospace industry is the single largest U.S. net exporter, with a positive trade balance in 1999 of $37 billion (figure 3). The industry exports over 40 percent of its total output and nearly 75 percent of its commercial products. Aircraft manufacturing and sales make up the largest component of the U.S. aerospace industry. U.S. manufacturers shipped 3,477 civil aircraft in 1999 with a total value of $45 billion, an increase

Figure 2
World Market Share of Large Commercial Transport Aircraft by Value of Deliveries

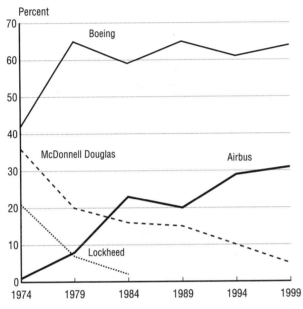

NOTES: In 1997, McDonnell Douglas became a subsidiary of Boeing. As of 1984, Lockheed stopped producing commercial transport aircraft.

SOURCES: 1974–1989—U.S. Congress, Office of Technology Assessment, *Competing Economies: America, Europe, and the Pacific Rim*, October 1991, available at http://www.ota.nap.edu/pubs.html.
1994–1999—The Boeing Company.

Figure 3
Aerospace Exports and Imports

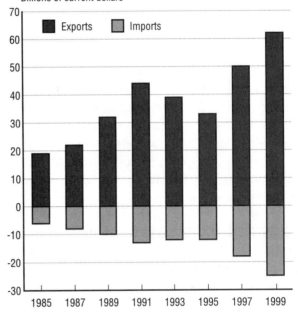

SOURCE: Aerospace Industries Association, 2000.

of 342 aircraft and $3.7 billion over 1998 levels. Civil transport production accounted for 620 aircraft valued at $38 billion [1].

While U.S. production of civil aircraft has been increasing in recent years, production of military aircraft continues to decline. In 1999, the United States produced 333 military aircraft, down from 811 in 1995. Of that total, 226 were exported and 107 were delivered to U.S. military agencies. Much of the decline in U.S. military aircraft production can be attributed to the end of the Cold War [1].

Sources

1. Aerospace Industries Association, *Aerospace Facts and Figures: 1999/2000* (Washington, DC: 1999).

2. Vilhauer, Robert, Aviation Affairs Office, The Boeing Company, personal communication, Sept. 28, 2000.

3. Aerospace Industries Association, Director of Aerospace Research Center, personal communication, Feb. 7, 2001.

Drug Smuggling and Interdiction

The U.S. government has identified drug smuggling as one of our nation's foremost national security problems. In 1998, an estimated 6.2 percent of Americans 12 years of age and older were illicit drug users [1]. To address this problem, $17.9 billion was spent on drug control programs in fiscal year (FY) 1999. Of that total, $3.2 billion was earmarked for drug interdiction operations (figure 1).

The increasing flow of trade and passenger travel means that more cars, trucks, and railcars are crossing U.S. borders, and more ships are arriving at U.S. ports from all over the world. Moreover, the growth in the use of containers to ship commodities has facilitated cargo transfers and increased intermodal transportation services, thus allowing an easier worldwide flow of goods from road to rail to sea. With increasing traffic and the flow of goods comes increasing opportunity to smuggle illegal drugs [2].

The U.S. Coast Guard (USCG) is the lead federal agency for maritime drug interdiction and shares the lead for air interdiction with the U.S. Customs Service. USCG patrols the Transit Zone, a 6 million square mile area, which includes the Western Atlantic, the Caribbean, the Gulf of Mexico, and the Eastern Pacific area. Cooperative agreements with nearly two dozen nations throughout the Transit Zone serve as the basis for combined U.S. and foreign counterdrug operations and enable USCG to exercise limited law enforcement authority inside foreign territory and aboard foreign-flagged vessels.

In FY 1999, USCG seized a record 111,689 pounds of cocaine—equal to 506 million drug doses, with an estimated street value of $3.7 bil-

Figure 1
Federal Drug Control Spending by Function: FY 1999
(In billions)

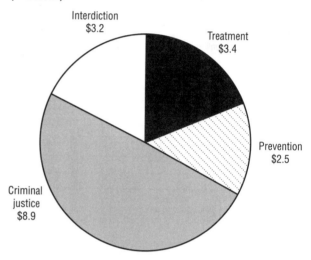

SOURCE: Executive Office of the President, Office of National Drug Control Policy, *Drug Data Summary*, April 1999, available at http://whitehousedrugpolicy.gov, as of Sept. 3, 2000.

lion (figure 2). USCG also launched a new counter-narcotics initiative in the Caribbean. This initiative, called Operation New Frontier, resulted in the confiscation of more than 6,900 pounds of narcotics [3].

Control of the processing and sale of illicit drugs worldwide is a continuous challenge. The United States has wrestled with drug control since the 1930s when the Federal Bureau of Narcotics was first established. Since then, increasingly rigorous antidrug programs have been established as demand has increased. Maritime trafficking of illegal drugs is expected to remain a global threat in the near future [1].

Figure 2
U.S. Coast Guard Drug Seizures: 1991–1999

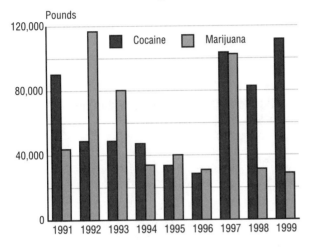

SOURCE: U.S. Department of Transportation, U.S. Coast Guard, *The 1999 Annual Report of the U.S. Coast Guard* (Washington, DC: May 2000).

Sources

1. Executive Office of the President, Office of National Drug Control Policy, *National Drug Control Strategy 2000*, chapter 1, available at http://www.whitehousedrugpolicy.gov/policy/ndcs00, as of Sept. 7, 2000.

2. Office of Naval Intelligence and U.S. Department of Transportation, U.S. Coast Guard, *Threats and Challenges to Maritime Security, 1999*, available at http://www.uscg.mil, as of September 2000.

3. U.S. Department of Transportation, U.S. Coast Guard, *The 1999 Annual Report of the U.S. Coast Guard* (Washington, DC: May 2000).

Alien Smuggling and Interdiction

Many alien interdiction cases begin as U.S. Coast Guard (USCG) search and rescue operations, and most occur in high seas in overcrowded and unseaworthy vessels. According to USCG, professional criminals vie for a share of the $10 billion a year migrant smuggling activity [1]. For example, as much as $6 million may be paid by a large boatload of migrants from the People's Republic of China (PRC) to be smuggled into the United States. USCG reports that PRC migrants pay between $35,000 and $40,000 each, and Cuban migrants pay between $3,000 and $8,000 each to smugglers [2].

From 1995 to 2000, the majority of USCG interdictions involved migrants from Cuba, the Dominican Republic, the PRC, and Haiti (figure 1). USCG estimates that approximately 20,000 illegal PRC migrants reach the Western Hemisphere by sea each year and most are bound for the United States. Often, Guam is used as a stopping point to gain entrance into the United States. Once in Guam, migrants can be sent to the United States for court hearings on requests for asylum or to address criminal behavior; once in the United States, they can disappear [3].

Cuban interdiction operations differ from those of other countries. Under the 1966 Cuban Adjustment Act (Public Law 89-732), Cuban migrants who reach U.S. shores can stay in the United States and obtain permanent residency status within one year. If captured at sea, they are returned to Cuba or taken to a safe haven [2]. Many Cubans are transported in regular high-

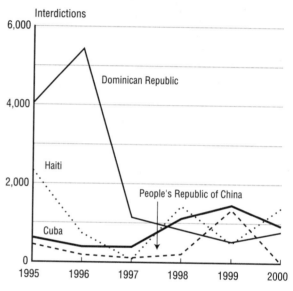

Figure 1
U.S. Coast Guard Migrant Interdictions by Sea: 1995–2000
(Top origin countries)

SOURCE: U.S. Department of Transportation, U.S. Coast Guard, *Coast Interdictions by Sea: Calendar Year 1995–2000*, available at http://www.uscg.mil/hq/g-o/g-opl/mle/amiostats1.htm#cy, as of March 2001.

speed boats that blend into normal boating traffic. Near the U.S. shore, migrants are transferred to small rafts that are difficult to interdict.

Overall, USCG expects illegal migrant activity by sea to rise. In 2000, Haitian and Ecuadorian migrant interdictions together accounted for 58 percent of the total USCG activity for the year (figure 2).

Figure 2
U.S. Coast Guard Interdictions by Sea: 2000

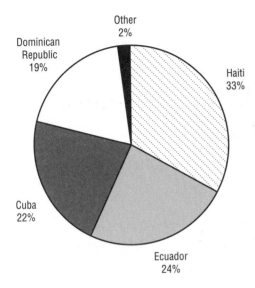

SOURCE: U.S. Department of Transportation, U.S. Coast Guard, *Coast Interdictions by Sea: Calendar Year 2000*, available at http://www.uscg.mil/hq/g-o/g-opl/mle/amiostats1.htm#cy, as of Dec. 3, 2000.

Sources

1. Office of Naval Intelligence and U.S. Department of Transportation, U.S. Coast Guard, *Threats and Challenges to Maritime Security* (Washington, DC: March 1999).

2. U.S. Department of Transportation, U.S. Coast Guard, *The 1999 Annual Report of the U.S. Coast Guard* (Washington, DC: May 2000).

3. ____. *America's Coast Guard: Safeguarding U.S. Maritime Safety and Security in the 21st Century* (Washington, DC: 2000).

Chapter 8
State of Transportation Statistics

State of Transportation Statistics

People and organizations make innumerable transportation decisions every day, including when, where, and how to travel and ship goods, what investments to make in equipment and infrastructure, and how to deal with the negative consequences of transportation. To make the transportation system work effectively and efficiently, decisionmakers in both the public and private sectors need good information. A wealth of information is currently collected, analyzed, and disseminated by a variety of organizations, but a number of questions arise about the data.

1. Do we have data on the right subjects?
2. Are the data reliable and accurate?
3. Are the data understandable, accessible, and timely for decisionmaking?

The Bureau of Transportation Statistics (BTS), established in 1992 as an administration within the U.S. Department of Transportation (DOT), has key data responsibilities in the domain of transportation. BTS's mandates, reaffirmed by reauthorization legislation in 1998, are to support the data-collection programs that already exist in DOT, to ensure that these programs provide data of adequate quality for the decisions they support, to identify data gaps, and to analyze all data pertinent to transportation in support of policymaking and evaluation.

Transportation decisionmakers need data that are relevant, high quality, timely, and complete, and ideally, the data should be comparable with other available data. Many reports over the years have pointed to the need for such data [1 ,2 ,3]. While improvements have been made, shortcomings remain. For instance, timeliness continues to be a problem. Much available data in key transportation areas may be a year or even several years out of date when they are publicly issued. Examples include the Federal Transit Administra-

tion's National Transit Database, the Federal Highway Administration's Highway Performance Monitoring System, and BTS's American Travel Survey. Data gaps remain in several areas, such as the location, mode, and other characteristics of U.S. imports and exports, congestion, and transportation's impact on groundwater, animal habitat, and land use [6, 7]. Some data currently collected fail the test of relevance for decisionmaking, particularly for local decisionmakers. For instance, the Commodity Flow Survey collects much national and state freight data, but many of the decisions about freight infrastructure are made locally. Information is also needed about freight movement at the metropolitan level.

To address these issues, BTS developed in 2000 a strategic five-year plan for transportation statistics (see box 1) and has undertaken several initiatives that fall broadly into three areas: 1) data collection, 2) data quality, and 3) data compilation, storage, and dissemination.

Data Collection

BTS and many other organizations collect data on myriad aspects of the transportation system, such as airline and motor carrier operations, freight flows, passenger characteristics and movement, energy consumption, environmental impacts, and makeup of the transportation system itself. The following areas are illustrative of some of these data collections.

Airline Data

BTS's Office of Airline information (OAI) collects and publishes on-time data for airlines, as well as more extensive operating data for both domestic and foreign airlines. OAI also collects detailed financial statistics for domestic airlines and various statistics on service quality. The data report-

Box 1: A Strategic Plan for Transportation Statistics: 2000–2005

This plan, released in February 2000, is aimed at improving transportation statistics needed for data and analysis. The plan identifies six key areas or attributes for data with goals for achievement of each.

- **Relevance:** the data needs of decisionmakers should be anticipated, and the information that is provided should directly address those needs.

- **Quality:** data for decisionmaking needs to be accurate, reliable, and objective.

- **Timeliness:** the lag between data compilation and reporting needs to be reduced, so decisionmakers have as near to a real-time view as possible of the transportation system and the factors that affect it.

- **Comparability:** transportation data should be consistent across modes and time periods to provide a broad perspective for program and resource decisionmaking.

- **Completeness:** all areas of transportation should be covered.

- **Utility:** data should be easy to access, understand, and use.

ing is mandated by law, and several issues are now driving changes in the reporting regulations. Public concern about airline delays led to legislation requiring better data on the causes of delay—a DOT/industry task force has made several recommendations and rulemaking will follow. The department also has been working for some time to modernize the data-collection program, bringing it up to date with changes that have occurred in the airline industry, and to take advantage of advances in information technology to reduce the data-collection burden.

Motor Carrier Data

BTS collects financial and operating data from for-hire trucking and passenger bus companies with annual operating revenues over $3 million (equivalent to a fleet of about 25 to 30 vehicles). BTS is undertaking an effort to improve the completeness, accuracy, and timeliness of the motor carrier financial and operating data. In addition, the database of trucking companies that might be subject to reporting has been updated. In December 2000, a series of outreach sessions was held to work with trucking companies toward better and more complete data.

Transportation System Data

Coordinated by BTS, the Omnibus Survey is a DOT-wide effort aimed at collecting information about the transportation system, how it is used, and how users view it. Information is gathered each month from a randomly selected sample of 1,000 households. In addition to a core set of questions, each month the Office of the Secretary and/or modal administrations can propose new questions for inclusion in that month's survey. Survey results are available within 30 days of the mailout, and the analysis is completed within the next month or sooner, if necessary. The results of the first Omnibus Household Survey were made available in August 2000, and the report that was issued highlighted safety. Targeted surveys aimed at specific topics are also planned. Omnibus Surveys are intended to provide timely snapshots of highly visible issues, but are not intended to substitute for more comprehensive data-collection efforts.

Freight and Passenger Data

Sample surveys sponsored by BTS in conjunction with agencies such as the Census Bureau and the Federal Highway Administration include the Commodity Flow Survey and the National Household Travel Survey. Freight data are collected by the Commodity Flow Survey, a survey of freight shippers that includes shipment variables such as mode, commodity, weight, value, and distance. Passenger data, both long-distance and local passenger travel by American households, are collected in the National Household Travel Survey (formerly the Nationwide Personal Transportation Survey and the American Travel Survey), sponsored by BTS and the Federal Highway Administration. The joint survey gathers trip-related data such as mode of transportation, and duration, distance, and purpose of trip. It also gathers demographic, geographic, and economic data for analysis purposes. These two surveys are conducted about every five years. While providing national benchmarking, the surveys have been too infrequent to track fast-moving changes in transportation.

Energy and Environmental Data

Most of the data needed to track transportation energy and environmental issues have long been outside the purview of DOT. Data on energy are collected or estimated by the Energy Information Agency (EIA) of the U.S. Department of Energy. The U.S. Environmental Protection Agency (EPA) provides a variety of data in the environmental area. Some examples are: estimates of air pollutant emissions from the use of transportation vehicles, emissions data from manufacturers of transportation equipment and petroleum refining, estimates of the disposed amount of some types of transportation equipment, and data obtained by monitoring air quality across the nation.

Both EIA and EPA make annual estimates of transportation's greenhouse gas emissions, which may contribute to global climate change. While both agencies use EIA survey data on energy consumption as a basis for their estimates, their coverage and methodologies differ, resulting in different datasets. Research in 2000 by the DOT Center for Climate Change and Environmental Forecasting led to a finding that some fundamental data on freight modes is unavailable leading to estimates of freight greenhouse gas emissions that are inferior to those on passenger vehicle emissions. The Center has initiated a study to determine the level of effort needed to improve these data estimations.

Data Gaps

Gaps in data may involve the absence of data, data that are of poor quality, or data that are collected but not provided in a timely manner or in a form that a decisionmaker can use. For example, a known major data gap is the absence of good inland U.S. origin/destination data for traffic moving in international commerce. A BTS project is currently underway to assess gaps in transporta-

tion data and the benefits and costs of possible solutions. This process involves consultation among major stakeholders including those within DOT and congressional staff, state DOTs, metropolitan planning organizations, the transportation industry, and research organizations.

Data Quality

DOT leadership and customers have identified data quality as a high priority, cross-modal problem. Data issues currently being addressed include safety, performance measures, and hazardous materials.

Safety Data Action Plan

One major effort is now underway in support of DOT's strategic goal to promote public health and safety by working toward the elimination of transportation-related fatalities, injuries, and property damage. This Safety Data Action Plan, developed with stakeholders and approved by the DOT Safety Council, has six recommendations for improving the quality, timeliness, and relevance of transportation safety data. They are to:

1. establish a lead agency to ensure intermodal collaboration,
2. develop an intermodal database,
3. develop data standards,
4. improve data quality,
5. expand transportation resources, and
6. conduct focused research projects to address data shortcomings (see box 2).

Performance Measures

Accurate, timely, and comparable transportation data will improve the credibility and thus the utility of statistics needed for performance measurement. The DOT fiscal year 2001 Performance Plan identifies performance indicators and goals that will be used to measure progress in achieving strategic goals [5]. To help in the performance measurement process, BTS is working with other DOT administrations to develop a framework to identify and implement best current statistical practices for data collection. A compendium of source and accuracy statements has been devel-

Box 2: Safety Data Action Plan Research Projects

The 10 research projects identified by the Safety Data Action Plan to improve data quality and fill data gaps will:

1. reengineer Department of Transportation data systems,
2. develop common criteria for reporting deaths and injuries,
3. develop common denominators for safety measures,
4. advance the timeliness of safety data,
5. develop common data on accident circumstances,
6. develop better data on accident precursors,
7. expand the collection of near-miss data to all modes,
8. link safety data with other data,
9. explore options for using technology in data collection, and
10. expand, improve, and coordinate safety data analyses.

oped for each of the data programs used in the performance report. Efforts are underway to develop departmental statistical standards and implement other steps to assure accurate data. The DOT Office of the Inspector General will verify and validate performance measures on a selective basis each year.

Hazardous Materials Data

The Secretary of Transportation delegated authority to BTS in coordination with the Associate Deputy Secretary to work with DOT administrations to determine data needs, collections strategies, and analytical techniques appropriate for implementing the department's hazardous materials program. This delegation of authority was recommended in a departmentwide evaluation of the hazardous materials transportation program co-chaired by the Office of the Inspector General and the Research and Special Programs Administration (RSPA) [4]. The report also recommended that BTS lead a project to identify data needs, identify and implement ways to improve the Hazardous Materials Information System and the Unified Shipper Enforcement Data System databases, and work with RSPA to design a process to more fully evaluate and analyze incident data.

Quality improvements must be made database by database.

Database Audits

At the request of Congress, BTS recently audited four transportation databases and found a wide range of quality issues and opportunities for improvement. The four databases audited were the Enhanced Traffic Management System (ETMS), the Metropolitan Intelligent Transportation Systems (ITS) Deployment Tracking Database, Office of Intelligence and Security (OIS) Survey of DOT Operating Administrations, and the Merchant Mariner Licensing and Documentation System (MMLD). The ETMS data were not subject to errors large enough to impair their primary use. Both the Metropolitan ITS Deployment Tracking Database and the MMLD system were of reasonable quality, but both contained some systematic errors due to missing, incomplete, or inaccurate data records. However, the data contained in the OIS Survey of DOT Operating Administrations were found to be unusable and possibly misleading because of high levels of sampling and nonsampling error.

Other databases to be assessed include the Highway Performance Monitoring System, motor carrier safety, seat belt usage, runway incursions, recreational boating accidents, and grade-crossing safety. Altogether, BTS has agreed to perform a quality review of about 80 major databases. The result in each case will be a report to the database administrator with specific recommendations for quality improvement.

Compiling, Storing, and Disseminating Transportation Data

Transportation data are of little use if they are not available and accessible to decisionmakers and others. Historically, decisionmakers have had to make do with datasets that essentially age between collection and publishing cycles. Now, largely because of the Internet, this static system is being replaced by one that offers highly dynamic capabilities. As soon as compiled data are checked for quality, they can be immediately shared with potential users worldwide.

A number of efforts are underway at BTS and elsewhere to make data more accessible. These include the Intermodal Transportation Database (ITDB), the National Transportation Library (NTL), geographic information systems, *Transportation Indicators,* and international trade data.

Intermodal Transportation Database

The ITDB will eventually provide one-stop shopping for a large number of transportation-related databases. Although current data programs will continue to collect and record data in their usual ways, the ITDB will create a unified interface that allows seamless integration of multiple datasets. Thus, users can obtain all the available information from a single source, in a uniform format, rather than having to contact multiple sources, some of which have data programs that many users may find difficult to manipulate. Additionally, the ITDB will provide standard-format documentation and a user-friendly front-end that will support an expanding array of statistical analyses, statistical graphics, and geographic displays.

The initial databases in the ITDB will be those called for by Congress in the Transportation Equity Act for the 21st Century (TEA-21): freight and passenger volumes and patterns of movement, the location and connectivity of transportation facilities and services, and transportation expenditures and capital stocks. Other transportation data related to areas such as safety, energy, the environment, and demography are expected to be available through the ITDB.

National Transportation Library

The NTL is an electronic "virtual" library, available only on the Internet, providing broad access to the nation's transportation research and planning literature. Congress directed the establishment of the NTL in TEA-21. Currently, the NTL contains over 150,000 documents and abstracts for another half million documents.

Geographic Information Systems

Geospatial data can be graphically portrayed in ways that are compelling for decisionmakers. BTS creates, maintains, and distributes geospatial data through the National Transportation Atlas Database program, outlined in TEA-21 legislation. These data are obtained from multiple sources and include the National Highway Planning network, a national rail network, public-use airports and runways, and Amtrak stations. In the near future, layers will be added for land use, waterways, transit, ITS, and satellite imagery. Together, these data comprise the transportation layers of the National Spatial Data Infrastructure. This program distributes transportation geodata and a number of geographic reference files including state, county, congressional district, and metropolitan statistical area boundaries.

Transportation Indicators

BTS has developed a set of transportation indicators published each month on the BTS website. The indicators fall into two broad categories: those that provide context about the economy and society in which transportation functions and those that convey interesting information about an aspect of transportation. Drawn from a wide variety of sources, the indicators are intended to provide decisionmakers with as timely data as possible, using quarterly, monthly, and in some cases, weekly information. The process of developing the indicators has helped to draw attention to data gaps, such as areas where data are out of date or where reliable data are unavailable. To address some of these concerns, research is planned to develop new indicators or to improve timeliness of data where practical.

International Trade Data

In an era of globalization, trade and transportation data are closely connected. BTS compiles, analyzes, and publishes information on U.S. foreign trade, variables that may influence U.S. global competitiveness, key international trends in transportation, and comparative statistics on transportation in various countries. These data provide context for understanding how the U.S. transportation system might be affected by exports, imports, and international travel, and set the stage for harmonizing international data. While the data may be published in printed format, much of these data are available on the BTS website. BTS also works closely with its statistical counterparts in Canada, Mexico, and many other countries, through a variety of exchange and collaborative activities.

Using Information Technology

Attention is also being focused on advances in information technology and its implications for providing timely data that can be collected unobtrusively. For instance, BTS currently collects a 10 percent sample of airline tickets sold by air carriers. Information on airline tickets is also processed through an industry clearinghouse to allow the allocation of revenues when travel is not completed on the ticketed airline. This clearinghouse information is a potential source of data on the patterns and prices of commercial airline travel in the United States. The advantages of using these data would include: the reduced burden on the airlines through elimination of the current survey; high-quality data because there will be no errors due to sampling or itinerary changes; and timeliness, because of the highly automated process. Another example of data derived from information technology is highway operational data automatically collected by traffic agencies as a result of the implementation of advanced traffic management systems. Such data could be used as a source of very timely information on metropolitan traffic patterns and performance.

Transportation Workers

To date, little attention has been focused on the transportation workforce that, like the population in general, is aging. As a result, the transportation industry has begun to forecast serious shortfalls of skilled labor. Some sectors may be hit harder than others, depending on the growth of the sector and the age distribution of the existing workforce. In order to provide data for decisions on workforce development, BTS is planning to improve the collection and analysis of data in this area.

Economics and the Transportation System

Another important topic that needs more attention is how to pay for the transportation system. Financing of the transportation system has been a central issue for many years, but there are still limited data spanning the entire system—including federal, state, local, and private sector investments. BTS is planning a project to estimate the demand for transportation funding at all levels of government over the past 10 years and the likely demand in the future. This will be matched with data on revenue to identify shortfalls or surpluses in the transportation financial system.

The Transportation Satellite Accounts is a joint effort of BTS and the Bureau of Economic Analysis (BEA) to provide a detailed picture of transportation in the nation's Gross Domestic Product (GDP). By enhancing the data used in constructing GDP estimates, BTS and BEA have been able to quantify detailed values for input-output models that allow in-depth resolution of the economic interactions between specific categories of transportation and other segments of the U.S. economy. A key feature of this work is the estimation of the in-house transportation sector, transportation services provided by firms in nontransportation sectors of the economy. This includes, for instance, trucks owned and operated by a grocery chain. Until recently, reliable estimates of this sector did not exist.

Furthermore, through a collaborative research effort, BTS and BEA have been developing a method for "capital stock accounting" to measure the value of the nation's transportation infrastructure, as directed in the TEA-21 legislation. This supports efficient asset management and enables other DOT modes to forecast remediation requirements. Initial data are expected in Fall 2001.

Conclusion

Advances in transportation and communications technologies have facilitated commodity production and consumption, allowing it to take place at greater speeds and on a global scale. In order to keep pace with these advances, decisionmaking must be increasingly rapid, flexible, and have broader geographical scope.

Data systems designed to support decisionmaking must provide the right data at the right time. Moreover, data must be accessible to a wide variety of actors with varying degrees of sophistication in data handling and analytical capabilities. Most daily operational transportation decisions are made at the state and local level. Federal agencies collect data from state and local entities largely for policy development and enforcement purposes, and the ways in which these data are ultimately presented and disseminated need to be made relevant to the needs of state and local decisionmakers.

Fast and flexible worldwide production and consumption has also raised the profile of intermodal transportation for both people and goods domestically and internationally. The increasingly intermodal environment must be supported with data that are comparable across modes and countries and measures movements from origin to destination.

Sources

1. Transportation Research Board, *Data for Decisions: Requirements for National Transportation Policy Making,* Special Report 234 (Washington, DC: National Academy Press, 1992).

2. Transportation Research Board, National Research Council, *The Bureau of Transportation Statistics: Priorities for the Future,* C.F. Citro and J.L. Norwood, eds. (Washington, DC: National Academy Press, 1997).

3. ____. *Information Needs to Support State and Local Transportation Decision Making into the 21st Century* (Washington, DC: National Academy Press, 1997).

4. U.S. Department of Transportation, *Departmentwide Program Evaluation of the Hazardous Materials Transportation Programs (HMPE,)* available at http://hazmat.dot.gov/hmpe.htm, as of April 2001.

5. ____. *FY 1999 Performance Report/FY 2001 Performance Plan* (Washington, DC: 2000).

6. U.S. Department of Transportation, Bureau of Transportation Statistics, *Bicycle and Pedestrian Data: Sources, Needs, and Gaps* (Washington, DC: 2000).

7. ____. *Transportation Statistics Beyond ISTEA: Critical Gaps and Strategic Responses* (Washington, DC: 1998).

Appendices

Appendix A: List of Acronyms and Initialisms

ADA	Americans with Disabilities Act
AFV	alternative fuel vehicle
APTA	American Public Transit Association
ATS	American Travel Survey
BAC	blood alcohol concentration
BEA	Bureau of Economic Analysis
BTS	Bureau of Transportation Statistics
Btu	British thermal unit
CAA	Clean Air Act
CAFE	Corporate Average Fuel Economy
CFR	Code of Federal Regulations
CFS	Commodity Flow Survey
CO	carbon monoxide
CO_2	carbon dioxide
CRAF	Civil Reserve Air Fleet
dB	decibels
dBA	A-weighted decibels
DGPS	Differential Global Positioning System
DNL	day-night noise level
DOD	U.S. Department of Defense
DOI	U.S. Department of the Interior
DOT	U.S. Department of Transportation
DWT	deadweight tons
EDS	Explosive Detection Systems
EIA	Energy Information Administration
EJ	environmental justice
EPA	U.S. Environmental Protection Agency
EPNdb	effective perceived noise level
ETC	electronic toll collection
ETMS	Enhanced Traffic Management System
FAA	Federal Aviation Administration
FARs	Federal Aviation Regulations
FARS	Fatality Analysis Reporting System
FHWA	Federal Highway Administration
FRA	Federal Railroad Administration
FTA	Federal Transit Administration
FY	fiscal year
GA	general aviation
GAO	General Accounting Office
GDD	Gross Domestic Demand

GDP   Gross Domestic Product
GHG   greenhouse gas
GPRA   Government Performance and Results Act
GPS   Global Positioning System

HAPs   hazardous air pollutants
HMIS   Hazardous Materials Information System
HPMS   Highway Performance Monitoring System
HSR   high-speed rail
HTF   Highway Trust Fund

ICC   Interstate Commerce Commission
INS   Immigration and Naturalization Service
IPCC   Intergovernmental Panel on Climate Change
ISTEA   Intermodal Surface Transportation Efficiency Act
IT   information technology
ITDB   Intermodal Transportation Database
ITS   intelligent transportation system

LNG   liquefied natural gas
LPG   liquefied petroleum gas
LTV   light trucks and vans

MARAD   Maritime Administration
MMLD   Merchant Mariner Licensing Documentation
mmtc   million metric tons of carbon
mpg   miles per gallon
mph   miles per hour
MPO   metropolitan planning organization
MSATs   mobile source air toxics
MSP   Maritime Security Programs
MSW   municipal solid waste
MTBE   methyl-tertiary-butyl-ether

NAFTA   North American Free Trade Agreement
NASS GES   National Automotive Sampling System General Estimates System
NDRF   National Defense Reserve Fleet
NEC   Northeast Corridor
NHIS-D   National Health Interview Survey on Disability
NHTSA   National Highway Traffic Safety Administration
NO_2 nitrogen dioxide
NO_x nitrogen oxides
NPIAS   National Plan of Integrated Airport Systems
NPL   National Priorities List
NPTS   Nationwide Personal Transportation Survey
NTL   National Transportation Library

OPEC   Organization of Petroleum Exporting Countries
OPS   Office of Pipeline Safety
ORNL   Oak Ridge National Laboratory
OSRA   Ocean Shipping Reform Act

PCCIP	President's Commission on Critical Infrastructure Protection
PFD	personal flotation device
PM-2.5	particulate matter of 2.5 microns in diameter or smaller
PM-10	particulate matter of 10 microns in diameter or smaller
pmt	passenger-miles of travel
PSC	Port State Control
PSR	Present Serviceability Rating
PTC	positive train control
PUV	personal-use vehicle

| quads | quadrillion |

RFG	reformulated gasoline
ROR	run-off-the-road
RRF	Ready Reserve Fleet
RSPA	Research and Special Programs Administration

SCTG	Standard Classification of Transported Goods
SO_2	sulfur dioxide
SSI	Supplemental Security Income
STRAHNET	Strategic Highway Network
SUV	sport utility vehicle

TANF	Temporary Assistance for Needy Families
TEA-21	Transportation Equity Act for the 21st Century
TEU	20-foot equivalent container unit
TICSA	Transportation Infrastructure Capital Stock Account
TREAD	Transportation Recall Enhancement, Accountability, and Documentation
TTI	Texas Transportation Institute

UNFCC	United Nations Framework Convention on Climate Change
USCG	U.S. Coast Guard
USGS	U.S. Geological Survey
UST	underground storage tank

| vmt | vehicle-miles of travel |
| VOC | volatile organic compounds |

| WTS | waste transfer station |

Appendix B: Glossary

14 CFR 121 (air): *Code of Federal Regulations,* Title 14, part 121. Prescribes rules governing the operation of domestic, flag, and supplemental air carriers and commercial operators of large aircraft.

14 CFR 135 (air): *Code of Federal Regulations,* Title 14, part 135. Prescribes rules governing the operations of commuter air carriers (scheduled) and on-demand air taxis (unscheduled).

ACCIDENT (aircraft): As defined by the National Transportation Safety Board, an occurrence incidental to flight in which, as a result of the operation of an aircraft, any person (occupant or nonoccupant) receives fatal or serious injury or any aircraft receives substantial damage.

ACCIDENT (automobile): See Crash (highway).

ACCIDENT (gas): 1) An event that involves the release of gas from a pipeline or of liquefied natural gas (LNG) or other gas from an LNG facility resulting in personal injury necessitating in-patient hospitalization or a death; or estimated property damage of $50,000 or more to the operator or others, or both, including the value of the gas that escaped during the accident; 2) an event that results in an emergency shutdown of an LNG facility; or 3) an event that is significant in the judgment of the operator even though it did not meet the criteria of (1) or (2).

ACCIDENT (hazardous liquid or gas): Release of hazardous liquid or carbon dioxide while being transported, resulting in any of the following: 1) an explosion or fire not intentionally set by the operator; 2) loss of 50 or more barrels of hazardous liquid or carbon dioxide; 3) release to the atmosphere of more than 5 barrels a day of highly volatile liquids; 4) death of any person; 5) bodily harm resulting in one or more of the following—a) the loss of consciousness, b) the necessity of carrying a person from the scene, c) the necessity for medical treatment, and d) disability that prevents the discharge of normal duties; and 6) estimated damage to the property of the operators and/or others exceeding $50,000.

ACCIDENT (highway-rail grade crossing): An impact between on-track railroad equipment and an automobile, bus, truck, motorcycle, bicycle, farm vehicle, or pedestrian or other highway user at a designated crossing site. Sidewalks, pathways, shoulders, and ditches associated with the crossing are considered to be part of the crossing site.

ACCIDENT (rail): A collision, derailment, fire, explosion, act of God, or other event involving operation of railroad on-track equipment (standing or moving) that results in railroad damage exceeding an established dollar threshold.

ACCIDENT (recreational boating): An occurrence involving a vessel or its equipment that results in 1) a death; 2) an injury that requires medical treatment beyond first aid; 3) damage to a vessel and other property totaling more than $500 or resulting in the complete loss of a vessel; or 4) the disappearance of the vessel under circumstances that indicate death or injury. Federal regulations (33 CFR 173–4) require the operator of any vessel that is numbered or used for recreational purposes to submit an accident report.

ACCIDENT (transit): An incident involving a moving vehicle, including another vehicle, an object, or person (except suicides), or a derailment/left roadway.

AIR CARRIER: The commercial system of air transportation comprising large certificated air carriers, small certificated air carriers, commuter air carriers, on-demand air taxis, supplemental air carriers, and air travel clubs.

AIR TAXI: An aircraft operator who conducts operations for hire or compensation in accordance with 14 CFR 135 (for safety purposes) or Federal Aviation Regulation Part 135 (for economic regulations or reporting purposes) in an aircraft with 30 or fewer passenger seats and a payload capacity of 7,500 pounds or less. An air taxi operates on an on-demand basis and does not meet the flight schedule qualifications of a commuter air carrier (see below).

AIRPORT: A landing area regularly used by aircraft for receiving or discharging passengers or cargo.

ALTERNATIVE FUELS: The Energy Policy Act of 1992 defines alternative fuels as methanol, denatured ethanol, and other alcohol; mixtures containing 85 percent or more (but not less than 70 percent as determined by the Secretary of Energy by rule to provide for requirements relating to cold start, safety, or vehicle functions) by volume of methanol, denatured ethanol, and other alcohols with gasoline or other fuels. Includes compressed natural gas, liquefied petroleum gases, liquefied natural gase, hydrogen, coal-derived liquid fuels, fuels other than alcohols derived from biological materials, electricity, or any other fuel the Secretary of Energy determines by rule is substantially not petroleum and would yield substantial energy security and environmental benefits.

AMTRAK: Operated by the National Railroad Passenger Corporation, this rail system was created by the Rail Passenger Service Act of 1970 (Public Law 91-518, 84 Stat. 1327) and given the responsibility for the operation of intercity, as distinct from suburban, passenger trains between points designated by the Secretary of Transportation.

ARTERIAL HIGHWAY: A major highway used primarily for through traffic.

ASPHALT: A dark brown to black cement-like material containing bitumen as the predominant constituent. The definition includes crude asphalt and finished products such as cements, fluxes, the asphalt content of emulsions, and petroleum distillates blended with asphalt to make cutback asphalt. Asphalt is obtained by petroleum processing.

AVAILABLE SEAT-MILES (air carrier): The aircraft-miles flown in each interairport hop multiplied by the number of seats available on that hop for revenue passenger service.

AVERAGE HAUL: The average distance, in miles, one ton is carried. It is computed by dividing ton-miles by tons of freight originated.

AVERAGE PASSENGER TRIP LENGTH (bus/rail): Calculated by dividing revenue passenger-miles by the number of revenue passengers.

AVIATION GASOLINE (general aviation): All special grades of gasoline used in aviation reciprocating engines, as specified by American Society of Testing Materials Specification D910 and Military Specification MIL-G5572. Includes refinery products within the gasoline range marketed as or blended to constitute aviation gasoline.

BARREL (oil): A unit of volume equal to 42 U.S. gallons.

BLOOD ALCOHOL CONCENTRATION (highway): A measurement of the percentage of alcohol in the blood by grams per deciliter.

BRITISH THERMAL UNIT (Btu): The quantity of heat needed to raise the temperature of 1 pound (approximately 1 pint) of water by 1 °F at or near 39.2 °F.

BULK CARRIER (water): A ship with specialized holds for carrying dry or liquid commodities, such as oil, grain, ore, and coal, in unpackaged bulk form. Bulk carriers may be designed to carry a single bulk product (crude oil tanker) or accommodate several bulk product types (ore/bulk/oil carrier) on the same voyage or on a subsequent voyage after holds are cleaned.

BUS: Large motor vehicle used to carry more than 10 passengers, including school buses, intercity buses, and transit buses.

CAFE STANDARDS: See Corporate Average Fuel Economy Standards.

CAR-MILE (rail): The movement of a railroad car a distance of one mile. An empty or loaded car-mile refers to a mile run by a freight car with or without a load. In the case of intermodal movements, the designation of empty or loaded refers to whether the trailers or containers are moved with or without a waybill.

CERTIFICATE OF PUBLIC CONVENIENCE AND NECESSITY (air carrier): A certificate issued by the U.S. Department of Transportation to an air carrier under Section 401 of the Federal Aviation Act authorizing the carrier to engage in air transportation.

CERTIFICATED AIR CARRIER: An air carrier holding a Certificate of Public Convenience and Necessity issued by the U.S. Department of Transportation to conduct scheduled services interstate. These carriers may also conduct non-scheduled or charter operations. Certificated air carriers operate large aircraft (30 seats or more or a maximum load of 7,500 pounds or more) in accordance with FAR Part 121. See also Large Certificated Air Carrier.

CERTIFICATED AIRPORT: An airport that services air carrier operations with aircraft seating more than 30 passengers.

CHAINED DOLLAR: A measure used to express real prices, defined as prices that are adjusted to remove the effect of changes in the purchasing power of the dollar. Real prices usually reflect buying power relative to a reference year. The "chained-dollar" measure is based on the average weights of goods and services in successive pairs of years. It is "chained" because the second year in each pair, with its weights, becomes the

first year of the next pair. Prior to 1996, real prices were expressed in constant dollars, a weighted measure of goods and services in a single year. See also Constant Dollar and Current Dollar.

CLASS I RAILROAD: A carrier that has an annual operating revenue of $250 million or more after applying the railroad revenue deflator formula, which is based on the Railroad Freight Price Index developed by the U.S. Department of Labor, Bureau of Labor Statistics. The formula is the current year's revenues multiplied by the 1991 average index or current year's average index.

COASTWISE TRAFFIC (water): Domestic traffic receiving a carriage over the ocean or the Gulf of Mexico (e.g., between New Orleans and Baltimore, New York and Puerto Rico, San Francisco and Hawaii, Alaska and Hawaii). Traffic between Great Lakes ports and seacoast ports, when having a carriage over the ocean, is also considered coastwise.

COLLECTOR (highway): In rural areas, routes that serve intracounty rather than statewide travel. In urban areas, streets that provide direct access to neighborhoods and arterials.

COMBINATION TRUCK: A power unit (truck tractor) and one or more trailing units (a semi-trailer or trailer).

COMMERCIAL BUS: Any bus used to carry passengers at rates specified in tariffs; charges may be computed per passenger (as in regular route service) or per vehicle (as in charter service).

COMMERCIAL SERVICE AIRPORT: Airport receiving scheduled passenger service and having 2,500 or more enplaned passengers per year.

COMMUTER AIR CARRIER: Different definitions are used for safety purposes and for economic regulations and reporting. For safety analysis, commuter air carriers are defined as air carriers operating under 14 CFR 135 that carry passengers for hire or compensation on at least five round trips per week on at least one route between two or more points according to published flight schedules, which specify the times, days of the week, and points of service. On March 20, 1997, the size of the aircraft subject to 14 CFR 135 was reduced from 30 to fewer than 10 passenger seats. (Larger aircraft are subject to the more stringent regulations of 14 CFR 121.) Helicopters carrying passengers or cargo for hire, however, are regulated under 14 CFR 135 whatever their size. Although, in practice, most commuter air carriers operate aircraft that are regulated for safety purposes under 14 CFR 135 and most aircraft that are regulated under 14 CFR 135 are operated by commuter air carriers, this is not necessarily the case.

For economic regulations and reporting requirements, commuter air carriers are those carriers that operate aircraft of 60 or fewer seats or a maximum payload capacity of 18,000 pounds or less. These carriers hold a certificate issued under section 298C of the Federal Aviation Act of 1958, as amended.

COMMUTER RAIL (transit): Urban passenger train service for short-distance travel between a central city and adjacent suburb. Does not include rapid rail transit or light rail service.

COMPRESSED NATURAL GAS: Natural gas compressed to a volume and density that is practical as a portable fuel supply. It is used as a fuel for natural gas-powered vehicles.

CONSTANT DOLLAR: Dollar value adjusted for changes in the average price level by dividing a current dollar amount by a price index. See also Chained Dollar and Current Dollar.

CORPORATE AVERAGE FUEL ECONOMY STANDARDS (CAFE): Originally established by Congress for new automobiles and later for light trucks. This law requires automobile manufacturers to produce vehicle fleets with a composite sales-weighted fuel economy not lower than the CAFE standards in a given year. For every vehicle that does not meet the standard, a fine is paid for every one-tenth of a mile per gallon that vehicle falls below the standard.

CRASH (highway): An event that produces injury and/or property damage, involves a motor vehicle in transport, and occurs on a trafficway or while the vehicle is still in motion after running off the trafficway.

CRUDE OIL: A mixture of hydrocarbons that exists in the liquid phase in natural underground reservoirs and remains liquid at atmospheric pressure after passing through surface-separating facilities.

CURRENT DOLLAR: Dollar value of a good or service in terms of prices current at the time the good or service is sold. See also Chained Dollar and Constant Dollar.

DEADWEIGHT TONNAGE (water): The carrying capacity of a vessel in long tons (2,240 pounds). It is the difference between the number of tons of water a vessel displaces "light" and the number of tons it displaces when submerged to the "load line."

DEMAND RESPONSIVE VEHICLE (transit): A non-fixed-route, nonfixed-schedule vehicle that operates in response to calls from passengers or their agents to the transit operator or dispatcher.

DIESEL FUEL: A complex mixture of hydrocarbons with a boiling range between approximately 350 and 650 °F. Diesel fuel is composed primarily of paraffins and naphthenic compounds that auto-ignite from the heat of compression in a diesel engine. Diesel is used primarily by heavy-duty road vehicles, construction equipment, locomotives, and marine and stationary engines.

DISTILLATE FUEL OIL: A general classification for one of the petroleum fractions produced in conventional distillation operations. Included are No. 1, No. 2, and No. 4 fuel oils and No. 1, No. 2, and No. 4 diesel fuels. Distillate fuel oil is used primarily for space heating, on- and off-highway diesel engine fuel (including railroad engine fuel and fuel for agricultural machinery), and electric power generation.

DOMESTIC FREIGHT (water): All waterborne commercial movement between points in the United States, Puerto Rico, and the Virgin Islands, excluding traffic with the Panama Canal Zone. Cargo moved for the military in commercial vessels is reported as ordinary commercial cargo; military cargo moved in military vessels is omitted.

DOMESTIC OPERATIONS (air carrier): All air carrier operations having destinations within the 50 United States, the District of Columbia, the Commonwealth of Puerto Rico, and the U.S. Virgin Islands.

DOMESTIC PASSENGER (water): Any person traveling on a public conveyance by water between points in the United States, Puerto Rico, and the Virgin Islands.

DRY CARGO BARGES (water): Large flat-bottomed, nonself-propelled vessels used to transport dry-bulk materials such as coal and ore.

ENERGY EFFICIENCY: The ratio of energy inputs to outputs from a process, for example, miles traveled per gallon of fuel (mpg).

ENPLANED PASSENGERS (air carrier): See Revenue Passenger Enplanements.

ETHANOL: A clear, colorless, flammable oxygenated hydrocarbon with a boiling point of 78.5 °C in the anhydrous state. It is used in the United States as a gasoline octane enhancer and oxygenate (10 percent concentration). Ethanol can be used in high concentrations in vehicles optimized for its use. Otherwise known as ethyl alcohol, alcohol, or grain-spirit.

FATAL CRASH (highway): A police-reported crash involving a motor vehicle in transport on a trafficway in which at least 1 person dies within 30 days of the crash as a result of that crash.

FATAL INJURY (air): Any injury that results in death within 30 days of an accident involving an aircraft.

FATALITY: For purposes of statistical reporting on transportation safety, a fatality is considered a death due to injuries in a transportation crash, accident, or incident that occurs within 30 days of that occurrence.

FATALITY (rail): 1) Death of any person from an injury within 30 days of the accident or incident (may include nontrain accidents or incidents); or 2) death of a railroad employee from an occupational illness within 365 days after the occupational illness was diagnosed by a physician.

FATALITY (recreational boating): All deaths (other than deaths by natural causes) and missing persons resulting from an occurrence that involves a vessel that is numbered or used for recreational purposes or its equipment.

FATALITY (transit): A transit-caused death confirmed within 30 days of a transit incident. Incidents include collisions, derailments, personal casualties, and fires associated with transit agency revenue vehicles, transit facilities on transit property, service vehicles, maintenance areas, and rights-of-way.

FATALITY (water): All deaths and missing persons resulting from a vessel casualty.

FEDERAL ENERGY REGULATORY COMMISSION (FERC): The federal agency with jurisdiction over, among other things, gas pricing, oil pipeline rates, and gas pipeline certification.

FERRYBOAT (transit): Vessels that carry passengers and/or vehicles over a body of water. Generally steam or diesel-powered, ferryboats may also be hovercraft, hydrofoil, and other high-speed vessels. The vessel is limited in its use to the carriage of deck passengers or vehicles or both, operates on a short run on a frequent schedule between two points over the most direct water routes other than in ocean or coastwise service, and is offered as a public service of a type normally attributed to a bridge or tunnel.

FOSSIL FUELS: Any naturally occurring organic fuel formed in the Earth's crust, such as petroleum, coal, and natural gas.

FREIGHT REVENUE (rail): Revenue from the transportation of freight and from the exercise of transit, stopoff, diversion, and reconsignment privileges as provided for in tariffs.

FREIGHTERS (water): General cargo carriers, full containerships, partial containerships, roll-on/rolloff ships, and barge carriers.

GAS TRANSMISSION PIPELINES: Pipelines installed for the purpose of transmitting gas from a source or sources of supply to one or more distribution centers, or to one or more large volume customers; or a pipeline installed to interconnect sources of supply. Typically, transmission lines differ from gas mains in that they operate at higher pressures and the distance between connections is greater.

GASOHOL: A blend of finished motor gasoline (leaded or unleaded) and alcohol (generally ethanol but sometimes methanol) limited to 10 percent by volume of alcohol.

GASOLINE: A complex mixture of relatively volatile hydrocarbons, with or without small quantities of additives that have been blended to produce a fuel suitable for use in spark ignition engines. Motor gasoline includes both leaded or unleaded grades of finished motor gasoline, blending components, and gasohol. Leaded gasoline is no longer used in highway motor vehicles in the United States.

GENERAL AVIATION: 1) All civil aviation operations other than scheduled air services and non-scheduled air transport operations for taxis, commuter air carriers, and air travel clubs that do not hold Certificates of Public Convenience and Necessity. 2) All civil aviation activity except that of air carriers certificated in accordance with Federal Aviation Regulations, Parts 121, 123, 127, and 135. The types of aircraft used in general avi-

ation range from corporate multiengine jet aircraft piloted by professional crews to amateur-built, single-engine, piston-driven, acrobatic planes to balloons and dirigibles.

GENERAL ESTIMATES SYSTEM (highway): A data-collection system that uses a nationally representative probability sample selected from all police-reported highway crashes. It began operation in 1988.

GROSS DOMESTIC PRODUCT (U.S.): The total output of goods and services produced by labor and property located in the United States, valued at market prices. As long as the labor and property are located in the United States, the suppliers (workers and owners) may be either U.S. residents or residents of foreign countries.

GROSS VEHICLE WEIGHT RATING (truck): The maximum rated capacity of a vehicle, including the weight of the base vehicle, all added equipment, driver and passengers, and all cargo.

HAZARDOUS MATERIAL: Any toxic substance or explosive, corrosive, combustible, poisonous, or radioactive material that poses a risk to the public's health, safety, or property, particularly when transported in commerce.

HEAVY RAIL (transit): An electric railway with the capacity to transport a heavy volume of passenger traffic and characterized by exclusive rights-of-way, multicar trains, high speed, rapid acceleration, sophisticated signaling, and high-platform loading. Also known as "subway," "elevated (railway)," or "metropolitan railway (metro)."

HIGHWAY-RAIL GRADE CROSSING (rail): A location where one or more railroad tracks are crossed by a public highway, road, street, or a private roadway at grade, including sidewalks and pathways at or associated with the crossing.

HIGHWAY TRUST FUND: A grant-in-aid type fund administered by the U.S. Department of Transportation, Federal Highway Administration. Most funds for highway improvements are apportioned to states according to formulas that give weight to population, area, and mileage.

HIGHWAY-USER TAX: A charge levied on persons or organizations based on their use of public roads. Funds collected are usually applied toward highway construction, reconstruction, and maintenance.

INCIDENT (hazardous materials): Any unintentional release of hazardous material while in transit or storage.

INCIDENT (train): Any event involving the movement of a train or railcars on track equipment that results in a death, reportable injury, or illness, but in which railroad property damage does not exceed the reporting threshold.

INCIDENT (transit): Collisions, derailments, personal casualties, fires, and property damage in excess of $1,000 associated with transit agency revenue vehicles; all other facilities on the transit property; and service vehicles, maintenance areas, and rights-of-way.

INJURY (air): See SERIOUS INJURY (air carrier/ general aviation).

INJURY (gas): Described in U.S. Department of Transportation Forms 7100.1 or 7100.2 as an injury requiring "in-patient hospitalization" (admission and confinement in a hospital beyond treatment administered in an emergency room or out-patient clinic in which confinement does not occur).

INJURY (hazardous liquid pipeline): An injury resulting from a hazardous liquid pipeline accident that results in one or more of the following: 1) loss of consciousness, 2) a need to be carried from the scene, 3) a need for medical treatment, and/or 4) a disability that prevents the discharge of normal duties or the pursuit of normal duties beyond the day of the accident.

INJURY (highway): Police-reported highway injuries are classified as follows:

Incapacitating Injury: Any injury, other than a fatal injury, that prevents the injured person from walking, driving, or normally continuing the activities the person was capable of performing before the injury occurred. Includes severe lacerations, broken or distorted limbs, skull or chest injuries, abdominal injuries, unconsciousness at or when taken from the accident scene, and inability to leave the accident scene without assistance. Exclusions include momentary unconsciousness.

Nonincapacitating Evident Injury: Any injury, other than a fatal injury or an incapacitating injury, evident to observers at the scene of the accident. Includes lumps on head, abrasions, bruises, minor lacerations, and others. Excludes limping.

Possible Injury: Any injury reported or claimed that is not evident. Includes, among others, momentary unconsciousness, claim of injuries not obvious, limping, complaint of pain, nausea, and hysteria.

INJURY (highway-rail grade crossing): 1) An injury to one or more persons other than railroad employees that requires medical treatment; 2) an injury to one or more employees that requires medical treatment or that results in restriction of work or motion for one or more days, or one or more lost work days, transfer to another job, termination of employment, or loss of consciousness; or 3) any occupational illness affecting one or more railroad employees that is diagnosed by a physician.

INJURY (rail): 1) Injury to any person other than a railroad employee that requires medical treatment, or 2) injury to a railroad employee that requires medical treatment or results in restriction of work or motion for one or more workdays, one or more lost workdays, termination of employment, transfer to another job, loss of consciousness, or any occupational illness of a railroad employee diagnosed by a physician.

INJURY (recreational boating): Injury requiring medical treatment beyond first aid as a result of an occurrence that involves a vessel that is numbered or used for recreational purposes or its equipment.

INJURY (transit): Any physical damage or harm to a person requiring medical treatment or any physical damage or harm to a person reported at the time and place of occurrence. For employees, an injury includes incidents resulting in time lost from duty or any definition consistent with a transit agency's current employee injury reporting practice.

INJURY (water): All personal injuries resulting from a vessel incident that require medical treatment beyond first aid.

INLAND AND COASTAL CHANNELS: Includes the Atlantic Coast Waterways, the Atlantic Intracoastal Waterway, the New York State Barge Canal System, the Gulf Coast Waterways, the Gulf Intracoastal Waterway, the Mississippi River System (including the Illinois Waterway), the Pacific Coast Waterways, the Great Lakes, and all other channels (waterways) of the United States, exclusive of Alaska, that are usable for commercial navigation.

INTERCITY CLASS I BUS: As defined by the Bureau of Transportation Statistics, an interstate motor carrier of passengers with an average annual gross revenue of at least $1 million.

INTERCITY TRUCK: A truck that carries freight beyond local areas and commercial zones.

INTERNAL TRAFFIC (water): Vessel movements (origin and destination) that take place solely on inland waterways located within the boundaries of the contiguous 48 states or within the state of Alaska. Internal traffic also applies to carriage on both inland waterways and the water on the Great Lakes; carriage between offshore areas and inland waterways; and carriage occurring within the Delaware Bay, Chesapeake Bay, Puget Sound, and the San Francisco Bay,

which are considered internal bodies of water rather than arms of the ocean.

INTERSTATE HIGHWAY: Limited access, divided highway of at least four lanes designated by the Federal Highway Administration as part of the Interstate Highway System.

JET FUEL: Includes kerosene-type jet fuel (used primarily for commercial turbojet and turboprop aircraft engines) and naphtha-type jet fuel (used primarily for military turbojet and turboprop aircraft engines).

LAKEWISE OR GREAT LAKES TRAFFIC: Waterborne traffic between U.S. ports on the Great Lakes system. The Great Lakes system is treated as a separate waterways system rather than as a part of the inland system.

LARGE CERTIFICATED AIR CARRIER: An air carrier holding a certificate issued under section 401 of the Federal Aviation Act of 1958, as amended, that: 1) operates aircraft designed to have a maximum passenger capacity of more than 60 seats or a maximum payload capacity of more than 18,000 pounds, or 2) conducts operations where one or both terminals of a flight stage are outside the 50 states of the United States, the District of Columbia, the Commonwealth of Puerto Rico, and the U.S. Virgin Islands. Large certificated air carriers are grouped by annual operating revenues: 1) majors (more than $1 billion in annual operating revenues), 2) nationals (between $100 million and $1 billion in annual operating revenues), 3) large regionals (between $20 million and $99,999,999 in annual operating revenues), and 4) medium regionals (less than $20 million in annual operating revenues).

LARGE REGIONALS (air): Air carrier groups with annual operating revenues between $20 million and $99,999,999.

LARGE TRUCK: Trucks over 10,000 pounds gross vehicle weight rating, including single-unit trucks and truck tractors.

LEASE CONDENSATE: A mixture consisting primarily of pentanes and heavier hydrocarbons, which are recovered as a liquid from natural gas in lease or field separation facilities. This category excludes natural gas liquids, such as butane and propane, which are recovered at natural gas processing plants or facilities.

LIGHT-DUTY VEHICLE: A vehicle category that combines automobiles and light trucks.

LIGHT RAIL: A streetcar-type vehicle operated on city streets, semi-exclusive rights-of-way, or exclusive rights-of-way. Service may be provided by step-entry vehicles or by level boarding.

LIGHT TRUCK: Trucks of 10,000 pounds gross vehicle weight rating or less, including pickups, vans, truck-based station wagons, and sport utility vehicles.

LIQUEFIED NATURAL GAS (LNG): Natural gas, primarily methane, that has been liquefied by reducing its temperature to –260 °F at atmospheric pressure.

LIQUEFIED PETROLEUM GAS (LPG): Propane, propylene, normal butane, butylene, isobutane, and isobutylene produced at refineries or natural gas processing plants, including plants that fractionate new natural gas plant liquids.

LINER CARRIER (water): A cargo-carrying ship operated between specified ports on a regular basis for an advertised price, versus a chartered ship that operates for single deliveries to a variety of ports.

LOCOMOTIVE: Railroad vehicle equipped with flanged wheels for use on railroad tracks, powered directly by electricity, steam, or fossil fuel, and used to move other railroad rolling equipment.

LOCOMOTIVE-MILE: The movement of a locomotive unit, under its own power, the distance of 1 mile.

MAINS (gas): A network of pipelines that serves as a common source of supply for more than one gas service line.

MAJORS (air): Air carrier groups with annual operating revenues exceeding $1 billion.

MEDIUM REGIONALS (air): Air carrier groups with annual operating revenues less than $20 million.

MERCHANDISE TRADE EXPORTS: Merchandise transported out of the United States to foreign countries whether such merchandise is exported from within the U.S. Customs Service territory, from a U.S. Customs bonded warehouse, or from a U.S. Foreign Trade Zone. (Foreign Trade Zones are areas, operated as public utilities, under the control of U.S. Customs with facilities for handling, storing, manipulating, manufacturing, and exhibiting goods.)

MERCHANDISE TRADE IMPORTS: Commodities of foreign origin entering the United States, as well as goods of domestic origin returned to the United States with no change in condition or after having been processed and/or assembled in other countries. Puerto Rico is a Customs district within the U.S. Customs territory, and its trade with foreign countries is included in U.S. import statistics. U.S. import statistics also include merchandise trade between the U.S. Virgin Islands and foreign countries even though the Islands are not officially a part of the U.S. Customs territory.

METHANOL: A light, volatile alcohol produced commercially by the catalyzed reaction of hydrogen and carbon monoxide. Methanol is blended with gasoline to improve its operational efficiency.

METHYL-TERTIARY-BUTYL-ETHER (MTBE): A colorless, flammable, liquid oxygenated hydrocarbon that contains 18.15 percent oxygen. It is a fuel oxygenate produced by reacting methanol with isobutylene.

MINOR ARTERIALS (highway): Roads linking cities and larger towns in rural areas. In urban areas, roads that link but do not penetrate neighborhoods within a community.

MOTORBUS (transit): A rubber-tired, self-propelled, manually steered bus with a fuel supply onboard the vehicle. Motorbus types include intercity, school, and transit.

MOTORCYCLE: A two- or three-wheeled motor vehicle designed to transport one or two people, including motor scooters, minibikes, and mopeds.

NATIONALS (air): Air carrier groups with annual operating revenues between $100 million and $1 billion.

NATURAL GAS: A naturally occurring mixture of hydrocarbon and nonhydrocarbon gases found in porous geologic formations beneath the Earth's surface, often in association with petroleum. The principal constituent is methane.

NATURAL GAS PLANT LIQUIDS: Liquids recovered from natural gas in processing plants or field facilities, or extracted by fractionators. They include ethane, propane, normal butane, isobutane, pentanes plus, and other products, such as finished motor gasoline, finished aviation gasoline, special naphthas, kerosene, and distillate fuel oil produced at natural gas processing plants.

NEAR MIDAIR COLLISION (air): An incident in which the possibility of a collision occurred as a result of aircraft flying with less than 500 feet of separation, or a report received from a pilot or flight crew member stating that a collision hazard existed between two or more aircraft.

NONOCCUPANT (Automobile): Any person who is not an occupant of a motor vehicle in transport (e.g., bystanders, pedestrians, pedalcyclists, or an occupant of a parked motor vehicle).

NONSCHEDULED SERVICE (air): Revenue flights not operated as regular scheduled service, such as charter flights, and all nonrevenue flights incident to such flights.

NONSELF-PROPELLED VESSEL (water): A vessel without the means for self-propulsion. Includes dry cargo barges and tanker barges.

NONTRAIN INCIDENT: An event that results in a reportable casualty, but does not involve the movement of ontrack equipment and does not cause reportable damage above the threshold established for train accidents.

NONTRESPASSERS (rail): A person lawfully on any part of railroad property used in railroad operations or a person adjacent to railroad premises when injured as the result of railroad operations.

NONVESSEL-CASUALTY-RELATED DEATH (water): A death that occurs onboard a commercial vessel but not as a result of a vessel casualty, such as a collision, fire, or explosion.

OCCUPANT (highway): Any person in or on a motor vehicle in transport. Includes the driver, passengers, and persons riding on the exterior of a motor vehicle (e.g., a skateboard rider holding onto a moving vehicle). Excludes occupants of parked cars unless they are double parked or motionless on the roadway.

OCCUPATIONAL FATALITY: Death resulting from a job-related injury.

OPERATING EXPENSES (air): Expenses incurred in the performance of air transportation, based on overall operating revenues and expenses. Does not include nonoperating income and expenses, nonrecurring items, or income taxes.

OPERATING EXPENSES (rail): Expenses of furnishing transportation services, including maintenance and depreciation of the plant used in the service.

OPERATING EXPENSES (transit): The total of all expenses associated with operation of an individual mode by a given operator. Includes distributions of "joint expenses" to individual modes and excludes "reconciling items," such as interest expenses and depreciation. Should not be confused with "vehicle operating expenses."

OPERATING EXPENSES (truck): Includes expenditures for equipment maintenance, supervision, wages, fuel, equipment rental, terminal operations, insurance, safety, and administrative and general functions.

OPERATING REVENUES (air): Revenues from the performance of air transportation and related incidental services. Includes l) transportation revenues from the carriage of all classes of traffic in scheduled and nonscheduled services, and 2) nontransportation revenues consisting of federal subsidies (where applicable) and services related to air transportation.

OTHER FREEWAYS AND EXPRESSWAYS (highway): All urban principal arterials with limited access but not part of the Interstate Highway system.

OTHER PRINCIPAL ARTERIALS (highway): Major streets or highways, many of multi-lane or freeway design, serving high-volume traffic corridor movements that connect major generators of travel.

OTHER RAIL REVENUE: Includes revenues from miscellaneous operations (i.e., dining- and bar-car services), income from the lease of road and equipment, miscellaneous rental income, income from nonoperating property, profit from separately operated properties, dividend income, interest income, income from sinking and other reserve funds, release or premium on funded debt, contributions from other companies, and other miscellaneous income.

OTHER REVENUE VEHICLES (transit): Other revenue-generating modes of transit service, such as cable cars, personal rapid transit systems, mono-rail vehicles, inclined and railway cars, not covered otherwise.

OTHER 2-AXLE, 4-TIRE VEHICLES (truck): Includes vans, pickup trucks, and sport utility vehicles.

OXYGENATES: Any substance that when added to motor gasoline increases the amount of oxygen in that gasoline blend. Includes oxygen-bearing compounds such as ethanol, methanol, and methyl-tertiary-butyl-ether. Oxygenated fuel tends to give a more complete combustion of carbon into carbon dioxide (rather than monoxide), thereby reducing air pollution from exhaust emissions.

PASSENGER CAR: A motor vehicle designed primarily for carrying passengers on ordinary roads, includes convertibles, sedans, and station wagons.

PASSENGER-MILE: 1) Air: One passenger transported 1 mile; passenger-miles for 1 interairport flight are calculated by multiplying aircraft-miles flown by the number of passengers carried on the flight. The total passenger-miles for all flights is the sum of passenger-miles for all interairport flights. 2) Auto: One passenger traveling 1 mile; e.g., 1 car transporting 2 passengers 4 miles results in 8 passenger-miles. 3) Transit: The total number of miles traveled by transit passengers; e.g., 1 bus transporting 5 passengers 3 miles results in 15 passenger-miles.

PASSENGER REVENUE: 1) Rail: Revenue from the sale of tickets. 2) Air: Revenues from the transport of passengers by air. 3) Transit: Fares, transfer, zone, and park-and-ride parking charges paid by transit passengers. Prior to 1984, fare revenues collected by contractors operating transit services were not included.

PASSENGER VESSEL (water): A vessel designed for the commercial transport of passengers.

PEDALCYCLIST: A person on a vehicle that is powered solely by pedals.

PEDESTRIAN: Any person not in or on a motor vehicle or other vehicle. Excludes people in buildings or sitting at a sidewalk cafe. The National Highway Traffic Safety Administration also uses an "other pedestrian" category to refer to pedestrians using conveyances and people in buildings. Examples of pedestrian conveyances include skateboards, nonmotorized wheelchairs, rollerskates, sleds, and transport devices used as equipment.

PERSON-MILES: An estimate of the aggregate distance traveled by all persons on a given trip based on the estimated transportation-network-miles traveled on that trip.

PERSON TRIP: A trip taken by an individual. For example, if three persons from the same household travel together, the trip is counted as one household trip and three person trips.

PERSONAL CASUALTY (transit): 1) An incident in which a person is hurt while getting on or off a transit vehicle (e.g., falls or door incidents), but not as a result of a collision, derailment/left roadway, or fire. 2) An incident in which a person is hurt while using a lift to get on or off a transit vehicle, but not as a result of a collision, derailment/left roadway, or fire. 3) An incident in which a person is injured on a transit vehicle, but not as a result of a collision, derailment/left roadway, or fire. 4) An incident in which a person is hurt while using a transit facility. This includes anyone on transit property (e.g., patrons, transit employees, trespassers), but does not include incidents resulting from illness or criminal activity.

PETROLEUM (oil): A generic term applied to oil and oil products in all forms, such as crude oil, lease condensate, unfinished oils, petroleum products, natural gas plant liquids, and nonhydrocarbon compounds blended into finished petroleum products.

PROPERTY DAMAGE (transit): The dollar amount required to repair or replace transit property (including stations, rights-of-way, bus stops, and maintenance facilities) damaged during an incident.

PUBLIC ROAD: Any road under the jurisdiction of and maintained by a public authority (federal, state, county, town or township, local government, or instrumentality thereof) and open to public travel.

RAPID RAIL TRANSIT: Transit service using railcars driven by electricity usually drawn from a third rail, configured for passenger traffic, and usually operated on exclusive rights-of-way. It generally uses longer trains and has longer station spacing than light rail.

REFORMULATED GASOLINE: Gasoline whose composition has been changed to meet performance specifications regarding ozone-forming tendencies and release of toxic substances into the air from both evaporation and tailpipe emissions. Reformulated gasoline includes oxygenates and, compared with gasoline sold in 1990, has a lower content of olefins, aromatics, volatile components, and heavy hydrocarbons.

RESIDUAL FUEL OIL: The heavier oils that remain after the distillate fuel oils and lighter hydrocarbons are distilled away in refinery operations and that conform to American Society for Testing and Materials Specifications D396 and 976. Includes, among others, Navy Special oil used in steam-powered vessels in government service and No. 6 oil used to power ships. Imports of residual fuel oil include imported crude oil burned as fuel.

REVENUE: Remuneration received by carriers for transportation activities.

REVENUE PASSENGER: 1) Air: Person receiving air transportation from an air carrier for which remuneration is received by the carrier. Air carrier employees or others, except ministers of religion, elderly individuals, and handicapped individuals, receiving reduced rate charges (less than the applicable tariff) are considered nonrevenue passengers. Infants, for whom a token fare is charged, are not counted as passengers. 2) Transit: Single-vehicle transit rides by initial-board (first-ride) transit passengers only. Excludes all transfer rides and all nonrevenue rides. 3) Rail: Number of one-way trips made by persons holding tickets.

REVENUE PASSENGER ENPLANEMENTS (air): The total number of passengers boarding aircraft. Includes both originating and connecting passengers.

REVENUE PASSENGER LOAD FACTOR (air): Revenue passenger-miles as a percentage of available seat-miles in revenue passenger services. The term is used to represent the proportion of aircraft seating capacity that is actually sold and utilized.

REVENUE PASSENGER-MILE: One revenue passenger transported one mile.

REVENUE PASSENGER TON-MILE (air): One ton of revenue passenger weight (including all baggage) transported one mile. The passenger weight standard for both domestic and international operations is 200 pounds.

REVENUE TON-MILE: One short ton of freight transported one mile.

REVENUE VEHICLE-MILES (transit): One vehicle (bus, trolley bus, or streetcar) traveling one mile, while revenue passengers are on board, generates one revenue vehicle-mile. Revenue vehicle-miles reported represent the total mileage traveled by vehicles in scheduled or unscheduled revenue-producing services.

ROAD OIL: Any heavy petroleum oil, including residual asphaltic oil, that is used as a dust palliative and surface treatment on roads and highways. It is generally produced in six grades from zero, the most liquid, to five, the most viscous.

ROLL ON/ROLL OFF VESSEL (water): Ships that are designed to carry wheeled containers or other wheeled cargo and use the roll on/roll off method for loading and unloading.

RUNWAY INCURSION (air): Any occurrence on a runway involving an aircraft, vehicle, or pedestrian that creates a collision hazard for aircraft taking off, intending to take off, landing, or intending to land.

RURAL HIGHWAY: Any highway, road, or street that is not an urban highway.

RURAL MILEAGE (highway): Roads outside city, municipal district, or urban boundaries.

SCHEDULED SERVICE (air): Transport service operated on published flight schedules.

SCHOOL BUS: A passenger motor vehicle that is designed or used to carry more than 10 passengers, in addition to the driver, and, as determined by the Secretary of Transportation, is likely to be significantly used for the purpose of transporting pre-primary, primary, or secondary school students between home and school.

SCHOOL-BUS-RELATED CRASH: Any crash directly or indirectly involving a vehicle that is used as a school bus, regardless of body design, such as a crash involving school children alighting from a vehicle.

SCOW (water): Any flat-bottomed, nonself-propelled, rectangular vessel with sloping ends. Large scows are used to transport sand, gravel, or refuse.

SELF-PROPELLED VESSEL: A vessel that has its own means of propulsion. Includes tankers, containerships, dry bulk cargo ships, and general cargo vessels.

SERIOUS INJURY (air carrier/general aviation): An injury that requires hospitalization for more than 48 hours, commencing within 7 days from the date when the injury was received; results in a bone fracture (except simple fractures of fingers, toes, or nose); involves lacerations that cause severe hemorrhages, or nerve, muscle, or tendon damage; involves injury to any internal organ; or involves second- or third-degree burns or any burns affecting more than 5 percent of the body surface.

SMALL CERTIFICATED AIR CARRIER: An air carrier holding a certificate issued under section 401 of the Federal Aviation Act of 1958, as amended, that operates aircraft designed to have a maximum seating capacity of 60 seats or fewer or a maximum payload of 18,000 pounds or less.

STATE AND LOCAL HIGHWAY EXPENDITURES: Disbursements for capital outlays, maintenance and traffic surfaces, administration and research, highway law enforcement and safety, and interest on debt.

STREETCARS: Relatively lightweight passenger railcars operating singly or in short trains, or on fixed rails in rights-of-way that are not always separated from other traffic. Streetcars do not necessarily have the right-of-way at grade crossings with other traffic.

SUPPLEMENTAL AIR CARRIER: An air carrier authorized to perform passenger and cargo charter services.

TANKER: An oceangoing ship designed to haul liquid bulk cargo in world trade.

TON-MILE (truck): The movement of one ton of cargo the distance of one mile. Ton-miles are calculated by multiplying the weight in tons of each shipment transported by the miles hauled.

TON-MILE (water): The movement of one ton of cargo the distance of one statute mile. Domestic ton-miles are calculated by multiplying tons moved by the number of statute miles moved on the water (e.g., 50 short tons moving 200 miles on a waterway would yield 10,000 ton-miles for that waterway). Ton-miles are not computed for ports. For coastwise traffic, the shortest route that safe navigation permits between the port of origin and destination is used to calculate ton-miles.

TRAFFICWAY (highway): Any right-of-way open to the public as a matter of right or custom for moving persons or property from one place to another, including the entire width between property lines or other boundaries.

TRAIN LINE MILEAGE: The aggregate length of all line-haul railroads. It does not include the mileage of yard tracks or sidings, nor does it reflect the fact that a mile of railroad may include two or more parallel tracks. Jointly-used track is counted only once.

TRAIN-MILE: A train-mile is the movement of a train, which can consist of many cars, the distance of one mile. A train-mile differs from a vehicle-mile, which is the movement of one car (vehicle) the distance of one mile. A 10-car (vehicle) train traveling 1 mile is measured as 1 train-mile and 10 vehicle-miles. Caution should be used when comparing train-miles to vehicle-miles.

TRANSIT VEHICLE: Includes light, heavy, and commuter rail; motorbus; trolley bus; van pools; automated guideway; and demand responsive vehicles.

TRANSSHIPMENTS: Shipments that enter or exit the United States by way of a U.S. Customs port on the northern or southern border, but whose origin or destination is a country other than Canada or Mexico.

TRESPASSER (rail): Any person whose presence on railroad property used in railroad operations is prohibited, forbidden, or unlawful.

TROLLEY BUS: Rubber-tired electric transit vehicle, manually steered and propelled by a motor drawing current, normally through overhead wires, from a central power source.

TRUST FUNDS: Accounts that are designated by law to carry out specific purposes and programs. Trust Funds are usually financed with earmarked tax collections.

TUG BOAT: A powered vessel designed for towing or pushing ships, dumb barges, pushed-towed barges, and rafts, but not for the carriage of goods.

U.S.-FLAG CARRIER OR AMERICAN FLAG CARRIER (air): One of a class of air carriers holding a Certificate of Public Convenience and Necessity, issued by the U.S. Department of Transportation and approved by the President, authorizing scheduled operations over specified routes between the United States (and/or its territories) and one or more foreign countries.

UNLEADED GASOLINE: See Gasoline.

UNLINKED PASSENGER TRIPS (transit): The number of passengers boarding public transportation vehicles. A passenger is counted each time he/she boards a vehicle even if the boarding is part of the same journey from origin to destination.

URBAN HIGHWAY: Any road or street within the boundaries of an urban area. An urban area is an area including and adjacent to a municipality or urban place with a population of 5,000 or more. The boundaries of urban areas are fixed by state highway departments, subject to the approval of the Federal Highway Administration, for purposes of the Federal-Aid Highway Program.

VANPOOL (transit): Public-sponsored commuter service operating under prearranged schedules for previously formed groups of riders in 8- to 18-seat vehicles. Drivers are also commuters who receive little or no compensation besides the free ride.

VEHICLE MAINTENANCE (transit): All activities associated with revenue and nonrevenue (service) vehicle maintenance, including administration, inspection and maintenance, and servicing (e.g., cleaning and fueling) vehicles. In addition, it includes repairs due to vandalism or to revenue vehicle accidents.

VEHICLE-MILES (highway): Miles of travel by all types of motor vehicles as determined by the states on the basis of actual traffic counts and established estimating procedures.

VEHICLE-MILES (transit): The total number of miles traveled by transit vehicles. Commuter rail, heavy rail, and light rail report individual car-miles, rather than train-miles for vehicle-miles.

VEHICLE OPERATIONS (transit): All activities associated with transportation administration, including the control of revenue vehicle movements, scheduling, ticketing and fare collection, system security, and revenue vehicle operation.

VESSEL CASUALTY (water): An occurrence involving commercial vessels that results in 1) actual physical damage to property in excess of $25,000; 2) material damage affecting the seaworthiness or efficiency of a vessel; 3) stranding or grounding; 4) loss of life; or 5) injury causing any person to remain incapacitated for a period in excess of 72 hours, except injury to harbor workers not resulting in death and not resulting from vessel casualty or vessel equipment casualty.

VESSEL-CASUALTY-RELATED DEATH (water): Fatality that occurs as a result of an incident that involves a vessel or its equipment, such as a collision, fire, or explosion. Includes drowning deaths.

WATERBORNE TRANSPORTATION: Transport of freight and/or people by commercial vessels under U.S. Coast Guard jurisdiction.

WAYBILL: A document that lists goods and shipping instructions relative to a shipment.

Appendix C: List of Figures, Tables, Maps, and Boxes

Index

ISBN 0-16-050853-3